AMAZING GRACE

AMAZING GRACE

With Charles Evers in Mississippi

———◄●►———

JASON BERRY

Saturday Review Press

NEW YORK

Published simultaneously in Canada by
Doubleday Canada Ltd., Toronto.

Library of Congress Catalog Card Number: 73–76488

ISBN 0–8415–0260–9

Saturday Review Press
380 Madison Avenue
New York, New York 10017

Printed in the United States of America

Design by Tere LoPrete

To my father and to Charles Evers

Acknowledgments

For advice in the writing of the manuscript: Hodding Carter, III; David Chandler; my agent at Lantz-Donadio, Hy Cohen; Wes Christenson; Steve Dwyer; Jeff Gillenkirk; Bill Minor; Berry Morgan; my editor at Saturday Review, Judith Sachs; and most gratefully, John Carr.

For insights into history: Harry Bowie; Hodding Carter, III; John Carr; Ed King; Bill Minor; Hunter Morey; and Jim Lowen.

For information in the last two chapters and epilogue: John Brittain; Frank Parker; George Taylor of the Lawyers' Committee for Civil Rights, Jackson; Charles Ramberg; Jackson-Hinds County Legal Services; and Douglas Schoen, Harvard, '74.

For giving time to allow me viewings in their film libraries, these reporters: Burt Case, News Director, WAPT, Jackson; Jack Hobbs, News Director, WJTV, Jackson; and Cliff Brown, News Director, WDAM, Laurel-Hattiesburg. Thanks also to Howard Lett, News Director, WJDX Radio, Jackson, for Point-Counterpoint tape, and to Steve Bell for election-night tape.

Thanks to John Messina for photography.

For miscellaneous favors: Clyde McHenry; Ed Cole; Skip Perkins; Cliff James; Cathy Adams; Joe Olree; Buddy Robichaux; Gil Jonas; Pic Fermin; Steve and Nancy Dwyer (for the typewriter); and Pat Dunn of New York City.

For permission to quote: The Delta Ministry.

Special thanks to Walker Percy.

Few books succeed without a whole lot of moral support, and that I received from Steve and Nancy Dwyer; Kenny Charbonnet; Lamar Berry; George Welch; Wayne Rester; Rich and Debbie Hluchan; Jack Berry; Beline Devine; Jerry and Kathy Meunier; Jack and Ann Parker; Lance LeLoup; L. J. Foley; Shirley Meunier; Albert Lamar; Paul Canonoci; and Tom Dullard.

And last but not least, to my parents, Jason and Mary Frances Berry, I owe deepest thanks. Their financial support and spiritual qualities will never be forgotten.

"Goodness. Yeah. Just plain simple goodness. Well, you can't inherit that from anybody. You got to make it. And you got to make it out of badness. Badness . . .

"Out of badness," he repeated. "And you know why? Because there isn't anything else to make it out of."

—Willie Stark, *All the King's Men*

AMAZING GRACE

Prologue

My earliest memory of southern politics is still vivid. When I was ten years old my father called me into the living room to see the late news. "Son," he said, "I want you to watch history-in-the-make. Look at that man—he's your governor. His name's Earl K. Long. Look out, now! Three men are holding him down in a wheelchair. Can you believe that? They're dragging him into a mental hospital and Channel 6 is beeping out his curse words!"

Old Earl was a year out of the Governor's Mansion and three months dead when I graduated from the sixth grade. Forgetting him was easy, but as more southern politicians came along I grew bewildered. Their vocation had a flexibility to it which was much like that of the deceased governor himself: it was never tied down by sanity, and rarely did the man holding the job appear to employ reason on purpose. But Long, at least, was a legitimate madman. That cannot be said of the rest of the southern leadership.

Through all of its years of insanity and fury, the South has been a region of sharp contrasts. The state with the starkest contrasts, the quintessential southern state, is Mississippi.

Mississippi is the original Cotton Kingdom, and today in the Delta that crop is the major economy. Tarpaper shacks totter in the wind less than a city block from palatial homes. Mississippi was the second state to secede from the Union. Jefferson Davis, the President of the Confederacy, once lived along the banks of the great river for which the state is named. His home, Le Beauvoir, stands as a museum on the Mississippi Gulf Coast. His birthday is a legal holiday for state employees.

With notable exceptions, most of Mississippi's figures of prominence have left: B. B. King, Willie Morris, Richard Wright, Stark Young, Bobbie Gentry, James Silver, Elvis Presley, Tennessee Williams. Those who stayed—William Faulkner and Hodding Carter (now both deceased), Charles Evers and Aaron Henry—are themselves testimony to the clash of emotions of the land. Mississippi has had more recorded lynchings than any other state, is considered the state most brutal in opposition to civil rights legislation and its implementation, and has an unparalleled history of racist demagoguery. Mississippi is the land where Pulitzer Prizes are anathema and where the nation's fourth Nobel winner in literature, William Faulkner, was hated even after he won the prize.

Mississippi is nevertheless a state of rare beauty. Springtime is a glorious experience, especially in the Delta, with its brilliant green kudzu, the ivy-vine enmeshing landscape and water; it is a sight of pure metaphysical wonder. Yet the beauty of Mississippi only underscores the terrible poverty of the state. Today Mississippi is the rock-bottom state in per capita income, and it pays less in taxes than it receives in federal aid. While bellies of black children swell with hunger each Delta winter, Senator James Eastland receives an average $150,000 in federal payments for not farming cotton on his vast acreage, which is part of perhaps the richest land in the hemisphere.

Mississippi is a state of diametric oppositions: black and white, rich and poor, quarterbacks and sorrow, misery and beauty queens. Even the word "Mississippi" evokes widely varied reactions from people who hear it:

Xenophobia, from 46,000 race-crazed fans at the Ole Miss vs. Kentucky football game in 1962 when Ross Barnett was introduced after he had blocked James Meredith from registering at the university.

A *shudder* from President Kennedy one night later, after he was forced to call out federal troops to maintain order on the rioting Ole Miss campus.

A *song*—"Mississippi Goddamn!"—from black entertainer Nina Simone, who understands what the word means to her people.

Silence, from my father, sitting in the den of his New Orleans home twelve years after he "introduced" me to Earl Long, as he listened to me on the telephone. I sat on the floor of my Washington apartment, letting the word sink in.

"*Mississippi!*" he said. "Of all the God-forsaken places to work for a black man runnin' for governor!"

"Dad, how can I explain it? What's the sense of going back South if I can't do something . . . well, just do something that I haven't done before? Something meaningful."

"Hell, I'm the first to admit *Mississippi* needs to be changed! I just don't like the idea of you doin' it. You could get your head shot off!"

"This isn't civil rights work . . . it's politics. And they haven't had anybody killed in five years."

"That doesn't mean they're finished shootin'."

His breath was heavy. "Son, I'm sure Charles Evers is a remarkable man. And you know your mother and I are opposed to racism. But we've got property in Mississippi . . ."

"The campaign office is in Jackson. That's over a hundred and fifty miles from our farm in Poplarville. You can't even get Jackson stations on the TV cable at the farm. Nobody'll know."

He breathed again. "When did you get the letter from his secretary?"

"Day before yesterday."

"She says they want you?"

"She said they're assembling a staff in Jackson and they need all the help they can get. I'll be going as a volunteer. I don't even know if I'll get a salary."

"It'll be dangerous over there, son."

"Maybe. Maybe not."

"But why in hell do you want to *go*?"

"Because I *like* Mississippi," I said blandly.

The conversation remained mutually unproductive and so we agreed not to talk about it until after commencement exercises, which he and mother were coming up for at the end of the week. On May 23, 1971, I was graduated from Georgetown *cum laude*, but it wasn't the most joyous of occasions. None of us talked much about Mississippi until they got ready to leave. Mother hinted at a trip to Europe, and then all three of us had a big argument.

The next day I went to Mississippi.

CHAPTER

1

To get to Lexington we took Interstate 55 north from Jackson for thirty miles until it stopped just above Canton, where the road crews were still at work. There was no completed four-lane running north–south through Mississippi. From Canton the next leg was Route 16 to Yazoo City, an old blacktop road repaved in the forties and untouched since. The crevices tear at tires of even mammoth trucks. The landscape is full and green but you don't have time to watch when you're at the wheel. The drivers on this road swerve back across the yellow line only at the last second. The lush expanse is a blur in the side of your eye. When dusk drains into night the road vanishes into the dark. It twists and turns like a snake through grass. Bad headlights when there is no moon mean trouble. Sometimes a car won't come at you for ten minutes running, and road and soil seem to merge.

Yazoo City lies on the southeastern fringe of the rich Delta land, and the last route to Lexington is northeast on 433, which takes you into Holmes County, whose seat is Lexington. It is located almost exactly in the center of the state. In 1955 the White Citizens' Council in Lexington tried to ruin Hazel Brannon Smith, editor of the town newspaper. The sheriff had shot a black man dead and was exonerated of murder. Hazel Smith raised the issue in print, and the sheriff sued for libel. The Council, usually violent in preservation of white supremacy, instead tried socioeconomic reprisal. Its members put fists on the town table and the paper's advertisers withdrew. The Council subsidized a new paper and the State Legislature passed a special bill allowing Lexington to publish its news outside the city. The House committee chairman who pushed the bill through observed that it "concerned some woman editor who's been writing things that don't go along with the feelings of her community." Hazel Smith made the permanent Council blacklist but her paper miraculously survived. However, her fight is ironic because she was never liberal to begin with. She merely refused to condone murder. She won the Pulitzer Prize that year.

But all of that was long ago and the word we had before leaving Evers' campaign office was that Hazel Smith was a "moderate." She was running for the State Senate and had made it clear to blacks that she didn't want them opposing her.

The day before, May 30, 1971, an eighteen-year-old black girl, JoEtha Collier, had been buried in Drew. She had been killed by a gun fired from within a speeding car. According to a family spokesman for the three drunk white teenagers being held for the crime, the shot had been accidental. Black folks from far-away hamlets and towns had risen early to drive into the Delta for midday services. Dr. Ralph Abernathy of the Southern Christian Leadership Conference had revised his schedule to eulogize yet another innocent black killed by whites. Cameras and newsmen converged once more on a hitherto unknown village to report the sorrow and the profoundly religious funeral.

As we left Jackson for Lexington, a white woman in the car next to us at a filling station said to her husband, "I hear all the cameras and them went up to Drew yesterday." The man had nodded impassively, saying nothing.

Ed Cole drove. He was a twenty-seven-year-old black man, Evers' campaign manager. His shirt hung so loose it made his flowered tie seem incongruously wide. He weighed no more than 155 pounds. The silver bracelet he wore on his left wrist gleamed in the headlights of oncoming cars. He said it was a soul ring. "Plenty things white folks don't know," he chuckled. It had taken me most of the day to realize he had an artificial limb from the right knee down, and that was why he limped. I learned later that when he was ten years old the leg had been severed in a grain elevator.

Next to Ed sat Dwight, the blackest person in the car. He was nineteen and lead singer of The Evers 4, the band that played at campaign rallies. He was blind and wore dark glasses all the time. Dwight's cousin Robert, who sat next to me in the back, was an albino with a deep purple rash on his neck. Robert's sight was poor but he was able to see things at close distances. Dwight caressed the radio dial, pressing his ear to the dashboard to sift music from the static. The tires thumped loudly on the road and it was impossible to talk.

We entered Lexington, and at the first light Ed turned off the blacktop onto a dirt and gravel road. "You can always tell where black folks live," he said. "Concrete ends and the dirt begins. When it rains, it floods, and then it's sho' some hell drivin'."

The parking lot of the high school where the rally was being held was jammed with old pickup trucks and cars with bent fenders and faded colors. A late-model Chevrolet was the only good car. Parking at the front of the gym, Ed opened the door and cupped his forearm underneath his right calf. He hoisted the bad leg out of the car and moved toward the policeman at the gym. Ed was the only man I had ever seen who could saunter with a limp. He carried a briefcase in one hand and a copy of *1971 Mississippi Budgetary Expenditures* tucked under the arm; Dwight held onto the other arm. Robert followed.

The three of them walked through the rear door of the gym. As I followed, on my first day in Mississippi, I thought, "This is the blind leading the blind." The black policeman at the door looked at me as we entered, looked back at Ed, and Ed nodded. When we reached the floor of the gym we were between the edge of the stage and the bleachers. It was impossible to see past Robert's head, but the lights overhead showed that the room was brightly lit. We walked very slowly but I still could see no one but Robert. A voice was speaking loudly and with frequent pauses. Others responded, as if part of a litany.

"Now you *know* a campaign cost money! Plenty money!"

". . . A-men!"

We walked toward the stage. It was somewhere to our left, but still impossible to see. Above the side tier of dilapidated seats the walls showed black smudges. The scoreboard was lit "99 All" and the quarters buttons were bright red.

"So, black folks, we can sit here till kingdom come, but we ain't goin' nowhere if we ain't got no money!"

". . . That's right! Yessuh!"

We stopped at the edge of the floor by the steps of the stage, and I peered over Robert's shoulder. Everyone in the room was black: black, brown, or a shade between.

"So if you want to talk big, black, and sassy—like *me!*— then you gotta *act* that way! And, black folks, you cain't do that if you ain't got no money!"

". . . Sho' 'nuf!"

"Black folks, they're only two things in this country that

make you free—money and votes. You cain't do nothin' without 'em!"

The speaker still was not visible. My heart was thumping loud and hard like a fuel pump. I had never been in a room filled with black people. Robert, plainly bored, was drawing circles with his shoe. I could feel the sweat under my armpits.

"All right now, we got our campaign band. Band, move out to the middle of the floor and let 'em take a look at you."

Ed, Dwight, and Robert moved, and so I followed. As we approached the floor, two young men about Dwight's age joined us. We stood in the middle of the basketball court, between two blocks of chairs. Five hundred people were seated before us, most of them old or middle-aged. The wall fans purred softly, a serene sound. Here were people whose hopes, sorrows, fears, and joys were not recognized by whites. I had never realized what it would feel like to stand in a room full of black people. I had passed black people daily, growing up in New Orleans, but had never seen them as other than inconsequential figures. I was sad and felt guilty about the color of my skin, even though I was excited about Evers and the new atmosphere. It would take time before I felt comfortable with these people.

"All right now, black folks," the voice continued, "while our band sets up, we want all our men to give five dollars each! Politics cost money! Here's mine!" They began to move. I turned and looked at Evers.

He stood, hands on hips, motionless, scanning the room— hair cut short and neatly cropped all around with no part, wearing a thin mustache, his age hard to guess because the hair had no white in it, his skin a smooth, deep black. Even from thirty feet away, the movement of his eyes was immediately noticeable: the whites were actually yellow, with a fluid motion to them that made the pupils glimmer as he peered beyond the podium. A lump the size of a fingernail caused a flutter of his right eyelid when he was not speaking. He was just about my height, six feet, but weighed close to 230 pounds. His shoulders were packed like cement blocks into his shirt and his biceps looked like tree trunks. Though his belly was big, he was more thick than fat, built solid as a ship.

He turned to one side. His shirt was a deeper blue where the sweat ran down his back: it looked like a butterfly inkblot. He turned toward us and loosened his tie. His face glistened with sweat. "C'mon, black folks. We gotta support our local candidates. You cain't win nothin' in politics if you ain't got no financial support!" The crowd echoed a chorus of "Amen!"

He ran a handkerchief over his forehead and squinted. "Where's Ed Cole?" he said in a loud whisper away from the microphone. "My campaign manager, Ed Cole. Anybody seen him?" Ed was already at his side.

The second man to put his five dollars on the table was Representative Robert Clark of Ebenezer, the next town over. He was the first black man elected to the Mississippi Legislature since Reconstruction. None of the white legislators would sit next to him. Polite applause rippled from the crowd. Everyone in Lexington knew Representative Clark.

"All right, now, black folks. Representative Clark and I have given our five dollars. Now you men gotta give yours. If you ain't a man don't bother comin'."

I stared at Evers in awe as men roused themselves to give money. These people had no money, yet they were falling into line to contribute five dollars each. It was almost as if his words had truth and meaning simply because it was he who spoke them.

The men fell into single file, shy and almost childlike at first. They were old, their brows furrowed and parched. The first man who stood up had silver hair and light brown skin.

He took his hat from his knee and self-importantly placed it on his fuzzy head. He buttoned the dark coat, which did not match his khakis. Smiling sociably to the men pressed behind him, he tipped forward in a slow gait, pausing only to nod at a tiny woman curled in the last seat of the row. Pushing himself forward, he arrived at the card table. Carefully he removed a chunky wallet and, after inspecting its contents for a half minute, withdrew a five dollar bill and placed it on the center of the table. More men fell into single file, some reluctantly, after others had chided. The first man returned to his seat, ever so slowly, with his ear bent to the floor as though there was something beneath it or within the humming of the crowd that he was trying to hear.

Evers swept a beefy forearm over the crowd, speaking from the edge of the stage without a microphone. "C'mon now, Holmes County! This ain't civil rights no more. Y'all got your local candidates. They gotta buy pla-cards, bumper stickers—that stuff ain't free! Ask Rep'sentative Clark, he'll tell you. Prayin' and marchin' ain't gonna get elected officials for *Holmes* County!"

The first man in the next row moved a little faster and those behind him hurried. The next man's lower lip quivered and his whiskers looked like pins sticking from a cushion. The man behind him was huge and heavy and smoked a green cigar: he laughed hard and his shoulders heaved. The man behind *him* had coal-black hair that was wet from sweat and looked like oil. The last man on the row was laughing so hard he began to cough and pound on his chest.

"Now the ladies! *Wives* of our men. C'mon now, wives and mommas—and girl friends, too!" A peal of giggles swept the room. "Naw, naw. The ladies have to come, too. We ain't gonna have no discriminatin'. They vote jus' like us men do. But since plenny o' you ain't got no jobs, ladies, we'll say you give one dollar." Lining the base of the stage were the young blacks, who found great humor in the call for girl friends. I noticed them only now for the first time, about one hundred of them, mostly adolescents and younger. They wore neutral-colored clothes, no dashikis or bright colors; Lexington was poor. Nearly all had Afro bushes. A few were my own age.

And so the ladies came. The first one was a huge soul, with breasts the size of basketballs. She panted as she walked. The dollar bill made a snapping noise when it hit the table. Evers said, "Now *there's* a sister!" The young blacks roared. "Look at that lady. She sho' 'nuf want that political power!" A girl yelled, "Right on, Brother!"

The band was playing "Treat Her Like a Lady," and from the way Dwight played the organ and sang you would never have guessed he was blind. Some of the young blacks were dancing, their Afros bobbing with the music. Evers moved into the crowd of older folks. One after another he met the men and women in the front rows, and by the time he was in the middle seats everyone had returned. He put his hand on an old man's shoulder and whispered something in his ear. They both laughed uproariously at the secret jest between them. The next man was younger, in his late thirties. He jumped to his feet and talked hurriedly, gesticulating with his hand. Evers began to laugh, loud and deep and straight from his stomach. He slapped a soul-shake on the man and they were immediately thick as thieves. With his left hand he embraced the woman sitting in the next chair, and kissed the hand of the next woman. He was like a finger on the keys of a typewriter: he touched them and they moved. They flocked to him like steel filings drawn to a magnet. He was laughing, mock-frowning, nodding intently. He hugged an old woman and then he hugged her husband.

The crowd began to disperse and I was suddenly aware of the person next to me. It was the lady with the basketball breasts, or someone looking very much like her. "How do you do?" she said. "I'm so *glad* to meet you."

"I'm glad to meet you, too," I said cheerfully, though a little unsure of myself.

"Are you a reporter?"

"No, ma'am, I'm a volunteer for Mayor Evers."

Her eyes lit up and she put her hands to her mouth and "oohed."

A hand was tugging at my coat. It belonged to a man with somber eyes deepset behind bifocals. "I wanted to shake your hand, suh. Martin's my name."

I swallowed. "How do you do? Please don't call me 'sir.' " As the campaign developed and I began to understand people, I would say "Jason Berry's my name" before black folks could say their names to me. The effect of introducing myself to them made them more at ease. They had been conditioned to tell whites their first names, since a white would never call them Mr. or Mrs. It was an understood rule among all campaign workers that we use courtesy titles.

The band stopped playing; I was introduced to two security men and together we packed equipment into a trailer. We were the last three out of the gym. The policeman at the door nodded pleasantly to me. Ed was conferring with two teenagers outside the bar and grill across the street where everyone had crowded in to eat. He called me aside.

"Did you see Hazel Smith?"

"No," I said. "Where was she?"

"Standing in the back, with a Catholic priest. They came in late. The priest is a real good guy. He's from Chicago. Hazel asked The Mayor after the speech to endorse her to the black folks."

"What did he say?"

"He said, 'We'll see, Hazel.' " Ed fished tobacco from a pouch and lit a handsome pipe. "The Mayor's inside. I told him we got a new volunteer. He wants to see you."

The bar was an intensification of the gym: darker lit, black people eating and drinking, younger ones dancing to a

James Brown song that blared through the rest of the din. I
saw a hand beckon to me. It belonged to Evers, who was
seated at a small table eating fried chicken. Two old men sat
with him; a security guard stood next to the table. He motioned to me again, quickly, and I walked across the room. I
sat for about five minutes while Evers listened to the story
of one of the men. He shook hands with me, listening to the
old man.

He was not concerned with me at first. He nodded as the
old man spoke, looked around the room periodically, and
nibbled at his drumstick. He seemed to be listening to the
man, but his eyes darted continuously to other parts of the
room. He ran a piece of crust over the chicken to remove
pepper. The music wailed on and wormed its way inside my
head.

Suddenly he whipped around, eyes squarely on me as he
lifted the drumstick to his lips. "You Jason Berry?"

The question caught me unprepared for some reason.
"Oh, yes. Yes, sir."

He chuckled. "You sure?"

I grinned. "Yeah. That's one thing I'm sure about."

He turned back to the old man. He was forty-eight and I
was twenty-two. I couldn't get over him: he was constantly
in motion—hands, head, eyes, all moving incessantly. The
old men, the bodyguard, myself, the opening-closing of the
door seemed to be in orbit around him. The only stable factor in the room was the plate of chicken.

My knowledge of him was rudimentary; most of it I had
learned reading his autobiography, *Evers*, which had been
dictated to a tape recorder and edited by Grace Halsell. He
was the first of his race to be elected mayor of a biracial
Mississippi town. Fayette (population 1,800) had never seen
a mayoralty election like the one in 1969. Incumbent R. J.
Allen—nicknamed "Turnip Green" because he won black
votes by giving folks vegetables—had been in office eight-

een years. He was not prepared for Evers' sweeping voter registration drive and house-to-house canvass, literally dragging black folks to the polls. Not only did Evers win, but he took in an all-black slate of five aldermen with him. The rest of Mississippi was enraged, but from outside the state came enthusiastic response. President Nixon sent a congratulatory letter, as did Hubert Humphrey, LBJ, Edmund Muskie, Edward Kennedy, and others. The inauguration took place on a blistering July afternoon. Fayette, once an irrelevant, dusty town along Highway 61, was now a symbol of the New South. The town was deluged by reporters and a galaxy of famous people who came for the ceremonies. Ramsey Clark, Paul O'Dwyer, Julian Bond, and Shirley MacLaine were among the notables who cheered the new mayor as he took office.

The celebrities left, the work began, and Mayor Evers found that Turnip Green Allen and the aldermen who had left had purposely spent every last cent in the town treasury. Fayette was broke. Evers made an appeal on national television, telling of his town's trouble. Within two weeks checks and contributions had come in from across the country. With the help of a New York NAACP fund-raiser, Gilbert Jonas, Evers founded the Medgar Evers Foundation, geared to raise money for a health-care clinic, multipurpose recreation complex, and day-care center. Evers became an aggressive lobbyist, and HEW, HUD, and various foundations soon made investments in the town. By 1971 three factories had been built. To whites who decried "outside influences" Evers said philosophically, "So what if the Kennedys or Rockefellers decide to help us out by buildin' a plant down here or givin' a grant—that means jobs. And Fayette's poor."

In the two years since he had come to office he had resurrected Fayette from a Klan-dominated, dirt-poor town to a safe and orderly place for blacks as well as whites. Speeding laws were religiously enforced. It was against the law to carry a gun in public now. And when children were caught playing hooky, they *and* their parents came to court. Fayette was the only town in the state with a compulsory school-attendance law. Unemployment was down 30 percent from its 1969 level, and the economy was at its highest point ever.

Fayette was no utopia, of course. When Evers was elected, a sign was placed in the window of a restaurant: "Every cent spent by a nigger to be donated to the Ku Klux Klan." Early in the Evers Administration a Klansman from Tupelo drove into Fayette with a trunkload of rifles, intent on killing the town's famous mayor. A tip from an anonymous caller—whom Evers believes was the man's wife—was passed on from The Mayor to the FBI, and the man was caught. Evers went to visit the man in the jail cell to show that he bore no malice. He said to the man, "Listen, I don't know your story, but why don't we jus' sit down and talk it over. You don't know me and I don't know you. How come you'd want to shoot me? I got nothin' against you . . . what do you wanna kill me for?" The man had glared at him and begrudgingly said, "You're fair, but I hate your guts."

One white woman had managed to profit by all of the changes in Fayette. Marie Walker, editor of the Fayette *Chronicle*, attacked Evers in her weekly paper. Her circulation outside Jefferson County shot up quickly. Mrs. Walker, ironically, had sold some land to Charles Evers. She and her husband, Jimmy, a colonel on Mississippi Governor John Bell Williams' honorary staff, had had The Mayor to dinner to finalize the sale. Evers was fond of the Walkers, however, and he always kidded the editor: "Marie, honey, you write all them bad things about me, but that's all right. Jus' keep my name in there. I need all the press I can get. Besides, where would black folks be if there hadn't been any reporters coverin' the civil rights movement!"

The six years preceding his election in Fayette saw him rise to national prominence through the civil rights movement. On the other hand, he also had money, something not usually associated with civil rights leaders. With some dismay, a white Mississippi friend of mine sympathetic to Evers' struggle had told of his accumulations in Fayette: a restaurant, lounge, gas station, hotel, and shopping complex. Later I learned he had additional outside business interests. To my surprise, I also discovered that he neither smoke, drank, nor gambled.

Before his involvement in the civil rights movement, Charles Evers was a Chicago gangster. He had moved there from his native Mississippi in 1955; whites had financially ruined him after he started voter registration work. In his autobiography, he told of numbers-running and of being proprietor of a brothel. But when Medgar was assassinated in 1963, he was so traumatized that he returned immediately and took over his brother's job as Field Secretary of the Mississippi NAACP. He discussed this in his book, too:

> After the funeral I went back to Mississippi. I haven't thought of living anyplace else since. I was born here, and I'll die here. . . .
>
> Secretly, I wanted to do what he [Medgar] and I had planned to do a long time ago [as children]. That was to organize a Mau Mau gang to kill two whites for every black they killed. I was going to do it myself. I planned to sort of float around in Mississippi and kill a white man once a week, in a different part of the state. . . . I was going to kill one big racist in every county.
>
> I secured some equipment, several guns, and I looked around. But something kept telling me, "That's not the way, Charles, that's not the way." This battle was going on within myself. Every day I'd go to the

office and sit at Medgar's desk; it was like he was there with me, and something kept saying "Medgar wouldn't want it like that. That's not the way, that's not the way." I began to get busy. Gradually I got away from the idea of killing white people physically. I decided I could kill them better by doing what Medgar had been doing. And that's when I got busy getting people registered. . . .

Medgar's death made one thing clear to me. I had to change Mississippi not by shouting at people, but by giving blacks the courage to get registered and start voting. I followed in Medgar's footsteps.

A Washington attorney who knew Evers had warned me before I left that working for him would be a struggle in itself. "He is a remarkable man," the lawyer had said, "but you have to take him on his terms. He is dictatorial and *you* listen to *him*. He is a complex blend of capitalist and Christian. There've been some idealists who couldn't handle him."

I watched Evers nod to the old man. His eyes continued to probe, search, and notice forms and movements around him. He continually glanced at the door. Whether it had been to check for Chicago thugs or Klansmen, I felt he had always looked at doors.

His eyes danced. I saw myself in the reflection of his pupils. He said, "Where you from, son?"

"New Orleans."

He put down the chicken and looked at me incredulously. "You got to be kiddin'." He laughed and shook his head. Then he looked at me sternly. "You wrote that press release this afternoon?"

"Yes . . . yes, sir."

"I heard it up here on the radio. You done any political work before?"

"Well, I worked part-time for a senator when I went to school in Washington."

"Who?"

"Lee Metcalf, Montana."

"I never heard of him. I tell you who I like. That Mondale. He's got a lot of black folks workin' on his staff. He's from Minnesota."

He turned away and started talking to the man next to him again. Then a lady came over and told him about her daughter having problems at Jackson State. After five minutes he was back to me.

"I don't know anything about you, son, but if you want to help, come on aboard. One thing you always gotta keep in mind. I'm the candidate and you do what the candidate says. When you're the candidate and I'm workin' for you, I'll do what you say. Down here, you follow me. You can see our office. All I got is Ed and two secretaries and my security men. We're all just learnin'. Politics ain't somethin' we gotta lot of experience in." He chuckled. "Yeah, but b'lieve me when I tell you—this campaign's already makin' white folks confused!"

He spoke seriously. "Lemme make one thing clear. You ain't gonna be givin' no directions. When I campaigned for Bobby Kennedy out in California I did whatever he wanted. I took directions from him even though he was my best friend. That's the way it is. You follow the candidate. Always. What kind of experience you got?"

"Well, I've worked in press . . ."

"P.R. That's somethin' I got to get plenty of. Every day. Write those press releases, radio statements. Set up press conferences. Feed tapes to the radio. Jus' keep my name in there, every day."

He started on another piece of chicken. "How much money you need?"

I was stunned. "You mean salary?"

"Yeah, you can't work free, can you?"

"No, I guess . . . well, I could do it on $75 a week."

He nodded. "All right. When my wife Nan comes into the office tomorrow, you and Ed sit down with her and get Social Security straightened out. We'll get you six bits a week. I sure as hell ain't got much more, though. I've already spent $10,000 of my own money, and this's only the first week of June."

So I became press secretary. The Mayor thereafter referred to me as his P.R. man. I sat there while he finished his chicken. The old man was starting another story. It would take Evers a week to remember my name.

When the last piece was bone, Evers stood up and announced abruptly, "Let's roll!" Within a minute, his car, three security men, the van with the band equipment, and Ed's car with me and Dwight and Robert in it shot off into the night. I told Dwight and Robert they sounded good; Dwight thanked me for helping load the band equipment. Ten miles out I realized I hadn't eaten since noon. But in another minute I was asleep and didn't wake up until we got back to Jackson.

CHAPTER

2

Campaign headquarters was a storefront fittingly located where the Jackson business district ended and the black community began. It was walking distance from Steven's Kitchen, famous for soul food, as well as from the Governor's Mansion. We outgrew the office by mid-June, but stayed there, cramped, nonetheless. A dilapidated bar occupied the store front adjacent to us. Every morning an old woman swept it out as we came to work, the smell of bourbon and burnt chicken wafting out into the sidewalk. Across the street was a deserted filling station where every morning twenty black men lined the curb, waiting for cars to slow down, hoping for a white man needing someone for a day's labor. Occasionally a young office worker slowed down, and when men approached, he roared off, howling with laughter.

We had a large main office with five desks. There were three back offices. The first housed the statewide long-distance phone, the WATS line, and a small library of research material. The middle office was Ed Cole's, his desk wedged between the walls. The Mayor had the last office; it was the largest. It had an air conditioner, wall-to-wall carpet, and paneled walls on which hung a few awards; otherwise, it was modestly furnished. The largest item was a life-size photograph of his brother Medgar.

We hung posters on the walls and in the windows of the office. One sign read: "Don't Vote for a White Man. Don't Vote for a Black Man. Vote for the Best Man. Vote Evers for Governor." A smaller poster, the picture of a withered brown hand placing a ballot in a box, read: "Hands That Pick Cotton Now Can Pick Elected Officials."

There were four desks in the main office besides mine. Magnolia Osborne, a beautiful black woman of twenty-eight, occupied one. Magnolia had just returned from the West Coast. Divorced, she lived in Jackson, the town where she grew up, with her four-year-old son. Her best friend was Lois Williams, twenty-five, mother of three. Lois had light brown skin, moving The Mayor to remark jovially, "That's all right, honey, that light skin means you got Choctaw blood. An' black folks and Injuns got lots in common."

Ed Davis, twenty-eight, nicknamed "Squeaky," was an advance man and security man—in the press's vernacular, a bodyguard. At least two men accompanied Evers wherever he went. With an average of five threatening letters reaching him each week in Fayette—letters routinely picked up by the FBI—no one doubted the need for security. Squeaky was six feet four and had been a Special Services medic in Vietnam. A champion tennis player before the Army, he was now going to Jackson State part-time. Richard Woodard, "Woody," was Director of Public Safety in Fayette and was The Mayor's Chief of Security. He was a forty-five-year-old New York policeman on a one-year leave. Martin Lias, a brawny former all-state linebacker from Fayette High, was The Mayor's driver. The three men wore guns under their coats, but their personalities didn't fit their roles; they were easily the most congenial members of the campaign staff.

Of the whites on staff, only Charles Ramberg had worked in Mississippi before. He had spent a year in Fayette before his last semester at Georgetown Law School. He once said to me, "I drove down in summer of 1970 just to sort of see where my head was, and I ended up staying a year." He received a small salary as an administrative aide. Ramberg did our scheduling in the campaign. He had a disarming candor that delighted everyone, probably because it was reminiscent of The Mayor's.

But Ramberg was always beautiful in the way in which he dealt with black folks. Old people came into the office because he took time to help with their legal problems. He had a slow, direct, honest approach that set everyone at ease. On a regular basis he directed black folks to Legal Services and Civil Rights offices in Jackson.

Alec Berezin, twenty-three, a small, solidly built law student from Cleveland, arrived four days after his phone call to "Mr. Evers, or anybody else in the office who needs an advance man." Alec had just finished his first year at Case Western Law, and had worked in Howard Metzenbaum's Ohio senatorial campaign in 1970.

Later we were joined by two of the most colorful people in the campaign: Joe Huttie, a twenty-eight-year-old white Northwestern journalism MA, and Barbara Phillips, a black just graduated from Macalester College. Barb had spent the early part of the summer at Saul Alinsky's Institute on Community Organization in Chicago. Huttie was six feet four, with blond hair drooped over his eyes; Barb was petite and shapely, with an Afro and wire-rims. I think more than any two people they typified the variety in our campaign: she a black Memphian schooled in community organizing; he a Northern white who knew how to coordinate a media campaign.

Fund-raising was done by a New Yorker named Gil Jonas. He and Evers had met through the NAACP in the mid-sixties; Jonas had helped in the 1969 Fayette mayoralty election, and also raised funds for the Medgar Evers Foundation. He was National Coordinator for the existent but largely symbolic Committee to Elect Charles Evers Governor of Mississippi. It included senators Kennedy, Humphrey, Bayh, and Muskie, national civil rights figures, prominent liberals like Paul O'Dwyer, and Black Caucus members.

The key member of the office was Ed Cole. He was the "in" to black Mississippi. If you said "McComb" he would state the name of the contact in that town, "Harry Bowie," and give you Reverend Bowie's number off the top of his head. He kept the numbers he didn't know in a fat notebook. Ed called us together each morning to discuss the day's work, and we evaluated it with him most evenings. He spent roughly seven hours a day on the phone, conferring with county contacts. He gave researchers important background information on Mississippi.

Closer to the rest of us in age than Evers, Ed Cole gave the campaign a special meaning, for he had a deep stake in Mississippi. Ed had grown up in Cannonsburg, a tiny Jefferson County town midway between Fayette and the Mississippi River. His family, he once told me, accounted for more than half of the registered voters in the town. His childhood in the fifties had been difficult, including the accident in which his leg had been severed. He had worked his way through Jackson State, and had also been "a body for a lot of the demonstrations and marches." After graduation he decided against law school, and worked for the Child Development Group of Mississippi. He had spent a summer at Harvard, but, as always, he went back to Mississippi. By 1970 he had been hired by SEDFRE—Scholarship, Education, Defense Fund for Racial Equality—and became an economic development counsultant in the rural southwest region of the state, where he was born and raised. He often wrote proposals for Fayette's grant applications. The Mayor freely admitted that Ed Cole was "the one person I'd want to be mayor if it couldn't be me." Ed had taken a leave of absence from SEDFRE to run the campaign. His wife, Kitty, frequently dragged him out of the office to have lunch. "You all have to make sure he *eats*," she said. We started fetching hamburgers for him in July. Nevertheless, he lost ten pounds.

It was understandable, I suppose, that Ed and The Mayor had different philosophies about the way the campaign should be run. As The Mayor put it, "This campaign's gonna shake everybody up!" Which meant traveling across the state in motorcades, speaking in black communities, seeking press and media exposure—in short, showing black folks that he was waging a serious, professional campaign, attempting to inject a political spirit into blacks so that the counties would come together by November and get out the vote. Jackson staff members routinely visited county meetings.

But Ed, and soon the rest of us, realized that The Mayor's approach left the odds stacked against us, for given the projected budget of $120,000, it left no room for the hiring of thirty skilled organizers like Barb Phillips or the SNCC workers of the sixties. A good organizer lived and worked in a community, went to church even if an atheist, and built a grass-roots canvass for election day. Voter education classes had to be conducted; illiterates shown how to vote; sample ballots distributed; a map divided into sections, with one person responsible for each small area; car pools and baby-sitters arranged; everybody taken to the polls on election day. This was going to be a Herculean task. Often it meant people were going to have to walk from homes, fields where they worked, or filling stations, across the plantation or center of town into the polling place, which was usually a white man's store where everyone knew who they were and where whites eyed them menacingly. Voting had a history of physical and economic reprisals. The ballot in the South had come through suffering and blood. Ed called the fear element "The Plantation Psychology."

To get the movers cost money and we had little of that. By mid-June, even before our kickoff rally The Mayor had spent $15,000 of his own money. Money went for office rent, basic operating expenses, rented cars for travel since flying was too expensive, and salaries averaging $60 weekly. Our hopes for community organization rested with the volunteers. The volunteers were stunning people. Our own age or younger, they were peripatetic philosophers who had grown up in the age of technocracy and Vietnam, packed their knapsacks and hitchhiked from all over the country to Mississippi. This was one of the few places where if one could *do* something it might effect a meaningful change by November 3. By summer's end over seventy kids had come and done voter registration work. On a frustrating day one had only to look up and see a new volunteer reading the Tolkien trilogy, waiting to see Ed, and it cleared the head.

But it was doubtful whether the small numbers of volunteers could forge a bond among black voters and surmount a century of oppression. More than 250,000 voters were necessary if Evers was to make a creditable showing and if blacks were going to be elected to local and county offices. Our campaign, without vital community organizers, simply quit thinking about the things we lacked: money, people, more volunteers, billboards. We resolved early to work twelve hours a day seven days a week, and we never let up.

Undeniably, each of us had his or her personal sense of mission, but no one belittled the importance of the individual job to be done. When we overdramatized our personal roles, The Mayor set things in order. Whenever he came through the front door, his first words were always "Everybody workin'?" Then, shaking hands with everyone, he kissed a secretary on the cheek and said, "Darlin', you workin' for me today? I can't be no governor if my secretaries don't keep the office runnin' right!" And then he called us in for a staff meeting.

"All right now," he said, "we all gotta understand this"— pointing his finger at each of us quickly—"you, you, you, you, and *you*—all you got your own jobs to do. Make sure you do 'em. Everyone has a different job and no job's more important than the other! I'm the candidate but I can't go nowhere wi'out my staff. But if y'all ain't gonna do things my way, *leave!*

"No one does advance work 'cept for Elix [Alec] and Squeaky. Elix, you're *advance!* You don't go messin' aroun' with none o' that P.R. Jason, you stick with P.R.—and no advancin'! Now, Squeaky and Elix, when y'all go, go together. We want black and white everywhere. And Elix, it don't make no difference if you're Jewish, 'cuz you're white first, and that's what folks notice.

"An' don't forget police escorts. We wanna start gettin' escorts in every town. I'm a candidate like all the rest of 'em, and when my motorcade comes in, I want the police there to make sure nothin' goes wrong. If a town says no, tell 'em we'll call NBC news on 'em!" The police escort was important to black folks because the all-white Highway Patrol in Mississippi and the local police symbolized the sadism and brutality of the last decade; law officers had worked in collusion with volatile whites in many areas during the movement. In 1964 police in Philadelphia, Mississippi, conspired with Klansmen in the murders of Michael Schwerner, James Chaney, and Andrew Goodman. A police escort for the Evers motorcade was a symbolic drama of the changing times. By midsummer most towns had become cooperative.

Whipping his head to look at another part of the room, he

said, "Lois!" And then lowering his voice, "Now, Lois here
is our financial secretary. She takes care of books-and-
buttons money. *No one* 'cept Lois has books-and-buttons
money." On campaign trips at least two car trunks held the
recently published autobiography *Evers*. The books sold for
$6.00—"that's a dollar less than store price, black folks, so
y'all buy 'em cheap." Campaign buttons sold for $1.00.

"Everyone helps Lois sell, but she keeps the money and
gives it to me. And when y'all sell, sell good! Can't run a
campaign if we ain't got no money.

"An' Magnolia, she's our main secretary, keeps the office
runnin' right . . . and Ed, Ed's my campaign manager. He's
in charge o' seein' that *everything* runs right. And I'm the
candidate—you gotta remember your candidate!"

He also made great sport of his candidacy. "Martin an' I
parked on Capitol Street today and these two businessmen
were standin' in front of us. They didn' know *what* to do.
Afraid to shake hands and afraid to run away. Yeah, we got
this boat some shook up! Got plenty white folks *confused*!"
Evers *was* shaking people up, for he was taking Mississippi
on in politics, not in civil rights. To whites he was alarmingly legitimate.

The Mayor had expansive ideas about the governor's race,
but, as with much of his thought, his perception of how to
enact concepts was remarkably small. It was nothing for
him to emerge from his office and say, "All right, Jason, we
don't have enough pictures up."

"But Mayor, we don't have money. I haven't even talked
to the billboard company."

"Naw, naw. I'm not talkin' about billboards, but posters.
Take forty posters like we got on the walls and go into the
black community . . . go walk down Farish Street and pin
'em up!"

"But I'm cutting radio actualities off the tapes from your
last speech to give to the news shows . . ."

"Oh." He would pause, move, and his voice would resurface elsewhere. "Lois? Lois! Where's Lois?"

Lois, shutting the bathroom door behind her, running into the office: "Yes, Mayor? I'm right here."

"Honey, you and Magnolia get posters and go pin 'em up all down Farish Street."

"But, Mayor, I'm countin' books-and-buttons money, and Magnolia's doin' a stencil . . ."

"Mmm . . . all right. Okay . . . Elix? Elix! Where's Elix?"

"He's out advancin', Mayor."

By now his mind would be off Farish Street, concerned about money for billboards. Before shutting his door, he would call out, "All right! But when Elix returns from advancin', y'all tell him to get down to Farish Street!"

The Mayor was in the Jackson office only three days a week during June and July. He campaigned on weekends and usually two weeknights in early summer. The rest of the time he was in Fayette or flying to New York, Washington, or another place raising money for Fayette projects, or giving a speech, the honorarium going into the impoverished campaign chest. A 7 A.M. flight meant he was off to lobby in Washington or Atlanta for some program. And he always attended the Thursday night mass meetings in Fayette. He *ran* Fayette, too, knowing everyone by name and knowing where each of his staffers was and what he was doing. No one acted without consulting him. If some minor crisis arose while he was in Jackson, off he and Martin drove to Fayette.

Everyone called him "The Mayor." As Charlie Ramberg put it, "It's a cultural thing. If he was only a civil rights leader he wouldn't mind being called Charles. But he's an elected official, and for years whites have called blacks by their first names. It was just another reminder of white superiority. Now, of course, courtesy titles mean a great deal to blacks. Things have changed since civil rights . . . besides, he *is* The Mayor." Even his wife referred to him as The Mayor.

The Mayor lived in a small apartment in the Medgar Evers Shopping Center in Fayette. His wife and children lived in a large house with a pool in a fashionable black area of Jackson. He hadn't wanted his family in Jefferson County during the dangerous days when he began organizing. His legal residence was Fayette, where he spent most working days; the rest of the time he was home in Jackson.

It was understood from the outset of the campaign that The Mayor was running as titular head of a slate of three hundred blacks seeking election to local, county, and state offices. His candidacy was geared to get the black vote out to the polls. History warned it was going to be difficult. On paper, blacks had roughly 37 percent of the vote; however, laying a political base would be an enormous task. Only since 1965 and passage of the Voting Rights Act had black Mississippians gained suffrage. On the other hand, the all-white Mississippi Democrats had been holding elections for a century. The last major role blacks had played was in the election of 1875. Reconstruction had left Mississippi destitute: the agrarian economy faltered; small farmers and planters sold out; sharecroppers multiplied; and the standard of living was rock-bottom.

Cotton-king Democrats resurrected the indomitable spirit of the region in 1875, crushing blacks and Republicans in a sweeping election day victory abetted by widespread violence and intimidation at the polls. The next fifteen years saw blacks purged from the offices they held, harassed, and lynched to ensure disenfranchisement. In 1890 in Jackson the official Constitution of the State of Mississippi was ratified by delegates to the constitutional convention who themselves declared it law; there was no popular vote. The

Jackson *Clarion-Ledger* explained the popular view: "The negro must be returned to his position of inferiority. We must pass such laws as will insure this. He must be made to *feel* his inferiority." The key passage of the document was a suffrage clause making each prospective voter read and interpret a section of the constitution. The white chancery clerk would decide whether one passed or failed. Despite protests from various newspapers and even certain delegates—the argument being that poor whites would have as much trouble as blacks reading the clause—the measure was adopted. The Supreme Court upheld its legality that year, commenting that the suffrage requirements "reach wicked and vicious black men as well as wicked and vicious white men." In 1962, when John Doar of Robert Kennedy's Justice Department brought lawyers into Mississippi to commence litigation against court clerks for denying blacks their suffrage, the men found less than 10,000 blacks registered in a state with over 500,000 eligible.

It wasn't until 1964, when the civil rights movement reached its crest, that the ancient system slowly and painfully began to change. Lynchings, bombings, fires, and the murders of men such as Medgar Evers had made blacks understand how deadly important their freedom was. For the civil rights workers and sharecroppers in Mississippi, there was no more poignant moment in the historic Freedom Summer of 1964 than when an indomitable black woman named Fannie Lou Hamer spoke on national television in Atlantic City at the Democratic National Convention, testifying for the Mississippi Freedom Democratic Party. The FDP had been the brainchild of the SNCC and CORE workers who staffed the Mississippi Summer Project.° The

° The Mississippi Summer Project was a community program in which white and black civil rights workers lived with black families. They organized voter registration drives and they conducted Freedom Schools, teaching black children a wide range of topics not covered in black public schools. Civil rights workers in-challenge party contested the seating of the delegation of whites from the state that viciously denied black suffrage. The small, heavy-set Mrs. Hamer told the world what it was like to live in Senator Eastland's Sunflower County, where blacks starved in winter, were paid fifty cents an hour in summer for planting cotton, and were cheated by whites from the moment of birth. And with an eloquence enhanced by twenty summers' work in a cotton field, she pleaded for the right to represent *her* Mississippi as a delegate.

The convention at that point went into a minor uproar. Telegrams poured in from across the country calling for expulsion of the Mississippi Democrats. State delegations began pledging themselves to the FDP. But Lyndon Johnson had problems with expulsion of the Mississippi Democrats. If Eastland's party was ousted, Johnson might see a walkout by other southern delegations, as had occurred in the 1948 Dixiecrat revolt. For a President from Texas up for election, that would not look good. To compound the difficulties, the Republicans had just nominated a man who was perhaps the most right-wing candidate of the century. Barry Goldwater had staunchly voted against Johnson's civil rights bill and firmly stated that he wanted to bomb Hanoi.

Hubert Humphrey, an early FDP supporter, was Johnson's rumored choice for Vice President. He delivered Johnson's plan to the FDP and to the Regular Mississippi Democrats. The gesture made both sides mutually bitter. Two FDP delegates, Aaron Henry and the white chaplain from black Tougaloo College, Reverend Ed King, were offered seats as at-large delegates. This was quite a blow to the regular party, but the FDP took it even harder. They turned the plan down and embarrassed Johnson by walking out of the convention singing "We Shall Overcome," with network

---

structed every black family about the new opportunities under the Civil Rights Act. The Summer Project was the first loosely structured attempt to see blacks utilize the new law and to improve their lives.

correspondents following them to the Boardwalk, where they commenced a vigil. Bob Moses, director of the Mississippi Summer Project, explained, "The FDP delegates were the only people at the whole convention who were free in any meaningful sense of the word. The President told everybody else what to do. All I cared about was the insides of those sixty-eight delegates and the future of the FDP in Mississippi. It wasn't my responsibility to worry about Humphrey or the backlash. We couldn't let the others single out two people and appoint them our spokesmen. The whole point of the Freedom Democratic Party is to teach the lowest sharecropper that he knows better than the biggest leader. . . ."

Eastland and the Mississippi Democrats were seated. The convention nominated Johnson, who won. Mississippi voted a thundering 87 percent for Goldwater.

Charles Evers was never on good terms with the FDP. In 1963 he took over his brother Medgar's work as State NAACP Field Secretary, but he soon began to clash with SNCC. Medgar, at the time of his death, was moving increasingly closer to the philosophy of the SNCC and CORE activists. They sought a sense of community identity, of blacks coming to grips with their own problems and aggressively working and demonstrating as a unified body. SNCC was also deeply opposed to the Vietnam War. SNCC workers were firm anti-capitalists as well. Evers was soon at odds with them. He feared the stigma of communism would be attached to the efforts and thus endanger future work. A bedrock capitalist, Evers felt that economic independence, achieved through boycotts, would be the way to suffrage and political power. Evers had wanted to build the movement around the middle-class blacks and reach outward into the community; SNCC workers started with the teenagers and built up. As a former civil rights leader living in Jackson in 1971 had said, "Charles had a different philosophy from us. He wanted demonstrations, but they had to be respectable. He saw our movement as anti-middle class, anti-respectable, anti-influencing whites. We advocated an ethnic sense of dependence on the black community itself, not to try to imitate whites. The kids understood it best, and they couldn't lose jobs they didn't already have. Evers wanted folks to look to the established black middle class. The trouble was that the black bourgeoisie—the preachers, ministers, and all—were scared they'd lose their jobs if they took any bold steps. They needed constant prodding from people like him; we [SNCC] provided the bodies for the demonstrations. His approach meant that a dominant leader was needed, and that's what we in SNCC didn't want. We wanted the movement, the people themselves, to be the focal point. What happened, of course, is that the movement eventually died. He stayed around . . . he became the focal point. Maybe he was right. Maybe the folks never could have looked to themselves as a movement of force with strength. It worked for a while, though. . . ."

For the FDP, politics, like civil rights work, came not in lengthy planning sessions but in hard emotional outbursts. In January 1965 they challenged the seating of the Mississippi congressional delegation, claiming blacks had been categorically denied the right to vote. Although the challenge failed, the attempt, along with the violent voter drive in Selma, Alabama, dramatized the plight of southern blacks, and the Voting Rights Act was passed.

In the spring of 1965 a white SNCC field secretary named Hunter Morey had organized groups across the state in an attempt to get an FDP charter in the National Young Democrats. This would give the FDP legitimacy with the national party. But the FDP met with more opposition. SNCC's bitterness about the war had intensified and that sat poorly with the Democratic National Committee. Then a handful of white moderates sympathetic to the cause joined forces with Evers and the NAACP; Evers' forces felt that most Mississippi blacks were concerned more about their own struggle than about a war in Asia. Organized labor, never a power in Mississippi, was at least on amiable terms with the NAACP, and the AFL-CIO joined the fray. The FDP lost the charter. Hodding Carter, III, liberal editor of the *Delta-Democrat Times*, was one white who became an Evers ally. Son of the former editor of the paper, Hodding III followed his father's ideological leanings. Unlike his father, who fought the Klan and white Mississippi only in print, young Hodding became politically involved as well. He began working with Evers in 1965 and later commented on this first involvement in Mississippi politics: "The Vietnam War was really a surface issue. What it boiled down to was a power struggle over party leadership between us—the white liberal, NAACP, labor crowd—and the SNCC kids." Hunter Morey later observed, "What happened was that we got shellacked."

SNCC's potency in Mississippi reached its peak in 1966 when John Lewis was ousted as chairman in an election; the office had traditionally been conferred. In 1970 John Lewis remarked to Pat Watters (in *Down to Now*), that "some people . . . were raising legitimate questions about where SNCC should go—how it should relate to the third world, to the black movement, whether nonviolence was still relevant. . . ." SNCC's new approach under Lewis' successor, Stokely Carmichael, surfaced explosively in the James Meredith march from Memphis to Jackson in late summer, 1966. Meredith was shot in the beginning of the march and SNCC forces undertook the task of completing the march. SNCC wanted to dramatize the organization's disgust for the "liberal" Democratic Party, which it saw as exploitative and racist; whites were thus excluded from the march. A new phrase, "Black Power," emerged; it was to have deep repercussions in the American psyche.

By 1968 the civil rights movement was dead and buried. The SNCC workers were gone; with them left the community sense of identity, the elemental spirit that had moved blacks to work as a cohesive group to see demands met. But while the organization, the movement-as-people philosophy, had diminished, a new political coalition had been forged. A challenge contingent from Mississippi again went to the Democratic National Convention; however, the FDP did not control the delegation. Included in this group, later to be called the Loyalist Democratic Party, were black veterans of the civil rights struggle: Aaron Henry, president of the state NAACP during the brutal years; Charles Young, a Meridian entrepreneur and black leader, who was the first of his race inducted into a Mississippi Chamber of Commerce; Robert Clark, the first black representative to the legislature since Reconstruction; and a Starkville physician named Douglas Connor, long involved in civil rights. Of the FDP holdovers, the most famous was Mrs. Fannie Lou Hamer.

And there were whites, too: Hodding Carter, III; a wealthy cotton planter, Oscar Carr, who with his wife was a member of a Delta NAACP branch—he and Evers had been state co-chairmen of Robert Kennedy's brief 1968 campaign; a thirty-seven-year-old Greenville attorney, Wesley Watkins; and the wife of a Jackson physician, Mrs. Patricia Derian, who led a group called Save Our Schools.

Evers had come into his own by this time, leading crushing boycotts in Natchez and Port Gibson and laying the foundation for a political organization in Fayette. As the Democratic National Convention approached, the Regular Mississippi Democrats anticipated a credentials battle at Chicago over the seating of delegates. They chose Evers and two other blacks for the delegation, hoping this would show "minority representation." But Evers rejected the offer, for he was a key member of the challenge delegation. In 1968 the credentials committee of the Democratic Party broke with tradition and applauded Evers as he concluded testimony on behalf of the new party. The Regular Democrats were unseated by the predominantly black challenge contingent. It was the first time in the history of the Democratic Party that an entire state delegation was expelled and a challenge contingent seated in its place.

The convention nominated Humphrey, who as senator had championed civil rights but who as Vice President and Johnson's heir now was scorned by the idealists and radicals who had labored so selflessly in the South. Outside the Mayflower Hotel they protested an immoral war and were besieged by sadistic police using tactics similar to those used by cops during the southern civil rights struggle of former years. The activists' concerns had shifted from civil rights to the anti-war movement, a challenge less in sympathy with America than civil rights had been. The new delegates from Mississippi were faced with a cruel irony. Long-lasting ties with Humphrey strengthened the Loyalist Democrats' case, enhancing their dramatic break from political bondage. Outside the convention, meanwhile, freedom was stomped to the ground. The Siege of Chicago, as Norman Mailer called it, was of all theaters the very one that saw the first victory in the struggle for black political power in Mississippi. However, in November, Mississippi voted overwhelmingly for George Wallace; Humphrey received only 140,000 votes, mostly black.

The Loyalist Democrats returned to Mississippi and at their state convention Evers consummated the death of the FDP and the birth of his own political career. Reverend Harry Bowie, then of the FDP, told me about the meeting: "Charles knew we [the FDP] wanted to nominate Representative Bob Clark for national committeeman. But before we had a chance to nominate anyone, the convention chair immediately recognized Reverend Allen Johnson. Now you have to understand Reverend Johnson. Here is a man who was like a brother to Medgar, and he was very close with Charles. He has a deep, powerful voice and he is one of the most popular ministers in all of Mississippi. He gave a nominating speech for Charles that nobody ever forgot. He talked about Medgar; he talked about Bobby and Martin; he talked about dreams we all shared; and he praised Charles like I've never heard one man praise another. He was crying when he finished the speech. I was for Clark and *I* was crying! The folks from the Delta, who had worshiped Medgar, were going crazy, calling 'Evers! Evers!' Johnson sat down and before anyone had a chance to second him or nominate Clark, a band walked out and started playing 'We Shall Overcome.' *Everyone* was crying at the end of the song. It was a religious experience! Charles was nominated from the floor. After it was over I walked up to him and I was fuming. He was grinning from ear to ear. He said, 'Harry, I beat you, but you gotta love me!' I shook his hand. I had to. It was a feat of sheer political genius . . . and I love the guy, too."

Later that summer Evers attracted national attention by running for Congress. A special election had been called to choose a replacement for John Bell Williams, who had just been elected governor. Evers swept the first primary but was defeated by Charles Griffin, Williams' administrative aide, in the runoff.

The activism of civil rights days over the next three years gave way to frustration and despair. The movement had been swept into the flood of congressional legislation, federal reforms, and Presidential incentives. But then the country had changed. With Johnson's retirement it had become painfully clear that the real sickness in America was Vietnam. Perhaps, as some historians have felt, if Martin Luther King had lived, he might successfully have dramatized the intrinsic bond between domestic upheavals and the terrible war that was consuming billions of dollars that should have gone into the trenches of urban America. But King had died, Kennedy had died, and candidates Humphrey and Nixon had convincingly led the American people to believe that Vietnam and "law and order" were separate problems.

Mississippi in 1971 was a broken place. On the surface, things had changed: political rhetoric was not inflammatory, schools were slowly becoming integrated, blacks had access to public places, and there was the ballot box in nonviolent sections of the state. But while the face of the system had been lifted, the body was barely touched. It was the white man's power, the white man's money, the white man's police force, the white man's racism. The frustration was most deeply felt by the young blacks. Many were apathetic, but many were attracted to a separatist group from Detroit, the Republic of New Africa, which was now organizing an "independent nation" on a farm outside Jackson. Either apathy or militant philosophy caused young blacks to avoid the Evers campaign office. The fact that several of us were white turned off more than a few potential volunteers.

Jackson State College was, in Magnolia's words, "like a huge teepee . . . everyone inside themselves, no one can feel what's happening outside. . . ." After the 1970 killings an iron fence had been erected at both ends of the Lynch Street campus; in 1971 it was a grim symbol of the spiritual fatigue of the place.

Perhaps the most disturbing reality of 1971 was that the failure of the civil rights movement had been prophesied by the brilliant black historian Harold Cruse. In *The Crisis of the Negro Intellectual* he had written that the movement was falling prey to its own myths. Cruse wrote that America traditionally absorbs waves of immigrants, absorbs their radical ideologies, and "Americanizes" them. Cruse drew a parallel between the 1930s and the 1960s. He said that the New Deal had stolen the programs of the Communist Party and had stripped them of vitality through patronizing, semi-official recognition. Of the civil rights struggle he wrote, "The future failures or successes will depend on to what degree the movement succeeds in mastering the imperative of the social dynamic."

Civil rights leader Bob Moses told SNCC activists that one of their tasks was to make America see Mississippi as a mirror. Mississippi was no isolated sickness of the nation; rather, it was the microcosm. And in the summer of 1971, Mississippi was indeed a microcosm of the morally bankrupt country that was torn by the long Vietnam War while the President callously ignored the nation's domestic woes. It now seemed that even capitalism, the system, had deserted Mississippi. Nixon's drastic de-escalation of Justice Department incentives in civil rights and integration litigation, coupled with his obvious courting of southern segregationist representatives and senators, had thrust on Mississippi's black people a task that was clearly theirs alone.

Evers was nominated for governor at a special convention of the Loyalist Democrats in April 1971. It was now evident that Evers was going to run and also that blacks in counties with potential voting majorities would seek offices. Two crucial court decisions were handed down before the August Democratic primaries. On April 28 a three-judge federal court in Biloxi ruled against implementation of an open primary proposed by the Regular Democrats. This decision was a victory for the Loyalists; it meant blacks could run as independents in the general election, avoiding arduous campaigns in the August primaries. Black leaders knew it would be hard enough getting blacks to overcome fear in going to the polls in November, let alone in August. But the second court decision was a setback for the Loyalists. On May 18 a federal panel including former Mississippi Governor J. P. Coleman affirmed a reapportionment plan that clearly diluted black voting strength. The approved plan called for multimember legislative districts. This meant that in areas of heavy black population, instead of one representative being elected from one district, a certain number of representatives would be elected collectively from a large district. Thus, in populous Hinds County, where Jackson is, the fact that blacks comprised nearly a third of the potential voters did not guarantee any measure of success. All the legislators in the county would be elected by voters from every area. A black man from area A would not win—even if A was 90 percent black—because voters from areas B and C could vote against him. In smaller counties, the chances for blacks were better. In general, an at-large race would give whites the overwhelming advantage since all they had to do was vote a straight white slate. The court had ruled there was "insufficient time" to give complete study to a single-member legislative reapportionment before the August 3 Democratic primary, despite the fact that civil rights lawyers had a plan ready to present to the court. Black candidates faced a decidedly uphill fight.

Mayor Evers announced on June 1 that he would run in the November general election. "I could probably get into the second Democratic primary, but I'd lose in the runoff. That wouldn't do us no good for November. All our folks got to be together for November." So, he would campaign throughout the summer, try to raise money for the November general election, and try to build a black political organization in the counties.

For both the Regular Democrats and the Evers-led Loyalists, 1971 was a time of the past and a time of the future. The present, clearly, was trying to understand where it fit. As the summer primary began, there was a new approach by candidates to their electorate. Many white candidates in areas with heavy black voter strength would need black votes to win; blacks would be running in great numbers. The new political complexion demanded updated politics.

With some 250,000 black voters, the white Democratic candidates for governor in the August primary had a simple choice: employ the ranting and emotionalism of past demagogues such as Ross Barnett (who once remarked that "God was the original segregationist") or be a moderate, which meant being a pragmatist about the state's sorry image. For Mississippi's last three governors had lived in the beautiful Jackson mansion while the land ran red with blood. And it was not only the blood of blacks. The grim reminder of the two whites killed at Ole Miss during the riots over James Meredith's integration had given "Ole Ross" Barnett an inglorious memory in the minds of Mississippians. His successor, Paul Johnson, was elected in 1963 largely because as lieutenant governor he and a tier of state troopers had blocked James Meredith's second attempt to enter the front gate of Ole Miss. Johnson had run on the slogan "Stand Tall for Paul, He Stood Tall for You." He remarked on the stump that the NAACP stood for "niggers, apes, alligators, coons, and possums." But in Johnson's first year in office three civil rights workers were shot to death and buried in an earthen dam near Philadelphia. Jackson cops and Mississippi highway patrolmen were blasted editorially in papers across the country. Mississippi was scorned again. Johnson's popularity was at a low ebb as his term neared an end. Unable to succeed himself, he ran for lieutenant governor, saying, "The time for a lot of bull-shooting is over," meaning both he and the state had to admit that segregation was dead. But the people of Mississippi invoked a long-standing political tradition against hegemony of old governors, and Johnson lost, drifting into the fog of the past.

Congressman John Bell Williams, a war veteran who had lost one arm in the service, was elected governor in 1967, running as a hard-line segregationist. Despite rhetoric, he was a total failure in attempts to thwart integration. And blood had spilled during his administration. The 1970 storming of the Jackson State campus, leaving two students dead, shot by highway patrolmen who opened fire on a dormitory, caused a Senate investigation. Williams also had little rapport with the Mississippi Legislature, and few of his attempts to push through laws succeeded. In 1971, John Bell Williams was a bitter man.

It is difficult to say whether the state's voters in 1971 were opposed to racism as a platform because of what its resultant politics had already done or because of what would occur if this platform was carried on by yet another firm-fisted bigot. Probably, the electorate's shying away from race as a political issue was due to both. One thing accomplished by the racial strides made by blacks was casting Mississippi, the anachronistic showcase of good darkies, plantations, quarterbacks, and beauty queens, into disrepute. An army of national reporters had trekked over miles of sun-baked roads recording the movements of some of the most spiritually powerful people ever to fight for freedom. White Mississippians were sensitive to their presence, for they had spread the stereotype of the state's image.

The fact that Charles Evers was running for governor further complicated the situation. Cameras and reporter coverage were unavoidable, and the choice to-bait-or-not-to-bait was the question to be resolved early and forcefully by each candidate. You could attack the first black man running for governor as viciously as you wanted, but for the sake of image it had to be done in a subtle, sophisticated manner.

The white candidates for the August primary left little doubt that this state, the ancestral holdout against the Second Reconstruction, was beginning to change. Mississippi was by no means restless for change, but one thing was certain. *The time for a lot of bull-shooting was over.*

Two candidates ran on racist platforms. The dominant figure was Jimmy Swan, a radio country-music entertainer from Hattiesburg. In 1967, "Little Jimmy" had emerged from relative oblivion and finished a strong third in the governor's race. He had built himself a statewide name and scared all hell out of William Winter, a Jackson moderate four years ahead of the electoral mood, by almost edging him out of the runoff. Winter was tagged a liberal—in Mississippi tantamount to Communist—by John Bell Williams in the runoff. Williams won with a closing racist appeal even more vitriolic than Jimmy's.

Swan was a balding man, about five-five. By midsummer the top of his head was the same ruddy complexion as his face. His face wrinkled when he spoke and his jowls sagged. In 1967 he had captured the hearts of the Klan, Americans for Preservation of the White Race, and the White Citizens' Council with his stern decrying of integration: "We must not allow our children to be sacrificed on the filthy, atheistic altar of integration."

All of that was changed by 1971. The children had been sacrificed, as every Mississippian knew, by one court decision after another. But Swan pretended to be a populist, and even if he could not revive buried dogma he at least gave it new dimensions of life. He would be a kicker. His approach was sure-fire and from the gut. Everyone already knew where he stood on segregation.

He traveled around the state in a huge metallic-silver bus with "Save Our Children" blazoned in red letters. A Confederate flag and an American flag were stamped on either side. A bandwagon, draped with flags, was hauled behind. The Swan entourage would roll into one town after another, replete with the country gospel music of the Sullivan Family, two cowboys and a girl who strummed songs of the backwoods, creeks, and crannies. Jimmy's wife, "Miss Grace," was the campaign manager. His thirty-year-old son Randy handled the Jackson office chores when Dad was on the road.

If you mentioned Swan's name to anyone intelligent, ethical, or black, he scowled. The temptation was to regard Swan as the last of a dying breed, the aging demagogue doing his damnedest to preserve the ideology of the sons of the earth who, like their standard bearer, took firm stands against the perfidies of integration, atheism, communism, legalized alcohol, and, with the Age of Aquarius, marijuana and drugs—all with overreaching affirmations of God, the flag, and the Dixie Way of Life.

But one could not write Swan off. He carried his gritty message from county to county, from the oily shores of the Gulf Coast to the cracked, red-clay hills along the Alabama border. He always carried a copy of the incredible book written by the late, infamous Senator Theo Bilbo of Mississippi, *Take Your Choice: Separation or Mongrelization.* He would jab a finger at the crowds and hold the book open, crying, "We're on the last page, friends! We've got to unite. Time has come to quit pussy-footin' around!" Yet even Jimmy was possessed of the unalterable knowledge that despite his ranting, despite the braying farmers who loved to hear his rhetoric fly, history had changed Mississippi, and Mississippi had not changed history.

This was evident when he spoke about schools. "Integration is here whether you like it or not. I never will like it. I never will accept it. I'm not sayin' we can go back to what Bilbo said—send 'em all back to Africa—but I can say that what he warned about has come true."

The other segregationist was a man for whom the term is actually too mild. The candidacy of Marshall Perry, a Circuit Court Judge, was a blatant violation of American Bar Association judicial ethics. Mississippi, however, was the only state that did not prohibit judicial involvement in nonjudicial politics. I saw Perry, a roaring, vengeful man, as the Albert Speer of Mississippi. He exuded hatred when he spoke. (Swan, an intractable racist, kept his jargon philosophically oriented: the problem's upon us, we hate it, let's work around it, hooray for Mississippi!) Perry was firmly convinced he could turn back the clock. He was totally convinced that he was the personification of Mississippi's salvation. He scared the hell out of me.

Perry was a rumpled fifty, and when the heat caught up to him, sweat streamed down his cheeks in great washes. He was demonic when he bellowed, "I had a black and white couple that came up to me in court the other day and said they wanted marriage. Well, I said no. *Of course I said no!* So they went down to Fifth Circuit Appeals in New Orleans, and they overturned me! *Now there's not much I can do about that, is there?* Well, I'm not quittin' yet!"

He opposed hiring blacks to state agencies: "I say you cannot take a race two to three hundred years out of the jungle and give them equal employment with whites who are three to six thousand years out of the jungle and maintain efficiency and order in state government." He also observed that public schools had become "federal training camps! Our public schools now exist for the sole purpose of brainwashing our children into suitable robots for a police state!"

But Perry, like Swan, was longer on rhetoric than on deed. Most voters sympathized with the dogmatic duo, but also knew that they simply could not produce. They became figures of a rapidly receding dream. Their bluff and swagger stood in contrast with some other Mississippi men who were talking in a lower key. And rather than make most of their noise on the stump, the others made their presence felt by buying prime time on TV. Modern politics demanded TV, and this was a political death warrant for the man depending on the stump. Neither Swan nor Perry purchased much TV time; they did not have enough financial support.

Four candidates ran as moderates. They were unmistakable departures from the past; however, they were very Mississippian in appeal. Roy Adams, from the start, had little

going for him. Highway commissioner for northeast Mississippi for twenty years, he was defeated for a sixth term in
1967. What, then, does a twenty-year highway commissioner do in 1971 but run for governor? But northeast Mississippi, alas, has the worst state highways of all, and none
are four-lane. When the white-haired Mr. Adams quiver-
ingly spoke of a "grass-roots movement," the lack of highway concrete made him look weak. Although he advocated
hiring blacks in state agencies, there was not much about
Mr. Adams to impress black folks. He bought little television time and did not get many votes.

The candidate with the most promising record in the August heats was Ed Pittman, a thirty-eight-year-old state senator from Hattiesburg. He was well respected in the Legislature and The Mayor even told me he thought Pittman was a
fairly decent man. Pittman had spearheaded a report on the
state's graft-infested supervisory system, and had discussed
reforms that should have been aired publicly long before.

The crux of the report was that Mississippi, fiftieth in the
nation in per capita income and standard of living, was
wasting millions of dollars each year in state government.
Dollars were lost on high construction bids, with jobs always
awarded to the same companies. There were subtle hints,
too, at what everyone knew: that the work of these companies was damnably inferior. But the real sore spot was the
county system of government. The report advised Mississippi to revamp its system of county supervisors, elected
officials who purchase road-building equipment, build and
maintain county roads, and levy county taxes. Most supervisors are notoriously inept in their duties, yet are skilled in
profiting for themselves while in office. A man elected two
to three terms generally becomes handsomely fixed financially. Half the roads in the state are awful. Pittman's study
recommended that the state employ a county unit system of
purchase for all equipment and building and for repair of

roads. The supervisors would be required to give up their cozy little fiefdoms, known in Mississippi as "beats."*

Pittman's report did not say that Mississippi governors and certain of their friends traditionally left the Mansion wealthier than when they entered. The Building Commission, whose chief administrator is a gubernatorial appointee, invariably allots contracts to gubernatorial campaign contributors. Nor was mention made of the unmitigated waste in the state: the gold-plated doorknobs and bathtub faucets in the Mansion installed by governors Barnett and Johnson, the $35 million in HEW grants Governor Williams had vetoed on racial grounds, the thousands illegally funneled into the Citizens' Council during the sixties by the State Sovereignty Commission, an agency still existing in 1971. But Pittman's report at least took a stab at the woeful economic practices inherent in the state machinery. Pittman was dead right on economy as an issue, but he had little money to promote his candidacy. He used television sparingly, and finished back in the pack.

Education was an even more important issue. The moderate candidates shared the knowledge that Mississippians bitterly resented Governor Williams' handling of the school crisis, not because of his worn-out appeal to white resistance and segregation-at-all-costs, but because his entire approach had been a lie. He had made his position clear in 1968 that he would try to siphon funds out of the public schools and into segregated academies, even though the courts had stopped the state's tuition grants to private schools. He had wanted Mississippians to believe he had not yielded an inch

* Each county in Mississippi is divided according to population into five districts, or "beats," each under the jurisdiction of one supervisor. The areas were so named in the last century because the supervisor, whose function was—and is—to act as road commissioner, would patrol his "beat" as a policeman did in urban areas. The division of "beats" is extremely unbalanced in Mississippi today because the population of an area is not necessarily in equal ratio to the number or condition of roads there.

to the pressures of integration *despite* the court decisions. Now it was hard to digest official promulgations from the man whose son went to the poshest Citizens' Council school in the state. For it was no secret that poor whites' children had suffered the most during the integration battles. Not that poor people abhorred mixing less than the wealthy, but they were intimidated and scorned by the Council, which would not *hear* of any white kids, even from impoverished families, going to integrated schools. Many poor families couldn't afford private schools, and in some cases their children just stayed at home.

The situation, of course, varied from town to town. Tupelo is probably the most progressive city in the state, and the city leaders resisted demagoguery over education during the sixties. Tupelo, with no private academy, actively sought federal grants and avoided most of the problems other places had; the city officials, while conservative, were at least enlightened about the realities of the time. Tupelo did not have a black majority; however, towns with fewer blacks had much violence. In Tupelo, integration went relatively smoothly.

In Jackson, meanwhile, a rash of private academies sprang up over night. The largest, Jackson Prep, drew students away from the previously silk-stocking white public schools. Prep even hired the successful football coach away from the old school with little problem. The school was endowed with $1 million the first month.°

° In this respect, one might best understand Willie Morris' *Yazoo: Integration in a Deep Southern Town.* Morris' book about his hometown had been an impassioned and largely favorable report; however, it embittered many people close to the situation. A Yazoo student told me, "Integration's split our town terribly. We're not even havin' a prom this year. If he wanted to write about what it's really like, he ought to write about the success of the private academy and how those kids' parents don't get along with my folks cause I'm in a public school."

Perhaps the most bitter reaction about the book was that of a white woman with the Human Relations Council; she was a long-time advocate of public education. "What's going to happen now is everyone up north will say to themselves, 'Hooray

Education, then, became the issue that the moderates had in common. For, unlike Swan and Perry, the moderates approached the dilemma over public/private schools with some degree of resolution over what was at hand. The two most skillfully presenting their identical planks on the issue were Lieutenant Governor Charles Sullivan and Jackson attorney and former Hinds County D.A. William Waller.

Sullivan took the school issue to bat from the very beginning. "In the public schools a little over a quarter of a million of the children this fall will be white, slightly less than a quarter million will be black. They must all be educated, and I mean *all* of them. I do not propose to have us continue the back-breaking tradition of having to support a large segment of nonproductive society when, by simply reaching out our hands and educating and training these people, they too will become productive, they too can support their families, they too can stand up with pride and dignity in my state of Mississippi."

Sullivan was also friendly to the private schools. "Let me remind you that when the school crisis came to Clarksdale in 1965, it was Charles Sullivan who signed the note from his bank to establish the private school. And it was at the home of Charles Sullivan that Coahoma County citizens met and conceived that school."

The significance of Sullivan's fence-walking was that he pledged himself outright to public school preservation. He said he saw no way to give private academies state money. He justified it by saying it was the law, which everyone knew was true. There was little to be done other than lend moral support to the private institutions. And, of course, he was for that.

for Mississippi, redemption at last!' That's *all* we need. Nixon's turned his back on civil rights, the Justice Department doesn't want to touch integration cases, and Yazoo City has its white racist establishment, private school, and that damned book!"

Sullivan had the strongest financial backing in the state. The only candidate with financial support to match was Bill Waller. Waller's approach to the school crisis was the same as Sullivan's; however, he had a different delivery. Understand, first, that Waller's accent is supremely rural, straight from the hills. He was born and reared in Lafayette County, Faulkner's home soil. His drawl brought immediate identification with the redneck. And Waller had been a participant in the annual Mississippi Tobacco-Spit Contest. The farmers had empathy for Waller as well as Swan.

In many places, Waller's maxim, "I will defend to the hilt the right of private schools," was impressive. Like Sullivan, he admitted that this excluded financial assistance from the state, but the implication—strengthened by the fact that his children went to private schools—was that if any Citizens' Council braintrust could discern legal ways to siphon money, well then, just maybe . . . But for all his elbow-rubbing with private school folks, Waller knew there was no way as governor that he could give them money. He was a successful lawyer who was not about to jeopardize his personal or political stature by saying that he would revive John Bell Williams' ploys. Nevertheless, the idea of "defending to the hilt" had the ring of past bluster, and plenty of whites liked to hear it. Waller spoke at rallies sponsored by segregated academies much more than Sullivan did. Waller had the top grade of financial bigots, and he also had, with accent and tobacco juice, an immediate appeal to rural folks.

His attitude on public schools was equally slippery, attempting to please everybody. "The growth and progress of Mississippi can be traced directly to the way we provide education for our youth. It is the responsibility of the people to provide every youngster with quality education. I will help our public educators utilize resources of the state in providing a quality education for our children that will be comparable to the public schools of surrounding states."

Waller and Evers had first come into contact with each other in 1963. As Hinds County D.A., Waller had waged what everyone considered a vigorous and sincere prosecution against Byron De la Beckwith, the Greenwood fertilizer salesman whose fingerprints were found on the weapon that shot Medgar Evers. Despite Waller's efforts and two trials— the best he could do each time was a hung jury (the juries were all-white)—Beckwith went free. The Mayor respected Waller and had even contributed to his 1967 gubernatorial campaign. He had traveled across the state that year endorsing Waller before black groups. "Bill *tried* to convict that dirty scoun'rel, Beckwith," he said. "He showed 'em where his fingerprints were *on the gun* and still they let him go free." Waller's strong prosecution had not helped him politically at the time. But after losing in 1967 he had as a private lawyer defended a Klansman in the murder case of a black voter registration worker in Hattiesburg. The man had been found guilty, but his family made contributions to Waller's 1971 campaign.

As the Democratic primary began and the candidates took to the road, Mississippi was a land in mid-passage. One tradition for certain was dying. The removal of race as an issue to be discussed was a foregone conclusion by the first of June. But the black vote, as every candidate knew, could hand-pick Charles Evers' November opponent if it voted in unison. As the campaigns began, the tone was clearly set. It would be low-keyed, with a somewhat sophisticated approach to issues. But the oddity of the new departure was that, for the first time in a century, race *was* the issue, though it could not be out in the open. White Mississippi wanted to elect a racist but he had to be sensible . . . he couldn't *act* like one. And what did it mean for white politicians to approach the segment of the population enfranchised only since 1965? No one knew, nor did anyone want to be seen actively searching for the answer.

Exactly what Charlie Sullivan, Ed Pittman, Roy Adams, and Bill Waller thought about the outcome of the summer primary can only be conjectured. Charles Evers gave his kickoff speech in Decatur on June 12, and from then on the size of his crowds was carefully noted by his opponents in an effort to discover how a white man might subtly woo the black vote. But the moderates as well as Swan and Perry shared the feeling of great relief that Charles Evers was running in November. This meant that two white men would face each other in the August runoff.

CHAPTER

3

A gubernatorial candidate in Mississippi traditionally commences his campaign by speaking in his hometown. Evers' birthplace is Decatur, in the eastern section of the state, in wood and farmland roughly fifty miles from the Alabama border. Decatur during the Depression was as lowly a place for a black boy to live as one can imagine. In his autobiography Evers recalled, "You know you're black from the day you're born. From the time your mother spits you out of her womb, you know you're different. We were born in our homes, in some old bed with some old woman midwife who pulls the baby from the mother's body. White boys and girls of my age were born in a nice clean hospital with sanitation. I was born in a house with flies."

For Charles Evers to stand on the courthouse steps and kick off his run for the governorship would be a historic break with tradition. The focal point of the civil rights movement had been the old churches. Black folks are deeply religious and the movement to them had had divine connotations; it was the beginning of deliverance. But blacks had never gathered in courthouse squares. Political rallies had always been white folks' stuff.

And Decatur's courthouse had symbolic importance. As boys, Charles and Medgar had sat on the court steps and watched Bilbo deliver one of his fiery speeches. The demonic little senator had pointed at the two future civil rights leaders and shouted to his excited crowd, "If y'all don't watch it, one day these two li'l niggers are gonna try and git the vote and rep'sent you!" On June 12, 1971, Charles Evers spoke to blacks on the same courthouse steps.

From Decatur the itinerary took us into southeastern towns: Newton, Bay Springs, Laurel, and Hattiesburg. These were towns where Evers had friends, relatives, and memories of his young manhood. He had, at various times, been a cabdriver, filling-station operator, driver of a funeral hearse, and, through it all, a handy bootlegger. "We used to put the likker under the back o' the hearse," he jovially told his campaign staff one night, "an' we'd tear down them ole roads like it was death if we got caught! We'd come to a town an' we'd slow down. The ole sheriff would wave an' say to himself, 'Weeelll, there go them ole niggers, totin' somebody off to git buried. . . .' We used to always wave back and try to look serious, but after we drove off we used to laugh clean across to the next town!"

Southeastern Mississippi was the most significant region for the campaign to begin. It is the poorest area of the state, predominantly rural, and blacks comprise less than 45 percent of the population of any single county. There is no city south of Hattiesburg for seventy miles, and then you are at Biloxi and the Gulf of Mexico. Veer slightly west, and the nearest urban area is New Orleans, over one hundred miles distant. The majority of white people in this area, like the blacks, are incredibly poor. This is the Piney Woods section of the state. Lumber and farming are the two principal resources, and neither makes for a wealthy populace. Soybean farmers and pulpwood haulers ride their battered trucks down dusty roads; guns sit on racks in rear windows.

The two cities of this region—Laurel and Hattiesburg— have histories of violent racial domination. The countless tiny towns along narrow roads house chapters of the Ku Klux Klan. Racist demagoguery flourished here for a century, and that image of Mississippi is the one still remembered by the rest of America.

This part of the state is justly called a brutal place, and its history is steeped in the ancient myths, but it is mostly a sad land because the people, black and white, have never had a chance. The white folks in these counties, after they have warmed up to you, will talk not so much of race but of the dread poverty. It has always been this way. Political racism and abject poverty grew at the expense of these very people. The career of Senator Theo Bilbo is a case in point.

At the turn of the century in Mississippi only the very rich and the very landed were able to live in comfort. Most of these people lived in the Delta, the plantation land along the river that stretches some two hundred miles from Memphis to Vicksburg. The Delta comprises only a small portion of the state, but it was, and is today, the area of the wealthiest whites and the greatest population of blacks. Many slaves stayed there after they were freed and their descendants live on there. The typical Delta planter, in addition to his land, usually owned a store where he sold necessary commodities against returns on future crops. He was politically influential, sometimes director of the town bank, and he had scores of blacks working for him. An expression among such men was, "Nigger is nigger and cotton is cotton, and that's the way it will always be."

Response and opposition to such landowners came in the Populist Movement; however, it swept the Midwest and penetrated only a few parts of southern border states. Despite agrarian roots, any suggestion of a coalition among the Mississippi poor—perforce, black as well as white share-croppers—was to kindle flames of reaction by attacking the cornerstone of the culture: nigger is nigger. Mississippi's populism grew literally from the soil itself.

In contrast to the small number of Delta planters, the average white man in Mississippi was dirt poor. He worked his fields as long as there was sun in the sky and he sweated like a workhorse until after supper, when he finally had time to cool his heels and perhaps drink enough still-made whiskey to make him forget temporarily that he was dead broke. He didn't mind the niggers as long as they stayed in their place. Every so often he worked with a few of them when one of the store owners or big farmers was paying for extra help. His life was like any southern road: an oven all summer and cold hell in winter. Sex excited him and if the opportunity arose he would get a little on the side; he'd even done it with a few black girls. He went to church every Sunday and was reverent to the howls and gesticulations of the preacher. Through it all was the one constant, his land. It may have been a diminutive patch on the peripheries of a large farm, but it was nevertheless his. Like himself, it was part of the grand expanse—the sloping hills and meadows, the burly pines, the brilliant blue streams, the vast flatbeds of rich soil, and then the poor earth. It was all the land, as much a part of him as he of it. He could not describe what it meant to him to a city creature. It would be like trying to describe air or perhaps his soul.

The first of his lot to scale the political peak was James Kimble Vardaman, elected governor in 1903. He paved the way for Bilbo. Son of a dirt farmer, Vardaman came up the hard way: he was a self-educated lawyer turned newspaper editor. A Mississippian to his marrow, Vardaman knew the rural electorate's mood and intelligence. Although a refined gentleman of sorts himself, Vardaman's appeal was to the redneck. He knew how to use emotion, and they loved the high hell out of him.

He opposed education for Negroes, and called for repeal of the fourteenth and fifteenth amendments. "The only way to control the nigger," he said, "is to whip him when he does not obey without it, or never pay him more wages than is necessary for food or clothing." With flourishing bows to ladies of his audience, he endorsed lynching as a means of preserving the chastity of Mississippi womanhood.

Vardaman traveled around the state in a covered wagon preceded by a procession of eighty oxen. Into a steamy dull town he would come, beckoning all to hear his message. Blacks knew to lay low when he arrived. He wore snow-white tailor-made suits, and he let his jet-black hair grow long. Pedantic and often rambling, Vardaman had a stimulating voice and used physical movement in such a dramatic manner that crowds clamored for him. One observer said, "He looked like a top-notch medicine man." Immensely popular, Vardaman was called the Great White Chief. (Apartheid notwithstanding, he was actually one of the state's better early governors, reforming the terrible lend-lease agreement planters had with the penitentiary for prisoners. He also improved education and facilities for the insane.)

But race had never been Mississippi's major problem; the major problem was poverty. And there was little a politician in 1903 or 1971 could say or do about that. But it was not issue, it was emotion that had always made sense to the poor and largely ignorant Mississippi electorate. Politics became more a romantic pursuit than a forum designed to produce the man most qualified to legislate and politick in Washington. Conjuring up glories of the Confederate martyred, Vardaman charged the country mind with bastard emotion. He used the image of the black discarding his cloak of submissiveness and becoming a potential plunderer-rapist to terrorize the white communities. By his own vilifying dogma, he made every yokel hearing him expect that venom toward the Negro was not only sanctioned, honorable, and consistent, but moreover *demanded* of the politician. Deeper still, Vardaman's hatred for blacks, far overshadowing his sincere efforts to improve the lot of poor whites, was an integrating force in the Mississippi mind: he gave hatred a social status that ignited feelings of magic in his followers. The earth on which they struggled to live held them captive, but the inner madness of racism was a strength. Vardaman condemned the Delta people as wild socialites and haughty intellectuals who inherited wealth, while the hill farmer worked his hands raw. Thus, hatred of the black man intensified pride in the farmer's struggle against the red clay. Rural brutality was tantamount to the planter's economic grip on the black man. The two groups having the most economic, sociological, and psychological dilemmas in common were of course the poor whites and the blacks, put asunder by Vardaman.

The Great White Chief became a hero. People heard him speak and reaffirmed their beliefs and handed them down to posterity. Towns competed for the honor of holding festivities for him. His name became a household word. People started naming their children for him, and Faulkner even named several characters after him. Even today there is a town (population 637) in Calhoun County named Vardaman.

Theo Bilbo built his career on Vardaman's popularity. In 1910 the Great White Chief was defeated by a Delta planter named LeRoy Percy in a bitterly contested election in the Mississippi Senate to choose the man to fulfill the remaining year of the term of the U.S. senator who had suddenly died. Just after January 1, 1911, the five-foot two-inch Senator Bilbo from Poplarville announced that he had taken a bribe from a Percy confederate for his vote! A special hearing was called to determine the veracity of his claim, and after a lengthy probe it was learned that Bilbo had lied. He had tried to shame Percy through perjury but had failed. A special impeachment session was called to review Bilbo's credentials. The Mississippi Senate then issued this decree:

> . . . in view of the unexplained inconsistencies and incoherent improbability in the testimony of Senator Bilbo, his established bad reputation, and entire lack of credibility, that the Senate of Mississippi does hereby condemn his entire bribery charge, and the statement of the role he played as detective and decoy, as a trumped-up falsehood, utterly unworthy of belief; resolved further, that as testimony produced in this investigation, the Senate renounces Bilbo as unfit to sit with honest, upright men in a respectable legislative body, and he is hereby asked to resign.

In almost any other state Bilbo would have been politically dead and buried, but in Mississippi, precisely because he *was* so outrageous, he became all the more popular. He promptly announced his candidacy for lieutenant governor. In 1911, Vardaman was running for the Senate against Percy in a popular election. The impeachment proceedings caused a stir, but most voters knew bribery and malfeasance were rife; Bilbo had tried to help the Chief by showing how the Delta planter had beaten him with bought votes.

"People of Mississippi," Bilbo cried, "the fight between the classes and the masses, between the corporate influences and the people, is on, and it will be a fight to the finish!" Bilbo dressed in white suits, with red socks, red tie, red suspenders, and he called himself, predictably, a proud redneck. Percy, something of a moderate on race, was no match for the colorful Vardaman. Bilbo often campaigned for the Chief. He goaded Percy into calling one unruly, Bilbo-inspired crowd "Cattle!" and from then on it was the masses who beat the classes.

Bilbo's populism was of the earth, to say the least. He claimed allegiances by inviting potential male supporters behind a barn to parley with him while he pissed. "There's nothing," he told a friend, "like going behind a barn to get votes in Mississippi." Bilbo also called one opponent a "cross between a mongrel and a cur, conceived in a nigger graveyard, suckled by a cow, and educated by a fool." The accused finally caught him and nearly beat him to death with the butt of a revolver. The politically expedient Bilbo then announced from his hospital bed (where he lay with a concussion and ten scalp wounds) that he had been attacked from behind! A perennial underdog, he brought out the color, crudity, and simple killer instinct of the region.

In his two terms as governor he was most remembered for his purge of Ole Miss, ousting many scholars and replacing them with campaign contributors. He retired to his farm in Poplarville in 1932, built a lavish "dream house," and in 1934 was elected to the Senate. A dozen years later, with the dramatic end to World War II, Americans were suddenly made aware of the dangers of his Mississippi morality. Having just fought a brutal war against the most insidious racist in history, Hitler, they could no longer tolerate Bilbo, who proposed that America deport blacks to Liberia. His crowning feat was his book *Take Your Choice: Separation or Mongrelization*. A key passage reads:

> If we disregard segregation in all relations, is it then possible that we maintain fixedly the marriage of the South's Sons and Daughters? The answer must be NO. By the absolute denial of the Negro, the barriers are firm and strong.

He was condemned by civic and national groups, but in Mississippi he was worshiped. Hodding Carter attacked him in print and was rewarded with crosses burned on his lawn. In 1946, with Bilbo at his zenith, Carter won the Pulitzer Prize. For the next fifteen years he battled Bilbo's legacy. The United States Senate brought impeachment proceedings against Bilbo in 1946, the last year of his second term. The charges—questionable financial gain and conduct ill-befitting a senator—little daunted him. He announced his candidacy for reelection, even though he was coughing blood and phlegm and rapidly thinning. His campaign was one of the most racist in Mississippi history, and he was overwhelmingly reelected. Reviewing Bilbo's victory, Hodding Carter wrote, in *Southern Legacy*:

> The outsiders who sought his defeat made certain his victory. Into Mississippi cascaded the scornful comment of the nation . . . a conglomerate of organizations who won fleeting publicity by insisting in advance that the Senate should nullify the decision of the electorate of a sovereign state. And on the street corners of Mississippi, citizens who never in their lives voted for Bilbo announced heatedly they were going to elect the little so-and-so just to show those damned outsiders that they could not run a Mississippi election.

But before impeachment hearings commenced, Bilbo was forced to retire to a hospital in New Orleans. He died that year, 1947, of cancer of the mouth. For four decades, from 1907 as a brash state senator until his death, Theo Gilmore Bilbo, perhaps the most hated man in the U.S. Senate, was spokesman and standard-bearer for the ignorant souls he represented. Before anything else, before cotton quotas or even industry that was so desperately needed but hard to attract, the Mississippi standard of white supremacy had to be upheld. If it meant electing a Bilbo, burning a cross, firing a shot at a pointy-headed newspaper editor, or hanging a nigger, it would be done. It was preservation, defense, the heritage. It was the southern man's sickest fiction, which he called truth, and which, if ever challenged, meant war.

In 1967 my father purchased some two hundred acres of sprawling woodland in Poplarville, seventy miles up the interstate highway from our home, New Orleans. I was eighteen, but this was the first time I had heard of Theo Bilbo, a Mississippi senator dead twenty years who had built a famous dream house (which since had burned) less than five miles from our small cabin. He had died in the same hospital where I was born.

Shortly before I left for my first year at Georgetown University, my father and I drove to the farm to spend an afternoon preparing the little house for remodeling. As we unloaded the car, I queried my father about Bilbo. His disgruntled reply was that "he was nothin' but a miserable little piss-ant."

I nodded, sensing he did not wish to pursue the topic.

Wiping his face with a towel, he stepped into the shade for a moment and looked at me. "Son," he reflected, "I wouldn't say what I just said to any of the folks around here. . . ." His voice trailed off and then he spoke again:

"Some of 'em knew him, I'm sure. Others might be related. No sense sayin' something unnecessary. These are good people. When we come up here on weekends, they'll be our neighbors. I like all the folks I've met. . . ."

He paused another moment and then said matter-of-factly, "Even so, all he was was a piss-ant."

In June 1971 my parents had not told our Poplarville friends of my new job, and we decided not to mention it. I called New Orleans the night before the kickoff speech to assure them that everything was all right. Mother and Dad were now interested in the campaign and I had sent home a copy of Evers' book. We talked briefly and my father said he was glad the motorcade was not traveling farther south than Hattiesburg.

A huge sun hung in the sky, and the heat pouring out was oppressive and smooth like an oil slick. Standing beneath the shade of the stores that were directly across from the small brick courthouse built before 1900, the forty or so white folks in Decatur didn't say much: they mostly watched. Two white policemen were roping off the street between the stores and the court. On one side of the building NBC crewmen kept flat against the wall and loaded a camera; the only relief from the sun was on that side. On the opposite side Dwight Ross was crooning "Watermelon Man" while his cousin Robert continued to soak, his hands palpitating feverishly on the bass guitar.

Two hundred black folks, their faces weathered and their clothes patched, huddled close in the middle of the lawn. They seemed listless. Most of the women fanned themselves. The young blacks stood together on the edge of the steps around the band, keeping time with the music. Everyone seemed interested in the song, but not moved by it. Perhaps they were more concerned about the heat.

A man called my name and I turned. It was Charles Gordon, the old political reporter for the Jackson *Daily News*. "This is Charlie Hills," Gordon said, introducing me to the chunky blond-haired man at his side. "He writes for the *Clarion-Ledger*. He needs one of your brochures." We shook hands and I gave him the press brochure that included The Mayor's picture, a brief biography I had written, and four position papers. The men ambled back to the shade.

There was no shade, however, on the lawn in front of the

courthouse, yet the old black people stayed pressed together. On the edges of the crowd an old woman held onto a telephone pole, gesturing at the camera team with her cane and smacking her lips up and down, communicating with an old man leaning on the other side of the pole. His straw hat was tilted forward and he sipped Coke through a straw in the bottle. The woman's dress looked like new cotton but the man wore fatigues with holes. She was yelling to be heard above the music, but from where I stood in the middle of the street it was impossible to hear. The old man nodded every so often.

The music lowered to a purr; Dwight only glided his hands on the keys. Two cars carrying The Mayor and his security men pulled discreetly into their places at the side of the courthouse. Ed McBride, a towering black man who doubled as security when not loading band equipment, leaned on the window of The Mayor's car and conferred with Woody. Then McBride made his way through the crowd.

The last notes of the organ lingered in the afternoon; the heat seemed to prolong them. Dwight smoothly transferred the microphone to McBride; the big man unraveled the line of wire as he stepped to the center of the courthouse steps. McBride was already dripping wet as he began to speak.

"All right, now. It may be hot, but we got business to tend to! We're showin' Decatur, *Mississippi*, that we're in politics for real! Now, repeat after me . . . I AM . . ."

The crowd repeated, half-loud, "Ah am . . ."

"C'mon, now! I cain't hear you! Once mo'. I AM . . ."

They were louder the second time. "AH AM . . ."

"SOME-BODDY . . ."

"SOME-BODDY . . ."

"WE ARE . . ."

"WE ARE . . ."

"SOME-*BODDIES* . . ."

"SOME-BODDIES . . ."

"*Loud* now, black people, be proud. I MAY BE POOR . . ."

"AH MAY BE PO' . . ."

"BUT *I* AM . . ."

"BUT AH AM . . ."

"SOMEBODDY!"

"*SOMEBODDY!*"

McBride ran his finger over his eyebrows, flicked the line of perspiration to the ground, and breathed heavily into the microphone. "Now, give yourselves a great *big* hand. . . ." They all applauded. There was more movement in the crowd and a steady hum of talking. Everyone was a little looser.

Then Martin cleared a path through the crowd. Woody stood next to the back of the car, one hand resting on the handle, the other over his forehead to shield the sun from his eyes. He scanned the crowd for about a minute, carefully sizing up the whites standing apart from the crowd, in front of the stores. McBride led the crowd in the chant again, and Woody opened the door. The Mayor jumped out, flashing the V sign. The reporters scurried to the porch of the courthouse. The NBC crew moved in close to The Mayor.

McBride spoke again. "And now, ladies and gentlemen, the next guv'nuh of the state of Mississippi . . ." Woody stood behind The Mayor, Martin in front, but The Mayor was immersed in the crowd, shaking hands and embracing people, many of whom he obviously knew well. I looked behind me at the whites; they had grown in number to about fifty. Most were lined up beneath the shade of the stores. Some men leaned forward, one knee propped on a truck; they craned to hear.

Then the crowd settled down. A tiny man, no taller than

five feet, stood on tiptoe, leaning to reach the microphone. "May we have silence?" There was a widespread hush; all heads bowed. "We will now heah from Rev'nd Willis Moore, who will give the invocations."

There was movement in the heat. It was quiet but we were aware of one another's breathing. A foot rustled; the motion was slight but palpable. Reverend Moore paused before the podium, then spoke:

"Oh Gawd, who has delivered us this day . . . in thy name we askith these blessings on all us heah, we are sin-nuhs . . ."

"Yesss . . ."

"We ask yo' grace on all who come today, Lawd. Especially on our speaker, who was bawn a li'l black baby in the red clay hills o' Decatur . . . an' we pray you bless him and watch over him and keep us all in your love, forever and ever, we pray and say . . ."

"Amen."

The Reverend moved aside; the people in the crowd jostled each other. The black people looked so awfully poor to me. Everyone was dusty from standing on the grass, which was as dry as fire. There was wide uneasiness despite the calm. They did not seem enthusiastic. The small man was now back on the podium.

". . . an' so w'out furthuh prelim'naries, I leave you wi' this word about our speaker, this black Moses o' Mississippi. The words o' Ruddard Kipplin'—'Though he hath the touch o' kings, he can walk wi' beggars.' Ladies and gentuhmens, the mayor o' Fayette and Mississippi's next guv'nuh, Charles—"

The applause was heavier but still restrained. The Afro kids in front stamped their feet. The old lady with the cane hit it against the pole. Her husband waved his hat. Ed Cole stood behind The Mayor as he peeled off his coat. Dwight was playing "Soulful Strut" and Woody and Martin stood close on either side of The Mayor, who told them to give him room to move his arms.

The Mayor's eyes were bright and glimmering, his teeth so white they formed an almost comic contrast with his skin, which seemed darker because it was wet. He loosened his collar and grinned.

"Look out now, white folks! In Decatur MISSISSIPPI we got a political rally—"

"Oh yeah!"

"In Decatur, Mississippi, where I was born . . . tell me somethin'? Is ole Miz Pace still aroun'? Remember ole Miz Pace?"

A high peal of "ooohs" comes from the crowd. "Yeah, black folks, we rem'mber ole Miz Pace, that ole *white* lady used to live in the back behind the store. Medg'r an' me used to steal all her pee-cans from her. Stolt *plenny* of 'em. Used to pick 'em up by day, an' put 'em into her barn and sneak in dere an' pick 'em up and put 'em back in our sack and run back away wi' 'em at night!"

"Dat's what dey did! Dat's exactly what dey did!"

"An' then we used to go sell 'em to dat ole Mac-Millan. Y'all remember Mac-Millan, ole white man used to *sell* pee-cans. We'd go steal 'em right back from him when he turned away and didn' look."

"Dat's de truf! A-men!"

He turned to Reverend Moore. "Ohh, but you gotta pray for me, Rev'nd Moore. I waddn't always a mayor or a mischiefous rascal in Decatur! Unh-unh, Revn'd. I was in Chicago . . . did bad things. I need them prayers, Rev'nd . . ."

The Reverend nodded three, four, six times.

The Mayor scanned the crowd. "Seems to me I see Miz-zus Tanner standin' out there in the hot sun. That you, Mizzus Tanner? I'm so glad!"

Recognizing her name, the old black woman blushed and threw her hands in the air, and everyone turned around to look at her and applauded as she lowered her head, blushing. The crowd giggled.

"Oh yeah, Decatur, we remember we had plenny ole folks that done died, too. Mr. Jim Tims, that ole postmaster —white man, real good man. Everyone knew him, liked him—"

"A-men!"

"Yeah, but black folks, they had plenny white folks that was *meannn.*"

"A-men! That's sho' 'nuf right!"

"Made us walk them dusty roads in summer—"

"Amen."

"Icy roads in win'er!"

"That's true."

". . . sometimes so col' we didn't have no *shoes* to wear to protec' our *feet!* An' we never had no coats for when it got col', neither!"

"Precious Jesus!"

"But we come far, black folks. Now we sayin' that a man born right here in Decatuh, Miss'ssippi—a *black*-skinned man—look out, white folks, he runnin' for guv'nuh o' this *state!*"

"I hear you!" The Afro kids on the steps yelled, "Right on!"

The Mayor was wet and burning in the heat. His words reached out to the folks he knew and to those he didn't. There was an electric pulse in the air, and the crowd felt it. They forgot about the white folks across the street. The Mayor was above the heat and everyone was with him.

"Look aroun' us, black folks. This the same Decatuh where that ole racist scoun'rel *Bilbo* stood—on these very courthouse steps—years ago! *Bil*-bo. He stood right here, and Medgar an' I watched him spit that ole racist fire. An' right where *you* standin' "—he jabs his index finger at a half-dozen parts of the crowd—"right where you are *this day* they had *meannn* white folks. *Three* times as many as there o' you! But look out, Bilbo, we comin' at you. You gonna turn over in your grave come November the second. In fac', you turnin' over in your grave right now!"

He sweeps his hand over the crowd. "Yeah, Decatur, I'm your prodigal son! This black man went off to Chicago, but when Medgar died, I said it's time to come back and change all this ole hate, all that racism got to change it into love."

"A-men!"

He gestured at the storefront. "Now, white folks, 'specially you boys and girls, you gotta talk to your mommas and daddies and tell 'em to do what's right. No mo' spittin' tobacco juice and cussin' us and callin' us names. We're runnin' for guv'nuh and we gonna teach everybody to change all that!

"Fuhst, we gonna change that seggurgated highway patrol. No more beatin' up black folks an' long-haired white folks . . . we gonna end all that!"

"I hear you! I *do* hear you!"

"An' we gonna end our ole two-school system. No more seggurgated, private schools. Unh-*unh*! We gonna have *black* children and *white* chil'ren all goin' in one school, with no more mean racism lockin' them doors up! Have our chil'ren learn *love* and *respec'* in addition to them ole a-b-c's.

"An' we gonna work hard to end that ole poverty, too. I've said it before, I'll say it again—I *hate* welfare! That's right. I hate it with a passion. Welfare's a sickness. Makes a man nothin'. I'll do as guv'nuh like I've done as mayor of Fayette—go aft'r those HEW grants, go after industry, go after HUD. We got ourselves a Manpower Trainin' Program in Fayette last year and we've already trained fifty men for jobs since the fuhst o' the year. As guv'nuh, I'm gonna *run* after all those millions o' dollars ole John Bell turned down."

"A-men!"

CRACK! Suddenly there was a shot, and three hundred heads turned toward the street.

But it was not a gun. A pickup truck driven by a white man had backfired and shot through the rope barricade. Two policemen ran after him, but everyone knew they wouldn't arrest him. The Mayor smiled. "That's all right, Mr. Truck Driver! You're part o' the past. Ain't no more guns gonna shoot at us in Decatuh. That day is *gone!*"

"Gone! Gone!" The crowd began cheering for itself. "Gone!" The clapping stirred the afternoon's heated stillness like leaves crackling underfoot in a silent wood. Evers' smile was radiant.

"Well, black folks, we gotta get goin' now. Thank you so much for comin' out today. An' remember, you cain't do nothin' unless you *vote!* So, all you young folks, if you mad, prove it! Git registered if you're ole enough, an' if you ain't, make sure mommy and daddy is registered!"

After the applause, everyone started moving, crowding around the speaker's stand, engulfing The Mayor. Woody tried to watch the whites across the street and stay close to The Mayor, but it was impossible to do both. He followed The Mayor deep into the crowd. Reverend Moore tried to hand him his coat, but The Mayor was busy kissing one of the Afro girls on the cheek. Then he hugged an old lady. Then clasped a young man's arm in a soul-grip.

The NBC crew stayed with us on the steps, camera high. Lois and Magnolia started through the crowd, selling books and buttons. The Mayor held a copy of the book high and reminded the crowd that the cost was $1.00 less than the store price. Reporters piled into cars to get to Raleigh, thirty miles away, where Jimmy Swan was scheduled to kick off.

According to press reports, the Swan rally was quite a show. A country band played for forty-five minutes. Five hundred whites got the red carpet: barbecued pork chops, fried chicken, potato salad, American and Confederate flags, country tunes, country girls, and finally Jimmy. He was introduced by a local woman who told of seeing the Evers motorcase a few hours before. "Thousands of 'em . . . all of 'em black, and a few long-haired white! Drivin' down the road like they owned it! We gotta elect a man to stand up for our rights! A man who knows when it's time to say NO! A man named Jimmy Swan!"

Swan went through his catalog of denunciations, though, as one journalist observed, "he didn't use the word 'nigger' once. I guess that's become taboo on the stump now that reporters are always around." Swan had promised a "blood and guts" campaign.

The Mayor, meanwhile, was telling a Newton crowd of one way to improve state economy. "When I'm governor, we won't have no dry counties. Why should Rankin County, which is dry and right next door to Hinds County, which is wet, git a share of tax money collected in Jackson. Don't make no *kinda* sense! An' so we'll cut out *all* dry counties, make 'em all wet, and git the extra tax money." °

Our next stop was Bay Springs; however, when the motorcade pulled into the rally site, there was no one around. Despite Woody's protests, The Mayor emerged from his car to meet the chief of police, a corpulent man with a long cigar, surrounded by four leathered deputies. "How do you do, Chief?" The Mayor said.

° In Mississippi, today, bootleggers do make small fortunes. Prohibition came in under Bilbo and many profited from it. State officials collected kick-backs from profiteering bootleggers; legislators voted dry and drank or abstained, according to their preference, knowing they were safe either way; preachers had both church and state in their corner. There are, even today, counties that opt dry. Bootleggers did well until, during the sixties, the Legislature began to have second thoughts about the revenue being lost on all the liquor trade and so the "black market tax" was levied. This meant that profiteers had to pay a percentage of their profits. This was, of course, a taxation of a practice that had flourished illegally so as to avoid taxation. It was eventually repealed.

"All right, I reckon. Ain't gonna be no rally today. The colored people decided not to come."

The Mayor looked at him and then gazed into the crystal blue sky as if to check for rain. "Well, nice meetin' you, Chief," he said, extending his hand.

The man looked at him icily and said, "I don't shake hands with colored people."

Evers looked him in the eye and said slowly, "That's all right, my friend. When you come to my town I'm gonna shake your hand anyway." The caravan drove deeper into southeastern Mississippi, toward Laurel.

Squeaky and I reached the town early. The street leading to the courthouse square could have been that of any quaint American city: rows of trees, carefully trimmed lawns, beautiful blooming shrubs, neatly kept cottages. Squeaky said, "This has been one bad-ass town. Violent. Mean Klukker chapter." He drew a puff on his cigarette and stared hard at the row of unassuming homes.

About a hundred folks stood around the steps of the Laurel courthouse. Most of them tried to get into the shade provided by one or two tall trees on either side of the marble porch. There was little talking. The motorcade pulled into Main Street, horns blaring and everyone waving at pedestrians. The Mayor's picture was printed on posters taped to car doors. As scheduled, The Mayor's car and the security escort had pulled from the parade entering the courthouse square, and now drove around the opposite block. McBride and the band were setting up when I reached the courthouse steps. Ed Cole was speaking to Dwight as he tested the notes of the organ. I waited until they concluded, and then approached Ed.

"Mayor's mad," he said to me.

"How come?"

"The band got here late and the folk haven't loosened up. They're scared to be at the rally. They're shakin' like leaves, tryin' not to show it." As in Decatur, young blacks crowded around the steps where the band was playing. They seemed less intimidated than the older ones, who were in clusters, talking timorously among themselves. Little by little, they began to move down into the middle of the lawn. Across the street stood fifty whites, grimly watching the proceedings. None of the blacks wanted to stand alone. They didn't want to be recognized.

I glanced at The Mayor's car, still unnoticed. "Why doesn't he come out? Wouldn't that loosen 'em up?"

Ed replied, "The Mayor's like any politician, Jason. He doesn't wanna spend time gettin' the crowd together. He doesn't wanna go to them. He wants them to come to him. Local leaders are drivin' through the community now, usin' the bullhorn to get 'em out."

"I didn't realize it would be so hard to get folks out."

"Damn sho' right it's hard. You saw Decatur—first time ever they stood on steps like that."

"How long will it take to draw them out here?"

"Few minutes, if they come. But that's not the important thing now. We've spoken to smaller crowds than this." There were close to 150 now. "Main reason we're waitin' is up in that window across the street. Look at the top floor o' that drugstore buildin'."

In the top window of the building across the street a man was peering from behind a curtain. Standing directly beneath the window was Martin, hands on hips, watching every move the man made.

"Jesus Christ," I said. "Do you think he's got a rifle?"

"No way to tell. He won't try anything, though. He sees too many people watchin' him. But look over at the other building on the opposite side o' the square—that white house on the corner."

On the upper balcony of a palatial home a man sat with binoculars, his chest resting on one forearm. He did not have a gun, however. Squeaky calmly stood on the sidewalk beneath him.

"I can see why these folks are scared," I said, scared myself.

But the presence of our large campaign force eased black folks' tension, and there was no trouble from the whites. After The Mayor finished, the band played awhile and a few people milled around the steps, shaking hands and talking. Most of the people left quickly, for it was growing dark. We went to an old restaurant and ate barbecued chicken and collard greens, and then drove south to Hattiesburg, where the last rally was held in a black high school gym.

We drove back to Jackson after the last rally. Ed dropped me at my apartment and as I fished for a key I asked what he thought of the rallies.

"Well," he said philosophically, "considerin' this was the first big day, I'd say things went pretty well."

"But most o' those folks were scared as hell."

"Yeah, but they came out, Jason. That's the important thing. Southeast Miss'ssippi's always been rough, rough territory. They came out. They'll be talkin', too. Next time we go back they won't be as scared. They'll all be talkin' about all the black folks that went to hear Evers *last* time he came to town. This is June, man, we're still buildin'. We gotta do more than just speak to our electorate. We gotta make 'em *realize* they're an electorate."

CHAPTER

4

My job was to get the candidate maximum coverage in the press and media. Every day I wrote a press release that was supposed to reflect Evers' views and quote him. Ordinarily, the daily news release is a routine part of a press aide's duties, but in my case the task had a creative dimension. The Mayor's English was unquestionably his own brand and I was reluctant to quote verbatim. Thus, with Ed's permission, I decided to change the statements slightly from the way The Mayor had actually spoken. For example, once he said, "I'll tell you what's been wrong with the sup'visor's system—them ole sup'visors ain't buildin' roads! Most of 'em don't do nothin' till election time and then they throw a slab o' blacktop over the bumps and say they been workin' hard. When I become governor, we gonna git a county unit system. Gonna git rid o' them ole sup'visors who don't do nothin' but dip n' chew, and we gonna get professional engineers who got the skill and know-how to fix our roads! No sup'visor's a born builder o' roads! He got to have the skill."

Perhaps it was my English B.A. that made me cringe, thinking I should write this for public consumption, but I decided that, although the duty of a press secretary was to present the candidate's words and programs in an official release, I would alter the statement for the reading public. The above statement read:

Jackson—Gubernatorial candidate Charles Evers today charged that "most supervisors don't work until election time, and then all they do is throw a slab of blacktop on an old road and say they've been working hard."

The Fayette mayor called for employment of the county unit system of government, which would replace supervisors with "professional engineers whose job would be to see we get our roads built and repaired the right way—and not the way our supervisors are doing it now."

Mayor Evers also said that supervisors "dip (snuff) and chew (tobacco)" but that they didn't have the necessary professional experience. "No supervisor's a born builder of roads," he said.

I usually read the releases to The Mayor, but he was always thinking about four other things. His only concern was that I not misquote him. Occasionally he would grin after I read the statements and say, "Couldn't be better if I wrote it myself!"

From the outset of the campaign we knew that national reporters would be following him periodically, stepping up their coverage in October. These journalists would check in with me and be given a press brochure, campaign itinerary, and weekly capitulation of major developments. Unlike national journalists whose stories were in-depth feature reports on the historic candidacy, Mississippi reporters were concerned only with covering the day-to-day developments of our campaign and those of the other candidates. Most of their news came from press releases and news conferences. When we were in Jackson I hand-delivered releases to the various news desks since we did not have enough staffers to leave the office on work unrelated to their own chores. I learned that it was a tacit rule for political campaigns to deliver statements, not to give them in on the phone. When we were on the road I called in news statements to the wire service desks, dictating the story to a correspondent on duty. Delivering releases in Jackson was not difficult and it also gave me the opportunity to talk with reporters with whom I would be dealing throughout the race. I was treated courteously everywhere except in the building of the large Jackson newspapers.

Most reporters liked Charles Evers. He was, of course, a hot candidate the national public was interested in. But he was also a fascinating personality and appealed to reporters. He called them by first names, slapped backs, and joked before and after the cameras and pens were still going. He was also religiously late for every meeting with the press. When he emerged from his back office or burst through the door just-arrived from Fayette, the impatient reporters perked up and grinned as he carefully waltzed around wires, lights, and chairs, saying, "Now don't go gettin' hot, fellas. One thing you cain't take away from us black folks . . . is the right to continue bein' late! We been late all these years, and don't go holdin' *that* against us!"

Our strategy in June was to establish a credible campaign by stressing Mayor Evers' stand on issues so that by the general election Mississippi voters would recognize Evers as a candidate with a legitimate platform of his own. Since the August candidates were discussing various issues, The Mayor's programs—which were decidedly more liberal than those of the white Democrats—received good coverage in the political roundup columns in daily newspapers across the state. The press releases I wrote dealt with specific problems and proposed solutions that would affect everyone, regardless of race. A half-dozen volunteers worked in the Jackson office vigorously researching platform positions that proposed sweeping changes in key bureaus and agencies. Mayor Evers himself repeatedly stressed that he was running not merely as a spokesman for blacks but for "black and white, rich and poor, young and old." (A detailed analysis of the Evers platform is presented in Chapter 9.)

The major outlet for news in Mississippi is television. Most of the newspapers are lax in news coverage. There are only nine TV stations in the state, and three are in Jackson. In some far-reaching rural counties, television sets cannot pick up Mississippi stations. Certain southern counties depend on New Orleans and Baton Rouge for programs. Assorted northern counties watch Memphis affiliates. Outside the mainstream of the state some of these areas are the most backward in Mississippi. They are certainly the most isolated.

TV reporting is superior to newspaper reporting for a number of reasons. TV reporters are for the most part younger than newspaper veterans, who have covered events for years "the Mississippi way." And there are few black newspaper reporters. In all my dealings with the press I found only one black newspaper journalist, a woman writing for Hodding Carter's *Delta-Democrat Times*. On the other hand, the Federal Communications Commission demands nondiscriminatory hiring for media outlets; most stations have at least one black correspondent and various black technicians. Moreover, the FCC has laid down strict rules governing news events: objectivity is a must. Mississippi TV stations have become especially sensitive to this, for in the early sixties a Jackson station, WLBT, was notorious for its slanted coverage of civil rights demonstrations and also for its sensationalized handling of the Ole Miss integration crisis in 1962. The FCC revoked their license and an interim station management was set up, subject to FCC scrutiny. Charles Evers, Hodding Carter, III, and a group of liberals filed a legal challenge to station ownership, and by 1971 five other parties had filed as well. In 1971, WLBT had a significant number of blacks; the ownership had bent over backward to change the image and the news coverage and was doing a creditable job.

Television had broken wide open in Jackson. It was a booming market. The WLBT case had not only seen two new competitive stations arise overnight but the advertising trade had also burgeoned. Young, probing, aware of their local ratings, TV reporters in Mississippi were a dynamic new breed of journalists.

Likewise, radio news coverage was more objective than press coverage of Mississippi events. Most stations read the AP or UPI wire reports on news programs. But by midsummer an enterprising group of men had started the Mississippi Radio News, an independent news bureau that recorded the news of the day and, for a fee, fed the taped broadcasts to stations across the state. This was an excellent service for small stations; by August MRN also had contracts with some large stations. Three to five times weekly I holed myself up in the WATS room and phoned MRN and fifteen radio stations in major population centers, feeding a recording of a thirty- or forty-five-second cut from one of The Mayor's speeches that day.

On the other hand, the Mississippi press was awful, with only a few exceptions. The UPI staff was fair in its coverage of the news, but it was undermanned. The AP staff was much less aggressive and had a tendency, especially in remote areas, to miss the point of a story completely. Stories in distant counties were covered for both wire services by stringers, local reporters with the confidence of the Jackson desk chief. But I discovered that a significant number of stories about black candidates—or blacks in general—didn't always make it into print. Some stringers, according to black county contacts and civil rights lawyers, were old-line Mississippians and didn't think of blacks as newsworthy.

Most major stories in daily papers were wire service pieces. Local stories by staff reporters rarely penetrated the surface of issues. As the campaign developed, it became obvious which newspapers were most slanted in covering Evers. Most papers would have preferred to ignore his candidacy, but the wire services supplied them with daily copy. His picture (if printed at all) rarely ran on the front page in any of the state's conservative dailys, and after his historic nomination, and its coverage by the national press, not one picture of him appeared in a spot check of eight of the twenty-odd dailys.

The average daily paper in Mississippi consists of a front page, with important state and national stories taken from the wires, and other pages consisting of news on the Chamber of Commerce, the mayor's office or the supervisors' doings, society, garden club, etc. There are few stories about black people since they are as a rule not members of such groups. Only in the last five years have most papers done away with the "Colored News" section; there were still some in 1971. Pictures of black political candidates in 1971 were printed in substantially fewer numbers than were photographs of their white opponents.

Editorially, most papers are arch-conservative. One need only observe titles to understand the thought contained in the essay. "Chappaquidick Teddy and Liberal Buddies Arrogant" was a defense of Nixon's choices for the Supreme Court. One paper said of the JoEtha Collier slaying in Drew that it was ridiculous to assume that "racism" killed the girl; "It could have happened in New York and nothing would have been said." One Delta leader told me that it was good the press had given wide coverage to the Collier slaying as "it means somethin' will get raised if they don't bring those bad murderers to court." The men were eventually convicted of manslaughter. But in West Point, Mississippi, in the latter days of summer, a white man who had slain a black leader a year before was freed by an all-white jury. Significantly, the only paper to cry foul was the *Delta-Democrat Times*.

The effect of the movement and subsequent court decisions had embittered certain papers. Commenting on one court ruling, John Perkins of the Meridian *Star* wrote on June 6, "Judicial tyranny is becoming a fact of life in the Deep South. . . ." Perkins' paper is a striking example of the problems a racist paper can cause a community struggling to change. Meridian had its quota of racial violence during the sixties. By 1971, however, things were looking up. The Chamber of Commerce was progressive and was the state's first to accept a black member. Integration was proceeding, although there were problems, relatively smoothly. Black leaders were optimistic. The TV station was a good one. But there was the Meridian *Star*, with its "Colored News" and slanted reporting. A white girl I met who was from Meridian remarked, "Meridian's getting a lot of problems licked. But you still have to contend with attitudes. People wake up every morning and read that newspaper. It's bitter, and people read it and become bitter."

During the entire race for governor only one Mississippi newspaper freed a man to spend a day with us on the campaign trail. He was a reporter from the Gulfport *Daily Herald*. But Mayor Evers was sick the day we agreed upon and the story never came off as planned. AP and UPI reporters in Jackson did stories on a typical day with the Evers campaign, but never did a Mississippi paper free a man to do what reporters from *Time*, *Newsweek*, ABC, CBS, NBC, *The New York Times* Washington *Post*, the *Village Voice*, San Francisco *Chronicle*, Baltimore *Sun*, and even *The Great Speckled Bird* were sent to do.

Mississippi's best newspaper, Hodding Carter's *Delta-Democrat Times*, was located in Greenville. In 1971 old Mr. Carter was long retired and in ill health; Hodding III was editor. The greatest virtue of the *Democrat*, aside from the enlightened editorials, was that staff reporters went into all communities of Greenville to write about life-styles, activities, human interest stories, and so forth. Greenville has interracial community organizations that are reported; the town knows what's happening. Greenville is no racial paradise; blacks there realize that most whites are segregationist in their social views. But Greenville's school integration is gradually beginning to work. The police force, in most areas praetorian, in Greenville is generally marked by even-handedness. Most people concede that Greenville avoided violence that beset other towns because the newspaper refused to play on the townspeople's emotions.

Nowhere was the contrast between newspaper and TV coverage more striking than in Jackson. The TV reporters were good; the newsmen for Jackson's papers were terrible. I learned the three don't's precluding at least a tolerable relationship with the press: no Saturday A.M. conferences; no calling in releases over the phone; and no airport conferences because Thompson Field is a fifteen-minute ride and a pain in the ass to get to. During June, whenever I broke one of these rules, press coverage lagged. It did improve by the end of the summer, however.

The bureau correspondents from the Memphis *Commercial-Appeal*, New Orleans *Times-Picayune*, and *Delta-Democrat Times* were committed to covering the doings in the state capitol. These men—A. B. Albritton, Wilson Minor, and Ed Williams—were among the best newspaper reporters in the state. They were compassionate men, but most of their in-depth pieces were about state-wide politics and government or major news events. The other newspapermen in Jackson (aside from the AP and UPI) wrote for the insidious *Clarion-Ledger* and its sister afternoon paper, the *Daily News*. Between these two different groups of journalists, the objective bureau men and the slanted Jackson papers' men, neither covered stories about the deeper workings of Jackson as a city. The bureau men did not have the time and the Jackson papers refused to do so.

The newspaper coverage makes Jackson appear typical of any southern community during the forties. Government is the major focus, followed by business, entertainment, and major civic developments. However, many of these stories are produced from press releases. Reporters lounged in their offices, waiting for a story to happen. They ignored the problems of legal services offices, welfare agencies, or the deeper human dilemmas in the public schools, stories that could be reported only after talking and listening to children. One never reads human interest stories that give a community some feel of itself. The only news from Jackson State and Tougaloo College, campuses with discontented student bodies, emerge from the institutions' press releases, which are relegated to the "nigger page" of the two dailies. The sad truth is that whites who are not fundamental racists never learn about the deeper and more subtle forms of discrimination, nor do they learn about the many accomplished blacks who live in their city. The black community is largely apathetic, no doubt in part due to its inferior or absent treatment in the papers. There is no sense of identity among blacks as Jacksonians.

It is impossible to understand Jackson without understanding the family that owns the two daily papers. The Hedermans are an old, racist, fundamentalist Baptist family of staggering wealth and power. The *Ledger* and *Daily News* are the two largest Mississippi papers and they wield awesome political clout. The papers have a tight-fisted monopoly on Jackson's advertising and the Hedermans hold large interests in banks and a TV station. Their political investments date back, too.

In the late fifties and early sixties the Hedermans gave roundhouse support to the White Citizens' Council and to Ross Barnett. The Citizens' Council was a community council that was organized to defy the 1954 Supreme Court Decision through legal resistance. The Council drew from upper- and middle-class whites. Senator Eastland was up for reelection in 1954 and barnstormed the state, thrilling councilites by crying, "The choice is between victory and defeat. Defeat means the death of southern culture and aspirations as Anglo-Saxon people. We will carry the fight to the victory. . . ."

The Council movement was given impetus by Tom Brady, a Brookhaven Circuit Court Judge who was later appointed to the Mississippi Supreme Court by Ross Barnett. Brady wrote a pamphlet called "Black Monday" in which he observed:

> We will not be integrated! . . . The fate of our great nation may well rest in the hands of the Southern white people today. If we submit to this unconstitutional judge-made integration law, the malignant powers of atheism, communism, and mongrelization will surely follow, not only in our Southland, but throughout the country.

The Council became the outlet for racist energies outside the Klan. In more excited moments, Council members were violent; for example, beating Fannie Lou Hamer in a Winona jail. In more restrained times, councilites conducted house-to-house canvasses. Through its social and economic powers, the Council ostracized whites who chose not to belong. Many belonging to the organization never went to meetings but paid dues respectfully. Members included doctors, lawyers, ministers, and store owners.

The most vocal opponent to the Council was the elder Hodding Carter. He wrote an article for *Look* condemning the Council. It was titled "A Wave of Terror Sweeps the South." He referred to the Council as the "uptown Ku Klux Klan," and was subsequently censured on the floor of the Mississippi Legislature for "selling out for Yankee gold."

The Hederman newspapers were staunch and fiery supporters of the Council. The *Daily News* editorial following the 1954 decision was called "Bloodstain on White Marble Steps." The paper had argued, "We are up against enemies who would destroy our way of life and put an end to the traditions of our people." The paper printed the names, addresses, and phone numbers of blacks who had signed a statement supporting the Supreme Court ruling . . . and the paper also printed the names and addresses of the blacks' employers! The Jackson *State-Times*, not nearly as outspoken as Carter, advocated some moderation on this issue. It lost its advertising trade to the Hederman papers and was soon bought out by them.

Then came the sixties and the primitive Ross Barnett. The Council was given massive economic help from the State Sovereignty Commission, the "watchdog of segregation," created by the Legislature. It was supposedly a public relations clearing house designed to publicize the peaceful co-existence of black and white Mississippians; however, the Commission existed mainly for the purpose of supplying money to the Citizens' Councils, and, in later years, of harassing civil rights workers.

By 1971 the Council had involved itself in the private school movement. One would see vestiges of the past on lawns of finely kept-up schools named "Council School 1," and "Council School 2." The Citizens' Council was now the bailiwick of the well-to-do, and the only sizable chapter was in Jackson. One could see newspaper ads in the *Clarion-Ledger* and *Daily News* with a white arm swinging a baseball bat; the caption: "Help Stamp Out Black Rule: Register and Vote, *Paid for by the Jackson White Citizens' Council.*"

The oppressive legislation, white blood lust, and plainly immoral doings of the White Citizens' Council were all part of the legacy perpetuated by the Hederman family. In 1971 the family's strength was still overwhelming. Jackson was virtually controlled by them. The few city parks were pathetically undernourished and by midsummer the grass was dry and dusty. Public swimming pools, ever a target of Hederman papers since the Civil Rights Act, lay dry and filled with weeds; broken beer bottles overran the floors of what used to be wading pools. White kids swam in motel pools for a quarter; by mid-June two black kids had drowned in canals. The main public swimming area was the huge Ross Barnett Reservoir on the outskirts of the county, yet it was grossly underdeveloped and had few recreational facilities. But the Jackson Yacht Club is there, and R. M. Hederman was the chairman of the Reservoir Commission.

In the middle of Jackson is a huge football stadium that seats upward of 46,000 people. It lies vacant throughout summer, winter, and spring. The city's progressive mayor was trying to upgrade recreational facilities (which are not good) for the young. Yet the soil remained untouched, save for an autumn schedule of big games. (Football is among the many traditions vaunted by the Hederman papers, and Zach Hederman is an influential member of the Stadium Commission.)

The city had suffered in other ways as well. In the 1960s, Jackson and the state lost millions of dollars in grants, federal appropriations, and factory and corporate expansion because of the terrible killings and the white rage. In 1970 the city was still riding on rough waters. A northern industrialist told the city he couldn't move a branch of his company there because of the white exodus from the public schools. In 1971, Mayor Russell Davis made earnest attempts with the school board to implement desegregation. But he was still battling the fear lagging from the sixties when the former mayor, Allen Thompson, allowed all his appointees to be carefully screened by the Hedermans, employed a councilite and Hederman family intimate as attorney for the school board, and ballyhooed to Jacksonians that he would preserve the traditions. It was a widely circulated political rumor that Russell Davis would be assaulted in the Hederman papers when he campaigned for reelection in 1973 . . . because he was the first mayor not to be dominated by the Hedermans.

The Jackson cops, lauded for their precision in the Hederman papers, are anathema to the black community. During the civil rights movement cops consistently beat up young blacks, gave them tickets for the sport of it, and taunted blacks in their own neighborhoods. Only with the arrival of two civil rights legal agencies in the late sixties did violence decrease in the "law and order" town that had sent the highway patrol onto the black campus to shell it into submission. Governor Williams, supported by the Hedermans, appeared on TV to pronounce the killings "justified."

The newspapers are an extension of the Hederman philosophy. The *Ledger*, for example made it practice to boycott Evers' news conferences. Such politics as burying an Evers press release in Section 4 beneath the comics were ritual.

One does not read what has happened in the Hederman papers; rather, one reads a monitoring of what has happened. Everything is predicated by ideological foundations. In the mid-sixties, when a vicious drive was underfoot to oust historian James Silver (*Mississippi: The Closed Society*) from Ole Miss, certain wire service articles carrying statements he made in a speech in Memphis were purposely doctored for print in Jackson; the sentence order was rearranged so as to convey a different meaning, something the man actually did not say.

Many people say that in terms of civility the papers fit the family. By summer of 1971 the *Commercial-Appeal* had higher circulation in the part of the state where it was sold, and the *Times-Picayune* was steadily gaining. The *Picayune*'s Mississippi bureau consisted of Bill Minor, one of the finest reporters in the South. An excellent journalist who had weathered all manner of difficulties in covering the civil rights movement, he had turned down offers to go elsewhere because of a deep spiritual investment in Mississippi. (The irony of his career is that the paper he wrote excellent stories for had been unflinchingly committed to segregation in New Orleans and was one of the worst papers in the nation, both in terms of its inaccurate news presentation and its stodgy, unrealistic attitude toward change.) In 1971, because of the *Appeal* and *Picayune* competition, the Hederman papers ceased referring to the papers by name, instead saying, "an article appearing in the Memphis [or New Orleans] newspaper owned by the Scripps-Howard Publishing Company, based in New York but owning papers in the South, said yesterday that . . ." Minor commented, "This is nothing more than a deliberate attempt to discredit me. They don't want to acknowledge the name of the paper. Why? Because they want to damage circulation and because they want to get back at me for not distorting the news."

But the Hederman papers cannot be characterized on the basis of their inaccuracy and venom alone. Indeed, not; there is much more to their propagandization of Magnolia mythology. Extensive coverage that summer went not only to politics but to the third most important cultural phenomenon (after football), which was, of course, the beauty queens. They came in bundles and clusters on the front pages of both papers, in color and black-and-white. They came seated on large tree trunks in Issaquena County and perched along the piers of the Gulf Coast, their hair waving in the spray. They came in pairs in front of the battle-grounds at Vicksburg where gray-uniformed boys had died to protect their great grandmas, and they posed in quintu-plet at the Miss Cotton Pageant at Raymond. The student homecoming court could expect to make the papers in Jack-son from as far south as Pearl River County. For here in-deed was the venerable southern institution of womanhood, seen in its logical extension.

The Miss Mississippi contest, held during one of the most dramatic weeks of the primary, received front-page cover-age, pictures, and articles for five days. And when Miss Mis-sissippi went to Atlantic City a special reporter called in sto-ries on her every morning and evening. And why not? For if Mississippi had blackened her own image, who, save an oc-casional football hero, could show what Mississippi was really like? Who could generate some radiance and beauty for this beseiged state? Who but Miss Mississippi?

Charles Hills, Jr., was the *Ledger*'s chief political re-porter, and he and I were at odds immediately. To my sur-prise, he wrote a most favorable article about the Decatur kickoff speech; he quoted four long paragraphs from "posi-tion" papers on prisons and taxes. Hills had quoted the "King's English" of the paper, which, given the way The Mayor spoke, was somewhat ironic. I wrote Hills a letter complimenting him on the article. The next day I received a call from the Jackson bureau correspondent of an out-of-state paper, a good reporter who liked Evers. "All of us who don't work for the Hedermans are wonderin' why you didn't write to us," he said.

I told him the truth: that I had assumed Hills would write a biased article, but that we were stunned with the fair one. "I feel like everyone else in the campaign," I told the man. "We think you all are good reporters who write fair stories."

He paused and replied, "Well, that's what we figured you thought, but you don't know the havoc that letter's caused. You see, John Bell Williams' press secretary got hold of it somehow—I can't imagine how—and that damned letter's been Xeroxed and is floatin' all around to reporters in town. Now they want to nominate Charlie for Sigma Delta Chi [the national journalism fraternity]. It's no big deal to join in plenty of places, but here we don't like to let racists get in. Williams' press secretary said to me, 'Well, looks like ole Charlie might have a chance now. . . .' "

I assured him I would write ten letters to Sigma Delta Chi telling about the boycott Hills and his paper had on our news conferences. As it was, Hills didn't make it into the office until late July, and then not again until late October.

Charlie, Jr. was a tubby, cherubic twenty-eight or so, and he sat at his deceased father's desk in the Hederman plant. He was generally disliked, both personally and professionally. One newsman said of him, "If you think Charlie's bad, you should have seen his daddy. He was just as much a bigot and equally as mean—only he was *smarter,* and that made him more dangerous!"

The first time I saw Charlie after the kickoff speech was in the lobby of the state Capitol. We stared at each other and I wanted desperately to fight him right there in front of God and the Mississippi Legislature. But to have done so would have been fatal for the image of the campaign. I had to let him smirk as I walked past.

The most notorious man on the *Clarion-Ledger* was not Hills or even the editor, scion Tom Hederman, who I suspect made it clear he wanted no coverage of Evers by his reporters. The shaping tongue of the *Ledger* was a cynical, ulcer-ridden old man named Tom Ethridge. Like Hills, he had never been accepted professionally by most other Mississippi reporters. Ethridge had been writing his "Mississippi Notebook" column for over two decades. A former

Jackson AP man told me that Ethridge was the "real brains behind the editorials—if you could call it 'brains'—during civil rights days." According to my informer, when Hederman's emotions so charged him, he would call in Ethridge, sit him at a typewriter, and pace up and down the floor, blustering, "Tom, ah don't know how to *write* it, but what ah want you to *say* is . . ." and Ethridge would exhale smoke from his cigarette and pound out another piece of Mississippi dogma.

In the fifties and sixties his column was a clearing house for the ideas of the Citizens' Council. In 1970, when the Mississippi State campus paper published an excellent issue discussing the "God is Dead" rage, Ethridge called the students Communists. In 1967, when a Congress-dispatched team of southern doctors published a detailed report about black babies starving in the Delta, Eastland, Stennis, and gubernatorial candidates Winter and Williams condemned the study as a Communist lie, part of a conspiracy. A Hederman editorial suggested that the state should purchase hearses to expedite things. Whether or not Ethridge actually wrote the editorial is anybody's guess.

But in 1971, Tom was growing old. He was still writing his tasteless column, but he came into the office only to deliver it. Though I never saw the man, a copy boy told me that "he looks like he's about to die when he walks in. I hear he's got a dozen bleedin' ulcers inside him. He shakes and jitters so gaw-damn' much he looks like he's about to puke." But that didn't stop Tom's pen.

The *Daily News* at least attended Evers' news conferences, and printed twice as much news about the candidate as the *Ledger*. The *Daily News* reporter covering us most of the time was certainly not partisan to The Mayor, but he never distorted releases. His name was Charles Gordon. He was a scratchy-voiced old man with a butch haircut, looking every inch the reporter apt to breathe fire. But there was something uniquely appealing about him. I liked him in spite of his views, and I believe the feeling was mutual. He took the statements I wrote and put them in with the others. Sometimes he would call and say, "Jason, I'm knockin' off early today. You got anything?" I would say, "Yes, I haven't had time to deliver them yet, but he said . . ." And Gordon would rejoin, "Hold on now, lemme get this piece o' paper into the typewriter. Now talk slow . . ."

I liked the old bastard because he was playing by the rules. He was fairly dependable, although in his personal columns he cut us to shreds. But Gordon actually helped us, and I think he knew it. For people reading the Hederman papers were either believers or cynics.[*] The believers of course liked the way the paper was written. The cynics, even the racists, recognized the hideous quality of the press. The Hedermans were unpopular nepotists. Evers hated the Hedermans, but had a more friendly attitude toward Gordon. One day, stepping out of the elevator in the Federal Court Building and finding Gordon, The Mayor grabbed his hand and shook it vigorously, saying, "There's my ole frien'. That's all right. Just keep my name in there. As long as folks keep talkin' about me, that's all that counts. Say anythin', just keep writin'." Mr. Gordon blushed.

I think what solidified my congenial relationship with Mr. Gordon was an exchange we had over an article he wrote early in the primary. The piece concluded, "There are better things a reporter has to do than stand in the hot sun and listen to this persiflage [meaning Evers' speech]." I sent him a letter—the second and last I would write to a reporter— saying that to comment on a speech was to destroy objectivity. To which he replied, "As for my approach and technique in journalism, I will follow what I think is the right way. . . . Mr. Berry, I suppose you fancy yourself a fine

---

[*] People referred to the papers as "The Hederman papers" or sometimes just "The Hedermans."

young liberal. I too once saw a great deal of hope in things and was a strong supporter of Norman Thomas during the Depression. All of that has changed now, as have I, and as I imagine in a few years, so will you." Nevertheless, from that point on, he did not write personal attacks outside his columns. Perhaps the reason I was really attracted to Mr. Gordon was that I knew he was the only one at the paper who would make sure my releases got into print. I assiduously placed them on his desk.

The *Clarion-Ledger* and *Daily News* were housed just across the hall from each other in a two-story building on Pearl Street in downtown Jackson. The newspaper building is part of the city block the family owns. The printing office is right next door, and the sign atop proclaims in red letters "Hederman Brothers." And from the front door of the printing company you can see a massive building towering over the rest of downtown Jackson one block away. A mere hundred yards from Hederman Brothers is a huge office complex with tree-size letters that say "Barnett Building."

In 1971, Ross Barnett was very much alive. One would occasionally see him sitting in the cafeteria of his building, sipping coffee, watching people go in and out the doors. He was a lumbering man in his seventies, with gray hair and a simple look on his face. Sometimes he would smile and wave to anyone looking at him. By July it became known that Ole Ross was supporting Waller, and this was a symbolic boost for Waller as it gave him a plus with old-line bigots, for Ross Barnett's career, so brief as an office-holder yet so astoundingly destructive, literally made Mississippi into the tragic place that it became during the sixties.

Barnett, elected governor in 1959 as the Council's candidate, had barreled through Mississippi proclaiming, "The Negro is different because God made him different to punish him. His forehead slants back, his nose is different. His lips are different and his color is sure different." But Ross was not all evil. Indeed, the last of ten children born in Standing Pine, Mississippi, he was more dumb than bad. Good-natured Ross had always said, "Whenever you're around, jus' kick open the door and ask for Ole Ross!" Which is precisely what job-seekers successfully did once he was elected.

And when Ole Ross mingled with the crowds there was empathy on all sides. For he was not a cynic like Vardaman or Bilbo. No less than human on the stump, he told one crowd in straight seriousness, "Hodding Carter is an *admitted* moderate!" And in his own peculiar way, he was somewhat gentle toward blacks. He frequently forked over bills to servants in the Mansion when they convinced him they were in need. And he once lent a black man with whom he hunted birds $1,500. To whites, of course, congenial Ross was the good old boy who grew up just a piece down the road.

Perhaps the most famous Ole Ross story concerns the time a reporter caught him in a harried moment and queried him about the United States problems with Communist China: "Governor, what's your view on Matsu and Quemoy?" Ross, nodding intently, replied, "Yes, they're both good men and ah'm sure we'll fahnd room for them in Fish and Game."

But beneath his gaping grin and the hillbilly twang was a metabolism geared for a touchdown on every try. From an impoverished childhood, Ross had worked his way through college and law school and was, by his fiftieth year, a $100,000-a-year damage suit lawyer. As governor, however, he relied on White Citizens' Council members as advisors, and, being an unenlightened man himself, the lack of good advice was responsible for his downfall. A rash of unconstitutional segregation bills swept through the Legislature in his term. But by mid-September 1962 a series of court rulings made it clear that James Meredith would have to be admitted to Ole Miss. As the Meredith registration loomed, Barnett did his damnedest to stop it. Twice he personally blocked Meredith's registration by physically standing in the black man's path; once, when Barnett's plane was held up in Jackson fog, Lieutenant Governor Johnson stood in Meredith's path. The Fifth Circuit Court of Appeals in New Orleans then issued a sweeping injunction against the governor, the lieutenant governor, and the university.

Barnett was now faced with a problem. Before Meredith's second attempt to register, Barnett had gone on statewide television and proclaimed, "We shall not drink from the cup of genocide!" But now, on the last weekend of September, he was forced to come to grips with the problem. He conferred with Attorney General Kennedy about the impending registration of Meredith. Robert Sherrill records part of the conversation in his *Gothic Politics in the Deep South*:

KENNEDY: Can I rely on you that there won't be any violence?

BARNETT: Yes, sir.

KENNEDY: I am taking a helluva chance. I am relying on you.

BARNETT: There won't be any violence. . . . No one will be armed. I will be in the front line and when Meredith presents himself, I'll do like I did before. I will read a proclamation denying him entrance. I will tell the people of Mississippi that I want peace and we must have no violence. . . . When your men draw the guns, I will step aside. You can walk in.

KENNEDY: I think it is silly going through this whole façade. . . . Your standing there, our people drawing guns, your stepping aside. To me it is dangerous and I think it has gone beyond the stage of politics.

The next day the campus was in too volatile a mood for any attempt. Barnett was honestly afraid of a riot and convinced RFK to wait until Sunday night, when the students would be crowded on the interstate highway coming home from the football game in Jackson. It was agreed that Meredith would move onto the campus Sunday night, October 1.

As was customary when the university played in Jackson, the college community descended en masse from Oxford on Saturday. And Jackson was white hot. The *Daily News* banner headline read, "Barnett: All Loyal Mississippians Support Him." Radios blared "Dixie"; fever raged. Barnett meanwhile spoke with President Kennedy on the telephone, assuring him that Meredith would finally be admitted the next day.

If the football game between Ole Miss and Kentucky was not enough to race the blood of the people of Mississippi, the unleashed frenzy vibrating through the stadium that night with the announcement of Barnett's name was. Forty-six thousand voices thundered in the warm night air as they sang the chorus printed in the morning *Clarion-Ledger*:

Never, Never, Never, No-o-o, Never Never Never
We will not yield an inch of any field
Fix us another toddy, ain't yieldin' to nobody
Ross's standin' like Gibraltar, he shall never falter
Ask us what to say, it's to hell with Bobby K
Never shall our emblem go from Colonel Reb to Old
    Black Joe.

Barnett slipped out of his executive box and stepped lightly across the turf. The sweat of the home bench settled in his nostrils. He gazed out at the screaming thousands. He knew what the next day would be like: no blocking the doorway, no more special proclamations—tomorrow Mere-

dith would enter the university. The screaming fans waited
for him to speak. Should he tell them the truth?

Ross Barnett looked into the vast black sky above as it
shimmered in the glare of the floodlights. Suddenly he forgot his misery. For this was Mississippi. He was Colonel
Reb, and despite tomorrow, this would always be Mississippi. Who knows whether it was cynicism, fear, relief, or
shrouded agony that rocked him when he lurched his fist to
the infinite night above and shouted: "I luvvvvvv Mississippi! I luvvvvvv her people! I luvvvv her customs!" The or-
ganic blast, foot thumps on autumn iron, the mesh of liq-
uored bodies could be heard in the next county.

The next night James Meredith quietly moved into Baxter
Hall. Barnett remained in Jackson; there was nothing more
he could do in Oxford. And the campus went to hell. By
dusk, hyper-keyed students were roaring in from the game.
The Mississippi senators and congressmen were called and
were begged to come to the campus to help restore calm;
none came. Carloads of burning-eyed bigots, Klansmen, and
rightest zealots flooded the campus. (Later it was discovered
that various groups had come at the behest of an uniden-
tified caller from a phone in the temporary Citizens' Council headquarters on campus; he had asked them to come and
"help Governor Barnett stand his ground at Oxford.")

The rioters merged with students and hurled bottles,
knives, rocks, and eggs at the federal marshals who had
been sent to preserve order. The crowd grew into an uncontrollable mob, and the marshals fired tear-gas bombs. Mississippi highway patrolmen, standing between the mob and
the marshals, withdrew when students pelted them. President Kennedy by now had spoken on nationwide television,
telling the university, "The eyes of the nation and all the
world are upon you and upon all of us . . . let us preserve
both the law and the peace, and then, healing these wounds,
we can turn to the greater crises that are without and stand

united as one people in our pledge to man's freedom." It was later discovered that, before withdrawing, Mississippi lawmen had showed armed outsiders various entrances to the campus. At 2 A.M. the U.S. Army, at the command of the President, moved onto the campus and battled the mob until the mania subsided.

James Meredith signed his name on the registration form the next morning. Twenty-eight federal marshals had been wounded by gunfire or cooking grease poured on them by irate sorority girls. A French journalist and a jukebox repairman from northern Mississippi lay dead on the Oxford coroner's table with bullets in their bodies. Federal troops occupied a Mississippi town for the first time since the Civil War. The nation and the world were shocked. And Ross Robert Barnett of Standing Pine, Mississippi, was a broken, defeated, and deeply confused man.

Each day I delivered press releases, I would leave the Hederman building, drive past the Barnett Building, and go to the state Capitol. The press room was on the fourth floor, directly above the Senate chambers. As one entered the second-floor rotunda of the Capitol there were four bright columns with niches surrounded by lights like the ones on dressing-room mirrors of movie stars. The two color photos facing the main hallway, which lead up the stairs toward the governor's chambers, were of the *first two Miss Mississippis to make Miss America!*

I had to climb one flight of stairs before reaching the beauty queens, however, and this meant passing the exhibit of the main-floor rotunda. Standing in the middle of the marble floor, flanked by hanging portraits of Paul Johnson and Ross Barnett, was the bronze statue of a small man, with one hand extended as though addressing some august body, conceivably the Mississippi Legislature. The inscription reads "Theo Bilbo, Governor and United States Senator from Mississippi." Who else, in the last analysis, better symbolized Mississippi?

Every time I left the Capitol and walked into the warm summer air, visions of Bilbo and Barnett swam in my head. They were as real to me as Jimmy Swan. I would think of what they stood for and remember growing up in New Orleans, oblivious to the savage moral logic that had existed for a century before the civil rights movement. Nothing had seemed wrong when black folks walked to the back of streetcars on St. Charles Avenue; as a child I had played with black kids who lived just around the corner but went to their own public school, while I never thought to wonder why. During my high school years, I heard older men at the golf club ruefully talking about "the business over civil rights." I began watching the proceedings on TV and became bewildered.

Bilbo and the acrid stares of Hederman employees reminded me of the bitterness I saw in faces of people screaming in front of the New Orleans City Hall in 1960; we had watched it on TV. My father had been morosely silent, my mother shaking her head and saying, "Nothing is worth all of that. Integration can't be so terribly wrong!" Now, as I descended the Capitol steps, *Barnett* etched across the horizon dedicated the sky to memories of my own early life that I tried to forget. Jackson, the raw, callous city forged out of loess wilderness between the Pearl River and the Natchez Trace, proof of civilization only in that it was made of steel and mortar, intensified the tearing inside me. This was a naked, brutal place where one would occasionally see a stir-crazed farmer roar into town on a Saturday night, drunk and ready to do battle with any creature in his path. And the difference between such a man and whites in the New Orleans where I grew up was very subtle. The lingering frontier culture of Mississippi made the quality of racism there rougher than it was in the city of jazz and Mardi Gras, where prejudice was manifested in a genteel, sophisticated way. Mississippians, at least, were more emotionally *honest.*

I had grown up in the kind of world Evers, Ed Cole, and every black person I knew had sought so desperately to set straight. But hadn't it been a white man named Faulkner who ascribed to this heritage a historical doom? Hadn't he shown the South its bloodied hands before they began to butcher? And all for what? I wanted to answer that question, if only for myself and my own expectations of the South.

CHAPTER

5

The most difficult problem I encountered working in the Evers campaign was not racist journalism, physical danger, or any form of harassment. The obstacle that was to take me most of the summer to overcome was the simple fact that I was a white working among blacks.

During the first days of June I was slightly uneasy despite the excitement of the new environment. I was different from the blacks. In retrospect, I am sure that Ed, Magnolia, and Lois were slightly uneasy about me. There is always a period of suspicion, distrust, and guarded feelings affecting both parties when a white person joins a black movement in the South. Southern blacks have lived under white rule for centuries, and the most important understanding a biracial effort must reach is that whites are in Mississippi not to lead but to follow. There is, too, the initial sentiment that most whites have when they first come to the state. That is to say, upon meeting the old black folks, one cannot help but be overcome by the simple goodness and beautiful spiritual quality of the people. Their religion is such a deep cultural foundation that it is, literally, a faith unto itself. The newly arrived white is often so overcome by the beauty of the black people that he tends to look upon them paternalistically—which is terribly dangerous. Though he may not feel the same way toward blacks his own age, there is nevertheless the compelling notion within the recesses of his mind which tells him that, with his experience, he can serve the cause by exerting influence. He may not understand that he is in effect becoming a white boss, but this is the image people soon get of him. Even the most radical—and inspirational—organization to work in Mississippi, SNCC, ultimately decided that the only way it could work successfully in the black community was to purge itself of white members who were social radicals with deep, philosophical commitments.

In this respect, my first week in Mississippi was a mixture of excitement, sadness, and, finally, bewilderment. Ed Cole and I drove to Vicksburg for a rally in a small church one night. As we sped along the interstate I asked him if the crowd would wait, since we had left the office an hour late. Ed laughed. "Don't worry, man, black folks been waitin' two hundred years. They'll wait an extra hour. Besides, you tell a black man to meet you somewhere at seven-thirty and that means come when it gets dark. And then you figure on him bein' a li'l late."

We arrived at the church as the crowd was filing in. After an opening prayer, the local minister introduced Ed, and he began to speak about The Mayor's campaign and what we were doing in the Jackson office. I looked around the small church, gazing at the worn people who were dressed in their best clothes and sitting on ancient wooden pews. Evers was not here, and I wasn't able to hear Ed; I was peering at the black people. Suddenly I was overcome with a great sense of awe—I had seen black people all my life but never gathered like this. They stared at me. The naked truth of what my skin meant was pounding inside my skull. This was a race that had been brutalized and my race had done the brutalizing.

For a moment a man gazing at me from the benches was Johnny, the ageless gardener who had presented himself at the rear door of my granny's house every Monday until the morning she died. It was not him, of course, but when I met his gaze I could not help resenting the understanding of all the kind old grannies, doling out dirt wages to men like him. I looked the other way.

In the last row was an even older man and I stared at him momentarily: Was that Freddie? That could not be him—the wizened caddy with only one eye who had drunk beer with me in a rickety bar on the levee the day I won the Audubon Junior Golf Cup. We had talked about my short game—no, it was not him.

In the first row was an old woman rocking a child and I remembered a woman about her age I had seen on television when I was young. She had tried not to cry and then she became embarrassed when the news cameras focused on her. She was at the funeral of a little girl who had burned to death in a church in Birmingham. Death and confusion had been very much a part of growing up in the South. It was inherited, nurtured during childhood, soon inherited by the young from their elders. It became clearer as one saw it unfold nightly on television: violence at the Walgreen's in Jackson, police dogs in Selma, sorrowful funeral processions in countless towns before Atlanta in 1968. NBC commentator Charles Quinn once said, "The South is schizophrenic." I looked away from the old woman in the first row.

The black people sat in the warm night and listened to Ed Cole speak. As on the first night in Lexington, I was overcome with sadness. But gradually I realized that these black folks did not see me as one making a spectacular break from the burdens of an old life. They had been meeting and working with young whites for a decade now. The low feeling began to lift, and I felt a rare, grand strength, the rev of the pulse upon arrival at a far-off place always previously out of reach. Everyone was smiling and clapping as Ed concluded his speech.

By the middle of June I was no longer feeling guilt. Although I was a white Southerner, I consoled myself with the fact that by being with Evers in Mississippi I had broken from the past, and that in itself meant something. But this was not such an important thing to the people with whom I worked. It was expected that everyone else shared a conviction about Mississippi; I had to prove myself as a person. From the outset, this proved difficult.

The night after Charlie Ramberg arrived we had a hamburger together and in the course of the conversation he told me pointedly, "It's going to be hairy for you for a while. It'll take time to get used to black folks' way of doing things."

I told him I didn't see how there would be any trouble and he responded very quickly, "Don't hand me that bullshit. You'll have to make adjustments to your way of thinking. Everyone does. When I went down to Fayette two summers ago after my second year in law school, I had to go through an incredible amount of changing and self-evaluation."

He cleared his hair out of his forehead and added, "I'd suggest that you start by stop worrying about getting everything done on time."

"What do you mean?" I asked.

"You're too hung up on time. Magnolia told me that you were pacing up and down the office the other day before you and Ed drove to Vicksburg. She said you nearly drove her up the wall but she didn't want to say anything since it was your first week."

"Yeah, but we were an hour late . . ."

"Time's irrelevant to blacks. They don't have rigid conceptions like whites do. Plenty of the country folk don't even have clocks. They go by the sun. Look at The Mayor. You know why he's always late? It's because he's *always* been late."

I suppose I began to realize a deeper insensitivity on my part when Magnolia told me, "You stand up when whites come into the office but you don't stand up for black folks."

"My job is to stand up for the press. They're the only people I talk to and get up for."

"You got up quick," she said icily, "when that blond-haired welfare worker came in the other day. If you get up for one person, get up for all."

Ed later told me in private, "When black folks come in, we gotta make them feel important. They gotta know it's their campaign. Nothin' does an ole black lady more good than when a white boy jumps up and says, 'What can I do for you?' " I started getting up.

There were similar reminders that, more than a political camp, the office was a social catalyst. There *was* importance to meeting and greeting black folks. One needed only walk down Capitol Street to see how whites generally regarded blacks. And it always disturbed me when the old janitor at the Capitol scratched his head when I entered the elevator to go to the press room. He would say, "You doin' okay today, Cap'n?"

Slowly, I was learning that it was simply not enough to look benevolently upon old black folks. In the office things were different. I had always been quick to react angrily when provoked, but now I had to find better ways to deal with conflict.

The women always reminded me, "Clean off your desk. You've got papers all over it. It looks like a trash barrel."

And I snapped back, "What difference does it make? As long as I get the job done, that's all that matters."

"It doesn't look like an office with your desk that way."

"It doesn't run like an office the way y'all keep the files!"

They fumed and I fumed and suddenly I remembered Ramberg's words: "It'll take you a while to get settled." Doses of learning came, just as he predicted. After Lois reprimanded me about the desk one day I glared at her. She warned, "Don't you give me that ole hate stare!" I apologized immediately and cleaned off the desk.

As usual, it was Ed who put things in perspective for me. He was quite a psychologist.

"Those radio cuts you did today were good. Keep it up. But about your desk. I've been wantin' to explain something to you—"

"Ed, they're always yelling at me about that and it's so irrelevant . . ."

"It might seem stupid to you, and I know they're not on top of what they're supposed to do all the time, but you gotta understand the importance of this. Every black person in this office knows that when a white man walks through the door he's jus' lookin' to find a dirty floor or messy desk so he can go say to his friends, 'Yeah, Evers' office looks like a bunch o' niggers work there—all dirty.' " I closed my eyes and nodded, and I started cleaning the desk regularly.

Another time Ed called me into his office while he was eating lunch. As he speared a french fry he suggested that I not ask Magnolia to type for me.

"Why not?" I asked.

"Well, at least for the present, she doesn't like the way you talk to her."

"Is she mad about the desk? I've been cleaning it off."

"No, she's just sort of up tight about the way you talk to her in general."

I pulled at my collar and shot back, "Look, I stayed here until 11 P.M. every night last week writing the position pa-

pers for the press brochure for the kickoff speech. She takes
a two-hour lunch break every other day. Why the hell can't
she type a few stencils for me?"

He looked down at his food and then spoke in a low
voice. "Yeah, man. I know that. But you gotta remember
something. She's a black woman and you're a white man.
No matter how important it is or how you say it, there's a
certain thing between you two that just ain't gonna jive—
until you get to know each other."

For the next week I tried to approach Magnolia cheerfully, but it was not always easy. I realized, as Ed said, that
winning her trust was not something that would come overnight.

Being a white Southerner made it even more difficult.
Both Magnolia and Lois asked me on different occasions if
my mother had a black maid, and appeared somewhat relieved when I answered that she did not. For the other
whites in the office the situation was different. Alec Berezin
had grown up in Cleveland and known blacks all his life.
Ramberg had worked in Fayette a year. Joe Huttie was dat-
ing a black woman. And I had grown up in New Orleans
and gone to Georgetown University, a pillar of tradition.

The turmoil of being a white among blacks remained with
me into July. I was constantly having to evaluate myself.
The worst thing to do was talk about it. It was properly assumed that I was working for The Mayor because I shared
the commitment everyone else there had—I simply had to
learn its application.

Sometimes I would drive out to the huge Ross Barnett
Reservoir late at night and sit on the white shell bluffs and
feel the warm breeze blow across the water. One by one the
lights of Jackson's fine waterfront homes turned off until the
shore was black. Cars of summer lovers parked on the other
side. I would sit and wonder what white kids in Jackson
thought about our campaign, whether it meant anything to

them at all. Occasionally I wondered about what I would be doing were I not in Mississippi—the trip to Europe my mother had suggested at graduation? But Mississippi was too real to even think about much else. College, only a month or so behind me, was a world removed.

I had difficulties, but slowly I felt changes. I was looking at a new dimension of myself for the first time. I was looking at houses I would never have looked at before and I was learning about the feelings that lived inside them. I read the police reports in the Jackson papers and was skeptical as I had never been before, remembering conversations with ACLU lawyers or young blacks who had been worked over by Jackson cops. I read glowing reports of Mississippi progress and had only to look across the street at the unemployed winos to know these statements were skirting the more important issues.

I had dinner with a priest one night, a white man who had been raised in Mississippi and who, in his own words, "was ecstatic when things began to change. I felt it was the will of God."

He spoke about a black woman he knew who lived in the Delta. She had borne twenty-two children. "It's something white people just can't understand," he said softly. "How do you explain to a white housewife on the pill that the Delta woman clings to sex and childbearing as *psychological* boons? The raptures of fornication and giving birth are the two dearest forces she knows. They give her joy."

In large quantities, the environment was sinking in. It was molding a foundation of the deepest objectivity.

I could not get over my striking dissimilarities with the black people and the fact that I related to everyday events in such a completely different way. Dwight and Robert would arrive in the office to sit for an hour or so before leaving for an evening rally. Phones buzzed and typewriters droned in the background, and the two of them would sit patiently and wait. Dwight would tap his palm on his knee while Robert gazed out of the large window. He jerked his head sporadically to catch the blur of a passing truck or the flurry of a mosquito. Their patience astounded me.

And sometimes, when the heat was overbearing, old women came in for the relief of the air-conditioning. They would wait, occasionally chatting among themselves, but often sitting without conversation, just waiting. Kids parked their bikes and came in to drink from the water fountain. Once an elderly brick mason opened the door and timidly pointed to the water fountain. After his drink he sat and said not a word, for fear of disturbing the office.

Sitting motionless, these people had a sadness and yet a nobility. Endurance was a fabric of their lives. As Ed Cole had said, "Black folks been waitin' two hundred years. They'll wait an extra hour. . . ." Some came more often than others, leaving as slowly and inconspicuously as they had entered when they just sensed it was the time to leave. It was almost as if they were letting time roar on without them.

I was most deeply struck by the humility of blacks on the afternoon I sat in the back of a Jackson church attending commemorative services for Medgar Evers. In between speeches, a choir of twelve-year-olds sang old spirituals that mean such a tremendous amount to the people's lives. The line of one refrain stayed with me: "The fault's not in the Lord, Oh no. The fault's not in the Lord, it's in me." The striking irony was that fault could hardly have been more removed from these black children. They were innocents who at long last had a slightly better chance than their parents. Their parents had lived in the shadow of the land for more than a century, raising their young, singing their joys, weeping their sorrows. Religion was more than a cultural trait: it was the foundation of the heritage, for they truly believed. "Freedom" had been the prayer before Emancipation and before the movement.

The choir stayed with me all summer, jelling thoughts of what Mississippi might one day be like. Visions of Jimmy Swan and Bilbo were banished when I sat in the churches of the black folks.

At one service, an old but powerful minister evoked the memory of Martin Luther King: "I have a dream that one day, the grandsons of slaves and the grandsons of slaveowners will stand together. . . ." I believed him.

CHAPTER

6

Charles Sullivan's headquarters on Capitol Street were twice the size of ours and two blocks closer to the Governor's Mansion. His name was embellished in red, white, and blue letters across the front of the building. His enigmatic slogan was "He'll Do It. He Said He Would."

Sullivan papered the state with glamorous billboards. A profile of his face was backed by an azure sky; a lone white star stood in a red square beneath the picture. "He'll Do It" was opposite the face. The face was golden, burnished by the sun, perhaps. But the real Charlie Sullivan had had acne as a youth and he looked noticeably different from the man on the billboard. And his hair, prior to the campaign, had been a dull gray. Now it was a bright metallic color. His press department disseminated releases of the "silver-haired lieutenant governor" and the press picked it up, but quick. Tough and lean, silver of hair and gold of skin, here was a man for Mississippi.

As lieutenant governor, Sullivan had the highest recognition factor of the August candidates. Although candidates ran independently of tickets, by his very association with

Governor John Bell Williams, Charlie Sullivan had to prove himself independent of the outgoing chief. Williams had become one of the most unpopular governors in the history of Mississippi. Even more than his hypocritical leadership and his vetos of sorely needed federal programs, Mississippians disliked his arrogant silence; he held virtually no press conferences and rarely spoke on TV. Something less than a teetotaler, Williams had also flown to Hawaii with seven aides on state money to attend the semiannual convention of the National Organization of Alcoholic Beverage Control States. When New Orleans *Times-Picayune* reporter Bill Minor brought this to the public eye, it evoked the ire of bootlegger and Baptist zealot alike. Minor was subsequently barred by Williams from gubernatorial press conferences. Minor's son, who for three previous summers as a college student had worked in the tax division of the state government, was immediately fired on Williams' orders.

But the worst of John Bell's mistakes was a huge wall of resplendent white brick that he had built around the Governor's Mansion. The only view of the Mansion, a truly elegant building, was through black metal rods in front. From the steps of the Capitol, two blocks away, all that lunching secretaries on the lawn could see were the oak trees rising above the wall. The wall had been built for "security precautions." It had cost $150,000 of state money. By the middle of his administration, the wounded-war-veteran-elected governor was referred to as "the one-armed bandit" because of the whiskey and wall moves. One journalist jovially told me that "they elected John Bell because they figured with one arm he could only steal *half* as much!"

Sullivan had to unharness himself from the Williams image, and The Mayor cackled when Sullivan began to appear on TV. "Lookit ole Cholly, he's sho' 'nuf tryin' to tell everybody he's a good ole Miss'ssippi boy!" Sullivan *was* trying. While other candidates labored to make themselves known and recognizable to voters, Sullivan struggled to change his image and seem his own man. He said he could not support Wallace over President Nixon. Nor could he support Kennedy, Bayh, Humphrey, Hughes, or McGovern. Thus, he was getting Republican money, and many observers felt he would change to the Republican Party upon inauguration. And his renouncement of Wallace not only impressed blacks, but won admiration of the white liberals. A long-standing enmity between Sullivan and Senator Eastland solidified the white liberals' support, for they hated Eastland to a man. Whites partial to Evers said they were going to vote for Sullivan in the primaries. Sullivan stressed his own political career as one of "independence, with my one tie being to you, the voter. In the past four years I have served as *your* lieutenant governor. And I can say to you without compromise that I have served in that office to the best of my ability."

He had a deep, emphatic voice, and his approach was slow, direct, and appeared to be well considered. When he said *all* of the children must be educated, you knew he meant Negroes. His ace line was "I have always, in all my years of public office, faced each issue squarely and with candor." Some people said it took guts to talk about schools in such a forthright manner.

Maybe Charlie Sullivan had guts; at least his political record was not one of paltry aspirations. He had come out of Clarksdale, a Delta town not far from Memphis, as D.A. in 1959, and had run for governor. He had made some impact, too, pioneering for legalized alcohol, a radical thing to do at that time in Mississippi. He was defeated, but some people at least remembered who he was, and so in 1963 he ran again. There was an adage in Mississippi that was applicable to Charles Sullivan: "Run for governor three times and if you've lasted that long you're sure a cinch to win." He got licked in 1963 but made the unprecedented move for a loser in Mississippi of endorsing another candidate, former Governor J. P. Coleman, in the runoff. In 1967, Sullivan was finally elected to statewide office, defeating outgoing Governor Paul Johnson in the race for lieutenant governor. (Sullivan had also run for President of the United States in 1960 on a right-wing ticket out of Texas, supported by oil money; however, it was more a protest against the two "liberal" candidates of the national parties than anything else.)

From the start I thought Sullivan had a modicum of savvy. Breaking loose from the Williams syndrome would be an accomplishment in itself, and he seemed to be doing just that in June. Rumors abounded of polls showing him far ahead of the field; he certainly had the best representation on car bumpers that first month of summer. And in addition to his heavy financial support, Sullivan was widely supported in the press. One Jackson reporter, a bureau correspondent who was a secret admirer of Ted Kennedy, said that Sullivan's refusal to support Wallace and his opposition to Eastland were the two most impressive things about him. Not only that: "I was followin' him on the trail last weekend and he shook hands with every black person in the shoppin' center that came up to him. Now that's *sayin'* somethin' about a man!" The oddity of Sullivan, the Mississippi progressive, was that he had the full support of the Hedermans.

Undoubtedly, the Hedermans figured he would win, and thus they went into his corner from the start. The members of the family wanted to retain their own appointments to agencies, and if they played a relatively significant role in the man's victory there would be the usual obligations to be paid off—and the Hederman strength would continue. By the second week in June large trucks from Hederman Brothers Press were parking in front of Sullivan Headquarters and Hederman drivers were unloading boxes of campaign literature.

Charlie Hills had covered Sullivan's announcement news

conference and his story set the tone of the Hederman coverage of Sullivan. Under the picture of the lieutenant governor, the only candidate to have his picture cover two columns in the center of the *Clarion-Ledger* front page, the headline read, "Liberals Hit at Sullivan."

> The probable trend of the forthcoming gubernatorial campaign emerged Thursday as Lt. Gov. Charles Sullivan made his formal announcement for governor in the August primaries.
>
> In a press conference in the Senate chamber of the Capitol where the lieutenant governor has presided over the past three and one half years, Sullivan was immediately bombarded with a rush of unfriendly questions regarding his base of political support and financing.
>
> Although there were plenty of information-seeking questions, mixed with a few definitely friendly inquiries, it was readily apparent that as the early leader in the race, Sullivan will be subjected to darts from reporters who differ drastically with the lieutenant governor's political position. . . .
>
> Plenty of barbs flew Sullivan's way but he fielded them all. . . .

Sullivan expanded on his theme of "my only tie being to you, the voter," and by July his advertisements had become ridiculous. One radio ad went like this: "In 1959, Charlie Sullivan ran for governor and the voters of Mississippi said, 'No, it's not time yet.' In 1963 he was a candidate once more, and the voters again said, 'No, you don't have the experience.' So in 1967 he ran for lieutenant governor and won. In the last four years he has gained that important experience. Now that he has it, let's let him use it. Let's elect him governor!"

Nearly every newspaper, even those not under Hederman domination, thought he had the experience. *The Deer Creek Pilot* endorsed Pittman, the Corinth newspaper gave Waller his lone endorsement, and Sullivan got just about all the rest.

Bill Waller was less flashy and had a lower-keyed campaign. He started out a decided underdog, announcing his candidacy only after William Winter decided in late May to run for lieutenant governor. Winter, who was finally paying off his campaign debt after losing to Williams in 1967, had a small though resourceful staff. Probably the most enlightened politician of statewide prominence, Winter eventually won the lieutenant governorship, sweeping the first primary.

Starting far back, Waller had billboards that were simpler than Sullivan's. The smiling candidate was looking up, and the caption read, "Elect Bill Waller. This Time, Let's Make a Change." Waller had come in fourth in 1967, behind John Bell Williams, William Winter, and Jimmy Swan. This year, however, he had more money. Most of Eastland's county supporters were lining up behind him and that in itself was strength (Eastland has never lost a Mississippi election and people he supports rarely lose). As opposed to Sullivan, who was seen on TV, billboards, or paid newspaper ads from the first week in June, Waller waited until the last three weeks of the campaign to flood the state with a media blitz. In June, however, the big question was whether Swan or Waller could take second place to Sullivan. Pundits felt that Sullivan might take it all in the first primary, August 3.

Waller's subtle punch line was "We need sober, efficient state government." Given John Bell's Hawaiian jaunt and rumors that Sullivan was no teetotaler, it hit home. The strong approach of Waller's campaign came into focus by early June. He would say, "Let's take the machine politics out of state government. I'm takin' on that Capitol Street gang. This time, let's beat the machine!" The machine, of course, was the unpopular Williams Administration and the Hederman family. The machine's candidate obviously was Charlie Sullivan. When Waller condemned the machine, people realized he was attacking Sullivan. He never had to identify "the machine."

The man who called the shots in Waller's campaign was one of the paramount political strategists of the South, De-Loss Walker, an advertising executive and pollster from Memphis. Walker had handled Dale Bumpers' media campaign in Arkansas. Bumpers, starting with a 3 percent recognition factor, defeated Governor Winthrop Rockefeller in a remarkable upset. It is generally conceded, however, that Walker did not provide the victory impetus: Bumpers, the candidate was dynamic. Nevertheless, the media campaign Walker designed for Bill Waller was excellent. The TV spots stressed issues and, always, the beat-the-machine slogan. Waller billed himself the "people's candidate." The Waller newspaper ads reflected the theme of southern political reform, but in a way even the most bigoted hill farmer could appreciate: "They did it in Georgia with a peanut farmer named Carter. They did it in Tennessee with a dentist named Dunn. They did it in Arkansas with an unknown named Bumpers. This time, let's do it in Mississippi with Bill Waller!" The concluding caption was "Let's Take the Machine Politics Out of State Government."

Not to be outdone, Jimmy Swan was stumping nonstop, for he had no media program. He was visiting the remotest hollows and farm fields in his "Save Our Children" bus. His battle cries were somewhat similar to Waller's, but were vintage Swan: "I say that Jimmy Swan and *only* Jimmy Swan can take the fat cats off the gravy train in Jackson! Who's the only strong candidate without some fancy, frilly advertisin' company from Capitol Street or up in Memphis somewhere? It's Jim Swan, that's who!"

One steamy June morning I stole away from the office to

hear Swan speak in Canton. I sat beneath a magnolia tree on the courthouse lawn; he spoke from a flatbed truck. The rest of the audience consisted of an ice-cream vendor and a small dog. Even the merchants stayed in their stores. No one seemed to care. "Oh they had a big one last week," he yelled. "The fat cats from Jackson. They were down there on the Gulf Coast havin' 'emselves a wild likker party! Ohh, they were havin' a doozie!" And if ever there was a scenario of the changing times, it was this morning, redolent with summer flowers, when Flonzie Goodloe of the Madison County NAACP marched across the courthouse lawn with thirty kids who cried mockingly, "Right on, Jimmy!" A truck roared past the speaker's platform and drowned his spiel about Bilbo's book. He cried louder, "We've got to save our schools!" One of the black girls cried, "Have mercy, Jimmy!" Swan scowled and hurriedly ended his speech. The black kids giggled. It seemed that even Mississippi had awakened to 1971.

But by the second week in June, The Mayor was concerned about Swan. He had decided on a strategy that would enrage liberals, racists, and blacks, not to mention members of his staff. He called a press conference in Jackson to announce his endorsement of a candidate in the August primary.

"I'm askin' all my supporters to join me in votin' for Jimmy Swan," he said.

While the press gulped and Charles Gordon's jaw hung open, The Mayor elaborated: "The only way for me to win in November is to make the choice between me and some other candidate the clearest-cut—between the best candidate, which is Evers, and the worst, which is Swan. I jus' don't believe there are enough hatin' white folks in this state who would vote for Jimmy over me. I think everyone knows he cain't do nothin' for the state."

After a long silence a reporter asked, "Mayor Evers, is

this to say you are going to seriously ask blacks to vote for Swan?"

"My supporters," he commented, "are not just blacks. And yes, I want them all to vote for him. So, we gonna back Swan. An' you watch us. We mean business."

Burt Case, a TV commentator, said, "Mayor Evers, not too long ago you told me that Charlie Sullivan was the best choice blacks could make in the primary. Have you gone back on that statement?"

"Well, Burt, we was jus' speculatin' then. Now I mean business. Chollie Sullivan's said he'll hire blacks to state jobs, but he ain't got a one of 'em workin' in his campaign. If he's for blacks, let him come out and show us!"

Bill Minor of the *Picayune* was fuming: "Do you mean to tell me that after all of the pain and insult and hardship blacks in this state have endured, you're askin' them to vote for a man like Jimmy Swan?"

"Bill, this ain't civil rights no more. This is politics. An' in politics you play to win. That means goin' after your greatest threat, which is all the so-called moderates, Sullivan, Waller, and Pittman, and crushin' 'em."

Minor countered: "A man named Machiavelli advocated the same kind of strategy you're talkin' about in a book that's since gone down as a philosophy of ill repute . . . and you're advocating the same thing?"

Evers looked at him. "Bill, I don't know anything about that book. I never read it."

The state went into a minor uproar. Pittman called it "political prostitution." Sullivan denounced it as hypocritical. Jimmy Swan grumbled, but finally, after no doubt a strategy session, said that he would take all the black votes that came his way. He added that he had known all along there were plenty of good colored people who would vote for him. Hubert Humphrey wrote a letter questioning the ploy and Evers responded with a note telling Humphrey to take care of his own politics. Hodding Carter, III, wrote a scathing editorial, calling the move cynical and bad strategy besides. Mrs. Patricia Derian, the Loyalists' white national committeewoman, told me, "It's horrible. He shouldn't do this." Perhaps the most conclusive statement was the remark of Mrs. Betty Carter, wife of Big Hodding: "It's not at all elegant."

For the first two months of summer, at every political rally, The Mayor explained the strategy in full, saying, "Black folks, this ain't civil rights no mo'. We got to give Jimmy every vote we can right now and then drop him quick like hot ice come November!" Black county leaders were most unhappy with the endorsement.

In retrospect, I am still not able to determine what The Mayor's ulterior motives were. Unquestionably, he arrived at the decision by himself. (No one else could have dreamed it up.) He had no advisors to speak of; the staff organized trips, worked with the counties, and handled the press, but he made all the decisions. The two men closest to him, his brother and Robert Kennedy, were long since dead. With The Mayor's intensely individualistic approach to life, he decided what to do and then went the hell ahead and did it. Some black leaders were calling it a boss tactic.

There were, of course, deeper political implications. Whites deliberating between Waller and Swan—the two men with the best chance to meet Sullivan in the runoff— would now think more seriously about Waller. Sullivan would indeed have a strong line in the second primary if he faced Swan: "Do you want a man who has served with dignity as your lieutenant governor these past four years, or do you want a man who got where he is because Charles Evers delivered a black vote to him?" Although at the time few people could predict the effect of the move, Waller won a swing vote the day of the announcement.

Certain observers took Evers' move to be a tacit support

of Waller. Reasoning that there was a sentimental tie because of Waller's prosecution of Beckwith, it was conjectured that Evers was supporting Waller. This view faded as Evers began hitting Waller especially hard because his children were in segregated private schools. Then, too, the endorsement made Swan look like something of a fool. The would-be giant killer now had to devote part of each speech to attacking Evers. The new stigma of Evers' support made Swan appear a clown, and this blackened his image. It is a terrible blow to any politician to be ridiculed.

In another dimension, The Mayor's strategy served as a test of black voting potential. If blacks supported Swan in the primary—even if he was defeated in the runoff—it would show every white in the state the strength of the black electorate. It would also be a test of Evers' strength as a political leader, or boss. But deep inside him, I believe The Mayor was convinced the strategy could actually work. (His staff didn't think so.) His career had been one of immense leaps and bounds. In less than a decade he had gone from Chicago racketeering to civil rights to Fayette and now to a run for the governorship. Odds meant nothing to him. His ideas were huge. When he interrupted a working day in the office to urge everyone out to pin posters on Farish Street, his mind visualized people seeing posters, standing underneath them, and soon after that, large billboards attracting more people—serving to remind them to register and vote. If blacks did vote en masse for Swan, he would be in the runoff with Sullivan, and then maybe the stunt could work. But as one paper noted, if by some chance Swan did win the Democratic nomination, an independent such as Ross Barnett or Paul Johnson would jump into the general election, knowing that neither Evers nor Swan truly represented Mississippi voters. Evers would need an incredible turnout in November to win. He could throw the election into the Mississippi House, but there his chances would die. Much criticism began to come our way.

One night, driving back from a rally, I sat in The Mayor's car discussing press coverage. As was his custom, he would ask a question, gaze out the window, nod vaguely as if uninterested, and then shoot back with another penetrating question. I was in the middle of a reply when he abruptly asked, "What do you think of the Swan move?"

I paused momentarily, remembering that the decision had been reached in a matter of days and convinced to a hastily called meeting of county leaders; critics said it had been railroaded through. "If you want my honest opinion, I don't think black folks like it at all."

"Dammit," he snapped, and his breath lingered as he stared into the night. "They just don't understand. The worst rascals of all are Ed Pittman, Chollie Sullivan, and Bill Waller. All of 'em are middle-o'-the-roaders, that's all. They won't be no different than John Bell. They'll hire 'em a few Toms and say, 'Lookit us down here in ole Mississippi. We sho' 'nuf changin'.' Jason, we don't need those kinda people."

"Mayor, I think what everyone's sort of uptight about is what it would be like if *Swan* won."

He looked at me incredulously. "You got to be kiddin'. B'lieve me when I tell ya, after all the people this state's had, that crazy redneck couldn' be worse than a one of 'em. Lookit Georgia—black folks got more in federal programs from that stupid ax-handler Maddox than they woulda got under some so-called moderate. Man, man. If we elect Brother Swan by some chance, there'd be more HEW programs comin' down here and foundations pourin' in *because* of him. Hell, he couldn' do no worse than John Bell!"

I was more disturbed than anything else about the Swan move, for I never felt blacks would vote for him to begin with. But sometimes I would meet liberal Jacksonians who saw a leader in Sullivan, the man who "signed the note for the Clarksdale private academy." I thought about the hypocrisy of Mississippi, vaunting itself as a land of noble traditions while everyone else thought of it as the asshole of the nation. The Mayor had a subtle point: why shouldn't Mississippi be represented by Swan? None of us discussed the strategy with The Mayor; it was done and he demanded complete fidelity through it all.

But the threat of Swan would not leave me. When we drove into the communities with pot-holed roads and ramshackle houses and tin roofs, and when I met the gentle, slow-talking black people, I tried not to think about Swan because it hurt. Sometimes it took a while before the black folks warmed up to me, and it was hard not to cry—these tender people who had lived all their lives in tropical heat and frigid winters, tied to the alluvial soil for life. And in a land that was so hostile, what else could be considered human besides the soil? I would think about Swan after we left the shanties and old churches and rust-colored roads with chickens and scraggly dogs and trash on the side. Whites stared at me and I thought about his ranting, waving the Bilbo book and yelling about the last page. I could feel him in the Jackson shopping center where a country band strummed tunes in front of the cafeteria where I ate.

Carrying our Swan endorsement across the state was only one difficulty at the outset of the campaign. Swan himself said in each speech that he would not speak on the same platform with Evers. But it was no problem, for Charles Evers was not invited to the political fairs and rallies that summer. And despite the influence of television, each candidate campaigned religiously on the stump. Only five cities in this state had populations of more than 50,000. County fairs were an ingrained part of the culture. A candidate did reach the majority of voters on TV, but if it was known that

he boycotted the fishing rodeos, barbecues, and old-time political rallies hosted by the people of the Great State of Mississippi, then look out.

One could always count on August candidates crossing
paths at the Maben Lion's Club rally or the Tishomingo
County Fair. As the chunky Jackson lawyer Waller descended the stage he would shake hands with Pittman, the
state senator from Hattiesburg, or with Perry, the tempestu-
ous judge from Grenada. At the rallies and eat-outs one
would hear the most colorful rhetoric. Judge Perry denouncing Sullivan and Waller for their well-financed campaigns: "They're the Gold-Dust Twins!" Or Mr. Swan, in
Lexington: "Too many pointy-headed liberal editors have
let Communism get a fist-grip on this state!" Or the silver-
haired lieutenant governor: "As your governor I will bring a
dignity to other parts of this land, for there is widespread
misunderstanding of our people in Mississippi." Or Elmore
Greaves, a Citizens' Council star of the sixties opposing William Winter in the lieutenant governor's race: "He's in cahoots with Charles Evers, I can tell ya that. He's goin' after
second spot on the nigra's ticket!"

It was discouraging to see this campaign composed of
such fragile issues called "unexciting" by the press. For the
most exciting of all candidates, the purest of populists, the
man the nation was most interested in, was not even invited
to the rallies. We received all of four invitations to fairs that
summer, and two came from the Gulf Coast, a traditionally
progressive area. (The tourist trade, hotel commerce, etc.
have hosted black groups in Biloxi and Gulfport since the
fifties.) Thus, one of my self-assigned duties was to try to get
The Mayor invitations to these all-white gatherings. Occasionally I would have luck, as when I called the Pontotoc
Fair Committee and caught speakers' chairman Wayne
Rains at his Pak-A-Sak supermarket just as he was about to
leave to see about tent poles.

"Charles Evers, you say?"

"Yeah, Mr. Rains [in my best southern accent]. The Mayor wants to speak before as many white Mississippi folks as possible."

"Weeelll, I never thought he'd wanna come up here. I didn' bother invitin' him. I guess I could take it up with the speakers' committee. . . . Aw hell, *I'm* the speakers' committee. Tell you what. If Charles Evers wants to come up here, well then come on up. He's a candidate like anybody else. . . ." But I had to call Wayne back the next day, and cancel with great thanks and apologies. The Mayor had to go to Washington to see about a sewage grant for Fayette. There were few Wayne Rainses that summer.

If The Mayor was concerned about speaking engagements or getting equal treatment with the other candidates, he never showed it. He spoke to the first white rally of the campaign in July at a Gulf Coast fishing rodeo. As he walked into a sea of white faces in the football stadium, there were some scattered boos and light applause. He told me later, "If you think those white folks were afraid, you shoulda seen me—I was shakin' like a leaf!"

As he began to speak, a man shouted, "Go home!"

Not batting an eye, he replied, "I *am* home!" And then he tore into Mississippi's taxes, prison system, and the "way all them ole politicians, year after year, go to Jackson, make money for themselves, and give us Mississippi folks nothin'."

But there were places like Mendenhall, where blacks and whites do not speak to each other. The Mayor spoke in front of a food co-op because town officials refused blacks permission to congregate on the courthouse square. Coming into the impoverished town, law enforcement officials could be heard on the two-way radio pickup in The Mayor's car. The sheriff was talking to his men.

"What are they doin'? Can you see 'em?"

"Just barely, Chief,"

"Who the goddamn hell is it?"

"It's the hippies. The niggers and the hippies."

(Third voice) "Naw. It's Evers."

"What'll we do, Chief?"

(Fourth voice) "Chief says to sit tight."

And there were communities where he spoke in churches because black folks feared a rally on the courthouse square. And towns where an advance man had to jump out of the street to avoid a roaring pickup truck. There was Charleston, where armed Deacons escorted black folks to the courthouse to register. One could not easily forget the past. A group of Wisconsin students, a nun among them, did voter registration work in Tallahatchie County, and were fired at with high-powered rifles. Highway patrolmen wrestled a black man against his car in that county, and began prying out part of his beard with pliers because he had an Evers bumper sticker on the fender. Two telegrams regarding Tallahatchie County were sent to Attorney General Mitchell, who did not even send a reply. (One reporter was discussing the state treasury candidacy of a John Bell Williams aide: "I've got plenty of reasons not to like the man. But he comes from Tallahatchie County, and that's reason in itself. 'Cuz nothin' *good* ever came out of Tallahatchie County!")

But these obstacles were not preponderant. By mid-July it was apparent that town officials for the most part were eager to show not only us but at times *themselves* that they were going to extend political courtesies to the candidate because he was a candidate just like all the others. There were no bombs thrown through the window of the campaign office; there were virtually no altercations involving staff members. Policemen even avoided ticketing cars in front of the office.

Ed Cole was always delighted to tell of an early problem Squeaky had with Jackson cops.

"Where ya goin', boy?" the cop had yelled as he stood over the sports car.

"I happen to be driving somewhere."

"I can see that. You know what time it is?"

"It's 3:30 A.M., and what's it to you, cop?"

"Get out of that fucking car! Just who in hell do you think you are?"

Squeaky said softly, "I'm Charles Evers' chief of security."

"I'm sorry, sir. We thought we had a stolen vehicle. We've made a mistake." He drove off before Squeaky started the engine.

My own brush with violence was marginal. On the way to my car after a movie one night, I was confronted by a drunken son of the earth stumbling out of a bar. He called me a "Mr. Smart-ass son-of-a-bitch with hair too long who thinks he can fandangle up our niggers, and I'm tellin' you somethin', that's plain *wrong!*" Whereupon he took a roundhouse swing at me and missed completely, which allowed me to plant my fist in his face and run like hell to my car.

For a time there was an aura of fortitude to the campaign trips, but it wore off quickly. A German journalist touring with us one Sunday kept looking out of the window to see if we were being followed. He couldn't understand the frivolity and havoc of our group. ("Lois, don't lose them buttons, they cost money. . . . Elix! Elix? where's he gone to? . . . Magnolia, they're servin' chicken at the community center. Make sure mine ain't got no pepper. I cain't take pepper. . . . Jason, take care o' our German friend here.") The trips were such a web of human spirits woven together, differing, holding to one another in moments of humor, reacting to and partaking of our various pasts, that we were often oblivious to thoughts that things might be unsafe.

Courage was one quality already imbued in each black person in the office, for all of them had gone through hard years before most of the whites knew who Charles Evers was. When Ed Cole talked about the days of SNCC, I tried to imagine myself walking into a restaurant with a group of blacks or trying to register voters in Philadelphia in 1965. I was a myopic teen-ager then, playing football and going to drive-ins. Sometimes I tried to imagine whether I would have gone down to Mississippi as a civil rights worker in 1964 had I been of age. I never was able to decide.

The blacks were consistently skeptical about the way whites treated us. Lois said to me one day, "Jason, jus' because things are goin' well doesn't mean they're gonna stay that way. You don't know white folks." Indeed I did not. For despite drunken rednecks, statues of Bilbo, and villains like Charlie Hills, down inside of me I simply could not believe that these people would do me harm. As a boy I had spent some summers on the Gulf Coast, and since 1968 I had known good people in Poplarville from weekends at the farm. But goodness was something I quit looking for in whites. A woman in Greenwood spat on me one day and after that I decided that people were good only as long as they thought you were part of their culture.

Everyone had different duties on the road trips, and my task was phoning in press releases to the Jackson AP and UPI desks. It had its difficult moments. Jotting a few notes on an envelope, I would compose a story and dictate it over the phone to the reporter on duty. This was always trying as there was not much free time between books-and-buttons collection and departure. But there was a second difficulty. I had to find a booth immediately, whether in the gas station next to the Holly Springs courthouse or two blocks away next to the Burger Chef in Greenwood. And there were always the stares. I would have to make my way through groups of four and five whites crowded next to a phone booth. They looked at me and I felt pity for them, for there was a forlorn resignation to their faces. They didn't understand me, but because of my connection with the press—carrying a tape recorder—they hurriedly moved out of the way. I represented freedom, something they didn't have. They feared standing in the crowd of blacks. They could not afford to be seen, and so they stood around the courthouse square, watching, trying to hear from a distance. But I, some strange creature with the same color skin, could stand right in the middle of the crowd of black people the whites had dominated all through life. Clustered around trucks, barbershop poles, and beat-up cars, they were obviously scared about what was going on.

Perhaps there was a deeper alarm within the white folks. For in 1971, with Evers bounding across the state attacking the August opponents for their lackluster platforms, the August candidates were tearing into each other like raving fools.

The man with the most troubles was Charlie Sullivan. He was working hard to shed himself of the John Bell Williams stamp when the governor called a press conference, dabbed a handkerchief on his brow to remove sweat caused by the flood of TV lights, and said to newsmen, "Gentlemen. I . . . uh, have been advised by city inspection officials that the Mansion is not fit for habitation. . . ."

"Do you mean the Governor's Mansion is condemned, Governor?"

"Uh, yes. This is correct."

The mood in Jackson was testy that week. People were mad. A fidgety man paying a lunch check at the Downtowner said to an associate that they ought to condemn the blasted so-and-so who was moving out. Which of course they could not do.

The Democratic contestants blamed Charlie Sullivan for being part and parcel of the disgrace in Jackson. (He had sat on the Building Commission, which okayed building the $150,000 wall.) Sullivan, with few means of recourse, promptly said he would move into the Mansion with his family as soon as he was elected, and then set about to have it repaired. Pittman referred to Sullivan sarcastically, "Don't you believe when it's unsafe for John Bell, it's unsafe for Charlie Bell?" Swan said the fat cats on the gravy train had built themselves a wall that worked fine, but a floor that was caving in. And Bill Waller kept plugging: "This is another example of the machine politics that's kept Mississippi under reins for so long. While we change the governor every four years, the political machine keeps the power. . . . This time, let's beat the machine!"

The Hederman papers ran an in-depth article on the Mansion, and then got back to the task at hand, which was pushing Charlie Sullivan's candidacy. Sullivan himself observed, "You didn't hear anybody talking negatively about your lieutenant governor until this year and then it was from people wanting his job."

Tactics in the various camps began to emerge. Everyone was attacking Sullivan, and Sullivan was talking about honest government. The Hederman press, in turn, led by Charlie Hills, was attacking Sullivan's opposition.

Though Mississippians read only sketchy newspaper reports about "organizational meetings" of the Evers campaign, by July The Mayor's presence was being felt. Fears common to Laurel and Decatur about coming out for rallies were not unique to those towns; but soon they began to ease up. From one town to another, word spread of how the drowsy summer afternoon had suddenly exploded with the caravan of cars, posters, books, buttons, Afro girls, and white boys with unkempt hair who accompanied the robust politician as he stood on the steps of the courthouse and talked to his folks, making them laugh when he mocked "tobacco-chewin' Ross" or "poor, do-nothin' John Bell." And then firmly, *politically*, driving home the message—register, vote.

The campaign had a psychological effect on blacks. It confirmed that the day was gone when congregating on the courthouse lawn was the white man's game. There was a thrill in the air that really hit home when The Mayor said, "We thank our local officials for lettin' us meet on the courthouse steps. But we all know it's *our* courthouse, jus' as much as it's theirs . . . and we gotta right to meet here."

We always drew good crowds, too. Bay Springs was the first and last place blacks were afraid to come hear him, and late in the race we returned there, to a crowd of four hundred. Black folks were excited about his candidacy. Alec Berezin's determined advance work before each speech ensured the large turnout.

The Mayor was aware of the good field work being done and whenever the staff met he attempted to give us directives of sorts. "All right, all right. We gotta make sure this is organized." He would take ten minutes to tell us why campaigns didn't need meetings: " 'Cause if everybody's workin', tell me what you need a meetin' for?" Then he would listen to our observations about the campaign's progress for about ten minutes, and suddenly we realized that this was indeed a meeting. Then he would grin and say, "But you know somethin'? Campaigns are always confused. That's one thing a good campaign's always got to have—*confusion*. If you ain't got no confusion then nobody's workin'. . . ."

In one such conference he queried me about my "P.R. work." I said, "I've been checking billboard advertising and the company gave me a list of prices on that pink paper I gave you—"

"*That pink paper*? Lawd, lawd. Son, that says it'll cost $28,000 to saturate the state. I ain't even spent that much myself so far. An' we don't have that much money floatin' around."

Lois: "No, indeed. Sho' 'nuf don't."

Magnolia: "I *know* that's true."

Jason: "Well, wait a minute. Mayor . . ."

Lois and Magnolia: "Jason, we don't *have* that kind of money."

The Mayor: "Well, wait a minute now. We gotta be fair and square. Let Jason say what's on his mind."

Jason: "I was going to say that if we want to build a sense of pride in the black communities, instead of saturating the state—which I realize we don't have the money to do—why don't we think about putting three or four billboards in black areas of certain towns, and maybe a few near college campuses or somewhere we've got a chance at a few white votes. . . ."

Mayor: "Well, that don't sound too bad. Mmmm, maybe thirty wouldn' be too much to afford, about $3,000. I could raise that after those two speeches in New York next week. We could put two billboard signs in Natchez near the River."

Squeaky: "Don't forget Tupelo."

Ed: "Clarksdale oughta have a couple."

Mayor: "Oh yeah, get two up there, Jason."

Alec: "Starkville, definitely."

Mayor: "Yeah, Elix, got to get 'em for Starks . . ."

Magnolia: "I think we should put one up near I-55 in Jackson."

Lois: "And one near Jackson State, too."

Mayor: "Yeah, but no more'n four for Jackson . . . let's get all this down on paper now. Magnolia, honey, write all this down."

And so we decided on billboards. It was a minor victory of sorts for me, even though we later junked the whole idea to pour what little money we had into extra TV time. But The Mayor realized the change of feeling that had gone on in the meeting. He looked at me and said, "You gotta keep pushin' like that, Jason. If you got somethin', go ahead and say it."

Then he turned his head and looked at Alec, then Ramberg, and then back at me. "Fellas, y'all got to understand somethin'. No matter how much you—whites in general—want to help, there's this thing inside us black folks that's hard to explain." He tried to smile but his mouth broke into a wry curve.

"Y'see, we jus' can't trust you." His eyes, which had been dreary from lack of sleep, suddenly came to life. "Don't get me wrong now. It ain't that Charles Evers don't trust Elix or Jason or Chollie Ramberg. Naw, it's jus' that black folks in general don't trust white folks. Y'all been mean to us all these years—not *you*, but white folks."

"That's right," Magnolia said.

"I know that's true," Lois said.

The Mayor continued, "But you gotta understand somethin'. B'lieve me when I tell you, we're learnin' from *you*. This is a campaign we're all workin' in together. We're all learnin' from each other. Ain't a one of us better than another. We got different positions, but we all learnin'. . . . *I'm* even learnin'—and I'm The Mayor!"

Money was a magical and nebulous factor in the campaign. Mrs. Evers brought us checks on Friday; however, The Mayor had to co-sign them. If he was out of town we had to wait for his signature before cashing. The Mayor himself had to give the word before any check was presented in advance of some service. Grimly I remember the first and only paid appearance of the Democratic primary.

As we left the TV studio, the manager said to me, "Mr. Berry, you're the press secretary?"

"Yes."

"Well, you owe us $760."

"Mrs. Evers didn't bring it over?"

"No."

"One moment, please." I caught The Mayor as he was getting into his car. "Man, man. We gotta pay these people."

He snapped, "Not one dime over $760. Not one cent more!"

"Mayor, that's the right price, but we haven't paid 'em *anything* yet."

"Oh." He loosened his tie and sat back. "Well, tell 'em we'll pay tomorrow."

"No, no. We can't do that. They won't air the tape."

Squeaky was getting irritated. "Come on, Jason. The Mayor's got to get back."

"I know, I know. Mayor, the tape won't go if—"

"All right, all right. I'll call Nan. Where's the phone?" And so for an embarrassing thirty minutes I waited at the studio until Mrs. Evers arrived, all smiles, with the check.

The Mayor followed every dollar that went in and out of the office. This was a natural product of his attitude toward money—which was to use it wisely and only when absolutely necessary, and at all other times to try to build on what he had. But the reason for his strict parsimony was, of course, that our campaign was running on a shoestring. We learned the hard way the drawbacks of our unfortunate financial situation after we convinced a man to print 5,000 bumper stickers. "Now when the man asks you for the check," Ed said to the two volunteers assigned to pick them up, "just tell him the truth—The Mayor had to lay over in New York because of bad weather, and he'll sign the check an' send it special delivery when he gets in tomorrow." But the man refused to give the bumper stickers. When The Mayor heard about it he howled, "What's that guy gonna do with all them bumper stickers?" What the guy did was make the volunteers return a second time, with a money order.

The campaign itself was often sustained on the books-and-buttons money we collected in black communities at the rallies—$400 if a large crowd, $100 if small—and this went directly into the Evers for Governor Campaign Fund. Sometimes the next day's deposit to the First National Bank of Jackson would be in the plastic bag along with the left-over buttons, which he would take home with him at night. One night The Mayor said, "Wheww, look at this." He held up the bag. "We got $300 overdrawn and $400 in the sack. Lawd, lawd. Who ever heard of runnin' a statewide campaign with four hundred bucks in the bank . . . and that hasn't even arrived yet!"

Once he told me, "You know, the real problem that black folks got to get over is with their money. I shouldn't have to be payin' for this campaign out of my own pocket. How many candidates pay for their own campaigns? Lookit the Kennedys. All that money they got, and after every one of 'em got elected, somebody'd throw a big ole $500-a-plate dinner to pay off the debt. Black folks should be payin' for me. They should make contributions to this campaign, to their local candidates' campaign. Well, black folks is jus' learnin' about politics." Then he reflected a moment. "O' course, they're plenny o' black folks that plain jus' can't afford to contribute."

The Evers campaign was not the only organization running on a threadbare budget. By mid-July, the Republic of New Africa was having troubles. The RNA was living on a small farm in Edwards, a town on the fringes of Hinds County. A cadre of blacks from Jackson State had joined the

group, seeing no redeeming qualities in a biracial gubernatorial campaign. Under the auspices of Imari Obidale, the
president, the group was not only attracting young blacks
from Jackson and outlying areas; it was getting heavy press
coverage, and nearly all of it was unfavorable. A main problem seemed to be money, and when Obidale announced
that Lofton Mason, the black farmer who owned the land
they were living on, would have to face a people's court, it
caused a stir. The purpose of the court was to decide if
Mason, a candidate for supervisor in the general election,
was in fact still owner of the land. Mason contended he had
rented the acreage to the group, for which he had been paid
$1,000. The RNA claimed the money was a down payment
on a deed to the land. Mason was demanding more money.
He said his soil was damaged and he wanted recompense.
Our office had no contact with the RNA and no one knew
which side was right.

Although I was not in sympathy with the RNA's separatist ideology, I was concerned about their plight. It was obvious Mississippi was raring for a fight. The state attorney
general had condemned the group as had Governor Williams; the press attacked them; everyone knew the cops
were just waiting for an opportunity to get them.

The Mayor was enraged when the RNA announced that
Lofton Mason was guilty of cheating the group, and he
promptly called a news conference to explain his position.
"I'm standin' right behind Mr. Mason. There ain't no reason
he should have to get only lip service from the RNA. This is
a black man, a Mississippian, who's lived all his life in the
state, and he don't have to give up his land to no kangaroo
court. I've said repeatedly, I'm against 'isms! That includes
racism, separatism, militantism—they're all in the same cradle, one as bad as the other."

A reporter asked, "Does this mean you're going to physically stand by him and evict the RNA, Mayor Evers?"

"That's for him to decide. If he don't want my help, that's his business. I jus' want him to know I support him . . . and will support him in person if I got to. If the RNA wants to take some land, why don't they take some o' my land . . . or some o' Big Jim Eastland's land?"

The questions shifted and they asked about the campaign's progress. Then I noticed for the first time that Charlie Hills was sitting in a corner; this was the first news conference he had covered. At a lull in the questioning, Hills said, "You're somethin' of a law-and-order man, but I hear if I drive in the streets of your town your cops will arrest me."

"No, that's not right. Thing is, you've never driven through Fayette, so how would you know?"

"I don't drive there 'cause I don't want to get arrested."

"Well that's you. You're jus' afraid. The law we enforce says *nobody*, not even The Mayor, drives over twenty-five miles an hour. We jus' enforce what's on the books. I say if it's a law, obey it."

Then Hills asked about The Mayor's plans for the approaching Neshoba County Fair, the biggest political rally in Mississippi held each summer in Philadelphia and widely attended by country people and politicians.

"Yeah," Evers said, "I plan to go to Neshoba."

Hills retorted, "You been invited?"

"Fair's open to all candidates."

"Have you spoken with law enforcement authorities up there?"

"*Up there*? You kiddin'? Hunh, those guys aren't gonna furnish me security and you know it."

"Do you carry security?"

"Yeah."

"Are they armed?"

"I carry security."

"Are they armed?"

The Mayor grinned. "What kind of security *isn't* armed?"

The reporters roared. "Sure they're armed. That's why they're security." Then The Mayor smiled and added jocularly, "I'm armed, too." The reporters laughed again.

I wondered if Hills knew that Neshoba Fair officials had steadfastedly refused to let him speak, saying the gathering was only for August primary candidates (which had never been the case in previous years).

The next day we felt repercussions of the RNA statement. Four members of the group came into the office and asked to see The Mayor. I was writing at my desk and didn't notice them until Magnolia nudged me on her way back to The Mayor's office. I walked over and introduced myself to the group, and none of them would shake hands. One guy pulled at his collar as if to get more air; another chuckled. I returned to the desk, sensing something bad was going to happen. The Mayor emerged from his office, Squeaky at his side. I followed them back to the front of the office.

"Hi, fellas," Evers said.

Obidale, wearing a dashiki, stepped forward. He spoke fast and didn't waste words. "You made comments about a nation of black brothers and sisters. You're runnin' for governor, man, and how can you be governor for black people of Mississippi if you condemn the only black nation?"

"Now look," Evers responded, "I'll tell you jus' like I tole reporters . . . an' I bite no bones about it—I'm against 'isms. Racism, separatism, any kind o' 'ism. I got no quarrel with your group, but I don't want y'all to go walkin' over some ole farmer who's so old he can't hardly even *hear*. An' all for some li'l piece o' land."

"We're an independent nation. He's been found guilt—"

"Guilty, hell. He don't owe y'all nothin'. That waddn' no court y'all ran."

"You're lyin'."

"Watch your tongue, mister."

Then Evers lost his temper in a way I had never seen. A

scowl split his face and he drew back his fist, but Squeaky, obviously prepared to destroy any of the men before us, stepped between The Mayor and Obidale, and said calmly, "Clear out. Now." They left, calling names behind them.

As quickly as he had become enraged, The Mayor calmed down. The men were still within sight of the window and he put his hands on his hips and drew a circle on the floor with his shoe. He smiled. "Ain't that somethin'? Ain't that somethin', now?" He walked back into his office and never said another word about the incident. But it had demoralized me. I hated to see factionalism in this state that could so poorly afford it. I had strong feelings against the RNA, however, because I knew their appeal was strong among young blacks, the people we wanted to attract.

The next morning (July 23), I forgot all about the RNA. Charlie Hills wrote an article for the *Clarion-Ledger* that ran on the front page. It read:

Neshoba Fair Could Become Hot Spot

The air at the Neshoba County Fair this weekend could be charged with more than the usual political rhetoric when Mississippi politicians take the podium.

Scheduled to speak are all but one of the candidates. . . . November candidate Charles Evers was not invited to speak at the historical political event because he is not running in the Democratic primary and [he] has vowed he will bring a contingent of armed guards to "protect" him.

Mayor Evers said, "I am going to shake hands and speak on the platform." Last week Evers told newsmen, "I'll be armed, too."

He said he would not even consider asking fair officials or Neshoba County Sheriff for whatever protection he might feel he would need.

Aside from the obvious tone, Hills had lied. Evers didn't "vow" anything; he never used such a strong word. He had responded to Hills' question about the fair, saying he planned to go. Playing up the "armed contingent," Hills didn't say what the press knew was true—that Waller and Charles Sullivan also had armed bodyguards. Everyone who had been at that press conference knew Evers carried body-guards because he received threats in Fayette each week. Moreover, Evers knew that the Neshoba Fair people didn't want him to go. Three civil rights workers had been mur-dered in Philadelphia, seat of Neshoba, in 1964; the police had been in on the plot. Nevertheless, I had passed the word to newsmen after the conference, for whatever it was worth, that we were in contact with the highway patrol.

Local law enforcement officials had done good jobs keep-ing problems from arising in their towns when he spoke on the courthouse lawns. Alec Berezin wrote letters of thanks to all sheriffs who had cooperated and in releases I stressed, "Mayor Evers was pleased with the wonderful cooperation of officials in ——— when he spoke there." And then we had Hills, writing of Evers, who would take his armed blacks to Neshoba.

The Mayor was in Fayette when Hills' story broke. I called him and he cursed. "They say I cain't go 'cause I'm runnin' in November. Then this article . . . they're trying to make me up as a fool."

The Sunday, July 25, edition of the *Clarion-Ledger* car-ried a schedule of speakers for the fair. To our shock, the first name on the list was that of Harold Gregory, a political unknown who was reportedly running as an Independent in November. The Mayor called me before noon. "You know what this means?" he said. "As long as one independent is speaking, I should be able to."

"Yeah, I've been workin' on a statement all morning."

We had to call their bluff. Evers didn't want anyone prohibiting him from going. The press release reiterated The Mayor's statement that he would go to shake hands, and that he intended to speak. With an Independent candidate on the podium, he assumed he would get a slot. The Hills article was attacked as "fallacious"; however, that charge did not appear in the brief mention given in the *Ledger* the next day. But on Monday the situation intensified. Fayette was deluged with threats and rumors of threats. Crank calls poured into the Jackson headquarters for the first time that summer.

The staff was about evenly divided on whether to go. Alec was for it; Ramberg was especially eager to "stuff it right down their Mississippi throats." Magnolia, Woody, Lois, and Joe Huttie were opposed to it. Squeaky was for it, as was Ed, although neither of them chose to press it. They wanted The Mayor to make his own choice.

I was for it one moment, against it the next. The Neshoba Fair would be a week-long nexus of spit contests, cattle shows, carnival rides, beauty shows, and then politics, the center-stage romantic interlude of the searing summer. This would be Swan's moment of glory; Marshall Perry would have a field day; Waller and Sullivan would draw large crowds. A Jackson attorney told me about the fair: "It's sort of a cultural extravaganza. But it's also a place where every redneck south of Memphis and north of Louisiana can drink his insides out, raise hell, yell at the moon, and go home dead drunk since he'll have his whole family with him and one of 'em can drive." I had visions of Schwerner, Goodman, and Chaney being shot to death, their bodies beaten with chains and lumber, and then buried in the swamp outside Philadelphia.

Suddenly I began to think about death.

I could not really believe that he would die. Death was something The Mayor did not discuss. Squeaky and Martin were always hurrying to catch up to him, but he was always moving away from them as if their mere presence reminded him that he might be shot. Even though he liked them and knew they were a necessity, he didn't like having security men. They slowed him down.

But I remembered the first night I had met him in Lexington, how he had looked at the door every minute or so. He had spelled out his notions of death to a journalist some time later: "So that's the way it goes down here—murder followed by whitewash, followed by more murder. And after a while, white folks get the idea it's no crime killin' black folks, 'cause they know they always get away with it. And for everyone of us we *know* gets murdered, how many others been killed and buried deep in the forests or fed to the 'gators in the swamps? So that's why I don't get as riled up at the thought of my own death as some of my friends up north do. When death been walkin' right behind you since you're a baby, you get used to it. I grew up with death. He's almost like one of the family now." All I could think was, *"someone is going to shoot Charles Evers at the Neshoba County Fair."*

The Mayor wanted to go, but he realized it would be uncommonly dangerous. His daughters were pleading with him not to go. Even newspaperman Bill Minor called: "Look, don't go. He's already getting a mountain of publicity by just *saying* he's going. Tell him not to. It's too dangerous. And what good would it serve?"

Finally, Mrs. Evers went to everyone in the office and, with glassy eyes and a shaking voice, said, "He's marched through walls of Klukkers before. It's not that he's afraid. It's just that this would be stupid. He can't win any votes down there. They're just a bunch o' crazy rednecks!"

The next morning The Mayor came into the office, a solemn look on his face. He went into his office immediately. About this time I had an idea. I knocked and entered his office. "Why don't we call the fair president, Norman Johnson, and *tell* him you're comin'? Make him force the decision out in the open. If they say 'no,' they have no reason and we can call them racists, which the press will eat up. All he can do is let you come, now that they've agreed to let that guy Gregory speak. Then you can publicly decline, after they've publicly invited you."

He grinned and the staff crowded into Ed Cole's office. We sat around the campaign manager's desk, The Mayor sat intently in a small chair next to the WATS line. I called the Neshoba Fair information booth. "Hello, this is The Mayor's office in Jackson callin'. It's very important that The Mayor speaks to Norman Johnson, pronto."

The man on the other end of the phone gulped. He thought it was Jackson Mayor Russell Davis' office calling—which I knew he would think. The man said, "Jus' a moment. Hold on. We'll get him. . . . Hey, Mort. Get your ass down there and call Norman. It's Russell Davis' office callin' him. . . . Hold on, sir. You tell The Mayor we're gettin' him. . . ."

I held the phone to my chest and all of us nearly split our guts laughing. When Johnson answered the phone I handed it to Evers. The two men had known each other as youths in Philadelphia. The Mayor was beautiful. "Hey, Norm, this your ole buddy, Mayor Evers." A long pause. "Tha-at's right, the mayor of *Fayette*. Say, how's your children doin', anyway? . . . Good, good . . . yeah, my youngest is in high school now. . . . Remember how you and me used to play in that red Neshoba mud when we was kids? That ole sheriff y'all had never knew it when I was bootleggin' in that ole funeral hearse."

Then he got serious. "Look, Norm, I'm comin' up there. Y'all let that ole rascal Harold Gregory git on the stand, and I got jus' as much right as he does. . . . Naw, naw. You lissen to me, now. Norm, I got the same right he does. . . .

Well, you make them arrangements quick, cause I'm coming. . . . What? All right, all right."

"What'd he say?" four voices blurted.

"He said, 'Dammit, Charlie, all right. But don't tell anyone I tole you. . . . I gotta clear it first and do some fast talkin'.' "

The Mayor slapped me on the knee. "Brother Jason, you're turnin' into a first-rate politician. When you run for governor of Loosiana, I'm gonna be right at your side, all the way."

The fair committee called him in Fayette Tuesday night to offer an official invitation. He thanked them, politely declined, and they released a statement to the press in an attempt to save face. But Evers had proven his point. It would be dangerous to go, the Evers press statement said. The Hills article had caused too much trouble; it was falsely written and aroused too many threats. The Mayor appreciated the belated invitation, but "since harmony and brotherhood are my ideals, I have no choice but not to go." The black man spurned the invitation because of a simple reason: the atmosphere at the fair would be lethal. This incident necessitated a sublime digesting of crow for the Neshoba Fair folks.

Once the excitement over the anticipated Evers' appearance subsided, the Neshoba Fair was Mississippi color at its best. The first speakers came Wednesday. Roy Adams was the first big name. He had used TV advertising sparingly, but a number of newspaper ads had appeared. The picture showed the candidate riding a black stallion. The ad read, "Roy Adams has been described as Mississippi's darkhorse candidate for Governor this year. He comes out of the Appalachia foothills of Tishomingo County with a record of public service which encompasses state government, education, and industry. He is the son of a school teacher . . ."

Roy came out of the hills to go the fair, and he brought a horse, too. The steed was a dun brown, however, and a local farmboy led it through the sloshy mud to the speaker's podium. Roy stepped onto the platform without getting himself muddied up. His speech, according to press reports, outshined the horse, but not by much. He charged that a group of twenty-nine influential Mississippians had recently met in Jackson to "decide on the future of Mississippi." He had the list with him, but for fear of hurting some of his friends on it, he would not release it for public consumption! He pledged his support for public schools, but noted that "we have had private schools in America since the Colonial days and we're not going to do away with them."

The Hederman papers' coverage of the fair was in keeping with the push-Sullivan philosophy. Of Waller, Hills wrote: "Waller . . . told the crowd, 'Mississippians will not stand for four more years of machine politics,' *which through the campaign he has claimed existed.*" (Italics added) His coverage of Swan was unnecessarily cruel: "Jimmy Swan delivered his standard stump speech which he has utilized throughout the campaign, and injected no new issues."

But the next day Sullivan spoke, and the press report was vintage Hills:

Biggest Crowd Hears Sullivan at Neshoba

Philadelphia—The spark of past political years that had been missing from the Neshoba County Fair appeared Tuesday as Lt. Governor Charles Sullivan's appearance attracted a huge crowd which jammed the speaker's pavilion and spilled out well into the sawdust covered fairgrounds courtyard.

The "feel" of the air was evident throughout the day, as the week's largest crowd reacted to the electrifying strains of "Dixie" and the "Star Spangled Banner" and the participants of the Jackson Day Program presented a professional yet folksy menu of entertainment.

An occasional Rebel yell, not heard since the last gubernatorial campaign, punctuated the festivities.

·   ·   ·

Briefly noting that most of his opponents have constantly issued personal attacks against him, Sullivan warned Mississippians do not need an "ugly, demeaning, negative type governor in your mansion."

"What I am concerned about is the future of this state," Sullivan said.

Sullivan said his white hair, which has been the target of barbs by various opponents, has turned that shade because "I've been about the people's business."

Hills changed tone when Pittman arrived:

State Senator Ed Pittman, whose arrival was delayed because of bad weather which cancelled his plane flight, immediately launched attacks against Sullivan and other opponents in the Governor's race.

Although not addressing as large a crowd as did Sullivan (many left after Sullivan's speech) Pittman drew cheers with his opening statement. "I'm not the man from Glad, even though I'm wearing a white suit (like Sullivan's). . . .

And that, more or less, was the Neshoba County Fair.

On August 3, Mississippians went to the polls to vote for the Democratic nominees. An overriding question was whether blacks would turn out, and whether they would vote for Swan.

By ten that night the results were in. Charles Sullivan led the governor's race with 38 percent of the vote, 268,000 votes. Waller was second with 31 percent, or 208,000 votes. Swan placed third with 17 percent, 115,000 votes. Later it was estimated he received only 27,000 black votes; he carried Evers' Jefferson County, however. Roy Adams finished fourth, Pittman was a surprisingly low fifth. Fiery Judge Perry was sixth. A seventh man, Andrew Sullivan, received few votes. (Everyone had heard a rumor that he was running at Waller's behest to confuse a few voters into voting for the *wrong* Sullivan; the rumor was never proven true or false.)

More important to the Evers campaign was the defeat of black candidates in Marshall and Noxubee counties. The slates had run to test black voting strength; the across-the-board losses were discouraging. The organizations had failed to get out the eligible votes; the whites voted a straight white slate. We had our work cut out for us between August and November.

CHAPTER

7

There was one element about the man Charles Evers that each of his campaign workers at one time or another had to reckon with: his ego. To understand him, you had to accept the ambiguities of his ego.

He was deeply religious but also ruthless. He was disarmingly candid, yet he maintained an aloofness that often frustrated those around him. He demanded complete fidelity from his aides while refusing to delegate authority to them in key areas. Yet his feelings for us were so strong that by late summer he periodically told us about them. He did not discuss salary with most aides until they had worked two or three weeks; acting on instinct, he hired me the day we met. He had a roaring sense of humor, but with bodyguards all around him one knew that he had an awareness of death.

His power of oratory was staggering, yet he was astonishingly ill-read. His charisma most affected old blacks and young whites, the two groups he enjoyed the most.

He liked people who, like himself, were activists and not intellectuals. His was a wide circle of friends, northern and southern, black and white, rich and poor. But he was a mysteriously private man at times who once said that, since the two people closest to him were dead, nothing could hurt him now. He was always at ease in social gatherings; he did not smoke or drink, and only in emotional moments (and among men) did I ever hear him curse.

He enjoyed power; his attitude about it bordered on the monarchical. But his power, like his speeches, was geared to the theme of social change. He was tender and aggressive, compassionate and materialistic. To understand him you first had to trust him, and that meant being willing to make sacrifices.

Charles Evers knew that his campaign was of symbolic importance to everyone in Mississippi, even to the most bigoted Klansman, but for different reasons, because Mississippi desperately wanted to erase its shameful image. Evers wanted to show that the past was buried, but his wish grew from deep and complex motives. Charles Evers' candidacy was an emanation of his ego. The campaign functioned on two levels, each wedded to a separate dimension of his ego.

Charles Evers was running out of a sense of dedication and *fulfillment* of his brother's death. The campaign was a spiritual mission. Medgar Evers, martyred eight summers earlier, was clearly the vital shaping influence on Charles' life. A marble monument in Medgar's honor stood on the lawn of the town hall in Fayette. Evers' interests in the town were located in the Medgar Evers Shopping Center. He frequently told reporters that one of the campaign's major objectives was "to bury the hate, to heal the scars." That had been Medgar's struggle.

The memory of Medgar shared in The Mayor's bedrock religiosity. His brother and his religion had been the focal points of his childhood. His sense of ritual, the understanding of the black man's cultural balance between God and life, was always apparent. "Amazing Grace" played in the background when he spoke; his speeches were like religious

sermons, and he always mentioned God. "I know that somehow, God's gonna see fit to let all that racist hate change
into love. But black folks, we gotta make that happen. God
don't give us nothin' unless we go out and work for it. . . ."

The controlling factor in Charles Evers' life was the
mythical importance of his brother's life and death. The relationship of the two, as Charles saw it, did not only derive
from their differences; rather, it centered on the spiritual
qualities of Medgar that Charles cherished and, ultimately,
emulated. In July he told a *Playboy* journalist:

> Medgar was always different from me; he was kind
> and gentle; he never wanted to hurt nobody. I was the
> rough one, the trouble-maker. All the fights and messes
> we got into, it was my fault, not his. . . . Medgar, he
> was a romantic, I guess. He was always considerate,
> worried about people's feelin's, whereas I was willin'
> to ride over 'em roughshod to get what I wanted. . . .
>
> I loved him. I was kind of fatherly toward him. I
> mean, he was my baby brother, and I'd try to take care
> of him, look after him. We went everywhere together,
> did everythin' together. We used to sleep with each
> other, and one of us was always kickin' the other one
> out of bed. I remember those cold winter nights . . . I
> always warmed the bed for him. God Almighty, was
> those old sack sheets cold! I'd warm up a spot for
> Medgar, then shift over and give it to him. I used to
> put my legs on him to keep him warm. It seems just
> like yesterday. It's hard to believe he's gone. . . .°

When we campaigned in Decatur, Newton, Philadelphia,
areas where he had lived before going to Chicago, he talked
at length about old ministers, people who since had died,

° PLAYBOY Interview.

folks he had remembered from church and youth, and always about Medgar. The two constants, his brother and his religion, interplayed throughout his rhetoric.

Even during gangster days, he had maintained his devotion to Medgar and an understanding about religion. He sent money home to his brother; however, "I never told him where it came from, how I got it. . . . I didn' want him to feel guilty takin' it." And late one night as I sat in a car with him coasting down the Natchez Trace, he told me with a wry grin that "in Chicago I didn' go to church as much as I should have—or needed to—but I did go." He told one crowd, "Us black folks, our religion is somethin' we learn when we're li'l children. It's somethin' that never leaves us —even when we know we're doin' wrong! It's the feelin' that, even as bad as a man might be, he knows somehow that God's let there be a little good in him." His feeling about religion was more direct after he left Chicago; it was less weighed down with hypocrisies. It also brought him closer to the memory of his lost brother, who had been very religious.

Talking about Medgar freed him from the guilt of his career in Chicago and cemented his ideals to his brother's. When he spit out the truth—"Oh, pray for me, Reverend, I was in Chicago and I was *ba-ad*"—he was confessing that he had changed because of Medgar's death. And this was very real to the black folks. They chastised themselves before God in emotional religious services each week. The Mayor's speeches—eliciting "A-men" or "Thaatt's right!" or "Jesus Saves!"—were a manifestation of the religious tradition. To black folks, Evers' politics came from the pulpit of southern experience.

His autobiography was dedicated to Medgar. He said that he didn't want anyone digging up his past during the campaign so as to politically damage him; he wanted to unveil himself by writing a book, and he challenged his opponents in the campaign to do likewise. (It was also suggested that he didn't want to be left open for blackmail by old Chicago people.)

The confessions of the book were part of his redemption. The people most enraged by the book were the Mississippi white liberals, virtually none of whom gave us any campaign assistance, including members of the Loyalist party. The book provided the excuse of The Mayor's questionable ethics vis-à-vis Chicago for those unwilling to lend support to the campaign. But the deeper dichotomy was cultural. The whites wanted to be called by Evers, to have their advice sought and listened to. The Mayor, a black man whose very life had been opposed to going around the back of the white man's house, refused to ask whites for their counsel. They would have to come into his campaign or call him at his house.

I think all of us in the campaign came to feel something of Medgar Evers' spirit in the late-night bull sessions we had with The Mayor in his office. After returning from a rally a group of us would crowd in, spilling off the couch onto the carpet. He would sit at his big desk. The huge photograph of his brother hung behind him: a taut face, firm and slender; the eyes were bright and the mustache pencil-thin. In his weary moments, The Mayor looked as though he might have been the father of the young man in the photograph. The resemblance was striking, but The Mayor's eyes had bags under them. At midnight his face was sadder and more burdened than during the day. He held a handkerchief tightly in his palm and ran it over his brow every minute or so. Each time we met this way he invariably said, "B'lieve me when I tell you, we're changin' Mississippi! This *campaign's* changin' Mississippi!"

As a politician he manifested yet another dimension of his

ego. Politically, he had shaped himself. An intense passion for freedom drove him every breathing moment. While the mythical presence of Medgar gave him ethical perspectives, it was his own thunderous spirit that gave force to his life and his politics. Medgar had been gentle as a youth, and as a civil rights leader influenced by Gandhi. Revered in life, Medgar became a martyr in death. The boy Charles had been the "rough one, the trouble-maker"; he had carried a gun for a time after coming back to Mississippi. Charles was never on good terms with the NAACP or SNCC. In the thin library of civil rights history, one book speaks of him as "Charles Evers, whose only distinction seems to be that he is the brother of Medgar."

Evers' victory in Fayette was the only logical end to the black movement in Jefferson County. Blacks had won suffrage through blood, their goal the politics of liberation. Laboring in his brother's shadow, Evers had been the catalyst. But upon inauguration as mayor he became a symbol to the nation. More important, he became his own man.

The gubernatorial campaign gave life to the deepest passion of his ego. His dynamism, quest for power, and sense of destiny generated the campaign. His gubernatorial candidacy was Evers' most important political accomplishment because he personally became the symbol of Mississippi in the midst of change. The national press covered the candidacy as a crusade, which in many ways it was. The campaign itineraries retraced the brutal geography of the civil rights movement. Black folks "sanctified" courthouses where there "used to be only white folks had rallies, but unh-unh, no more!" The religious element, the conviction that "this *campaign's* changin' Mississippi," the staff's attempts to draw in young whites, the gradual awakening through the state media that a black man was seriously contending for the governorship, the "new Mississippi" that was being presented to America through the national media—this was the stuff of Evers' politics. The campaign was a social phenomenon. The candidate made his presence known daily in Mississippi. *He* was the issue of the 1971 campaign. Whether he won or lost was irrelevant; his candidacy and Mississippi's response to it were the crucial factors.

Each of us who was close to him saw a constant interaction of his two selves. The spiritual awareness of his brother, the religious element, was one side. On the other side, as a political creature, he lived by his own visceral drives: he was proud, ruthless, hard, materialistic, intensely individualistic, but, beneath it all, honest. He used to say, "I got to make my own decisions. I can't be bossed *nor* bought!" Although he understood the people's need for religious belief, he indicated the necessity of separating religion from politics. He admonished his audiences: "Now, black folks, we can go out and pray all we want, but that ain't gonna get our local candidates elected. Prayin's fine, but we need votes. And you don't get votes unless you get out and work for 'em!"

One always knew that as a person he was the balance of the two drives: the human Charles tempered by the mythical force of Medgar. His movements reverberated from one sphere to the other. And one could not understand him without recognizing his own perception of past and present. He knew he was a Mississippi son, an ex-gangster, a civil rights leader, and a politician. Accordingly, he wanted his audiences to know him as such. He wanted those who came in contact with him to be illuminated by his brighter and darker impulses.

The focal point of his political self was his own history. The lessons of Chicago, like the memory of Medgar from youth, had laid a firm foundation for his thinking, feeling, willing, and distinguishing himself from other men. He was unflinching when he said, "They're those who are with you and those who are against you. The ones against you, you crush. That's the only way." He had needed this instinct for survival in Chicago's cavernous northern ghetto, where life had always been vicious and combative. He told Elizabeth Drew in a televised interview, "I believe in nonviolence, but only up to a point. If a man takes a swing at me, I'm gonna hit back!"

Mississippi, where his life began, had made him what he was long before Medgar's death. He had grown up in dirt-poor Decatur, where "your momma and daddy tell you how the white folks hate you and how you got to be careful how to deal with 'em or they can kill you jus' as quick as they'd step on a bug."

Evers' family was a stabilizing force in his childhood. By all indications (as revealed in his autobiography) Charles was shaped more in the image of his father; Medgar, "the gentle one" who later excelled academically, seems to have been influenced more by his mother:

My Momma was strong and my Daddy was strong, and they influenced my life the most. I got my religion from my Momma and my Daddy taught me not to be afraid.

Daddy was a mean man. He couldn't read or write, but he didn't back off of any man—white or black. His name was Jim Evers, he was tall, over six feet, like me. He didn't have the kind of trouble many blacks had, because Daddy was so mean. He'd just raise all kinds of problems. He worked hard, but he wasn't a bit scary. He taught me that most white folks are cowards. If they haven't got you outnumbered, you can back 'em down. So I've always thought that I could outwit most white folks. Being black, you gotta learn that just to survive. The only thing I didn't agree on with my

Daddy was when he'd say, "That's a white man's job." There's no such thing. . . .

My Momma was a bright woman and she wanted the best things in life for her children. After I got elected Mayor of Fayette, I had one thought: *I wish Momma was here.*

She read the Bible a lot and had an understanding about it. She knew the time was coming when we were going to have to have an education. She just poured it into our head.

The Mississippi of his youth was a world of juxtaposed extremes: his family and religion, the white folks and hatred. But an early dilemma having little to do with race was to have a lasting effect on Evers. When he was fourteen his father had an affair with another woman. The incident, in his own words, "left scars." He discussed it in depth in the *Playboy* interview:

I mean, a mother is closer to a son than to anybody else, even his daddy, and it did somethin' bad to me to see her hurt, even though she tried to put a good face on it. . . . I know it don't make no sense, but I came to identify all women with Momma's pain, and I wanted to get back at 'em. I made a solemn oath to myself then that I'd never give a girl flowers or candy or a valentine, or treat her with anythin' but contempt. And even though I know it's not right, that attitude stuck with me. I've used women, I've made 'em pregnant and dumped 'em, I've put 'em in whorehouses, but I've never respected 'em.

PLAYBOY: Not even your wife?

EVERS: No, Nan is different. I love Nan, jus' like I loved Momma. I'll admit I have my own fling now and then, but I never allowed any other woman to come between us. I told Momma that my wife would never suffer because of some other woman, and she hasn't. I may have somethin' on the side now and then, but nothin' serious, nothin' that will endanger our marriage. And I'd never come between another man and his wife and family.

PLAYBOY: Isn't your attitude toward women—your mother and your wife on a pedestal and all others dirt —unhealthy as well as irrational?

EVERS: It may be, but I can't change the way I feel. Momma used to say to me, "Now, Charles, don't you go round tryin' to hurt women." But I disobeyed her there. I always tried to get even with women for Momma's sake, to avenge her; and right down to this day, I have a hard time likin' most women. That's why I've never been too popular with girls. But I'm bein' frank with you, and healthy or unhealthy, that's the way I am, and it's too late to change now.°

The statement about women, which late in the campaign he was forced to discuss at some length on television, certainly belied his charity and ideals. I believe when he answered the question he was referring to an emotion that had remained with him all his life. In both his book and the *Playboy* interview, he discussed an affair with a white woman that had had obvious effects on him.

Before I met her, when I had in mind I hated all white people, I thought: *Every white woman I find I'm going to take and I'm going to do everything to her to make up for what they've done to us.* My intentions were not to rape them, but I knew how they felt about blacks, so I was going to use them. I changed my mind.

° PLAYBOY Interview.

If a woman loves you, it's not the color of her skin. It's the feeling she has for you, and the feeling you have for her. Period. . . .°

I think she helped defuse some of that hate that had been growin' up inside me, and I'm grateful to her for that.°°

During the campaign he never once showed himself to be disrespectful or hostile toward women. He was chauvinistic in that he thought all of the women on staff were secretaries, when most were doing research and other vital jobs. He always insisted that women go on the road trips. "Our campaign," he said repeatedly, "is black and white, young and old, male and female." Men and women shared in selling of books and buttons, but women bore the brunt of the task, and *they* had to account for the money! He repeatedly stressed that he would, as governor, appoint "a black, a youth, an ole person, and a female to every board I got the power to appoint." His Fayette staff had more women than men. He actually spent more time talking to new female volunteers. Once he said, "We cain't let those girls come all the way down here to Miss'ssippi and have 'em think that no one cares. Bein' the candidate, it's sorta like I'm the father."

He discussed his attitude toward women as he did other facets of himself. In speeches, interviews, and in his book, he first mentioned the past—his past, Mississippi's past, the country's recent past (the civil rights movement)—and then he talked about change. He said about his own life, "It's not what a man was yesterday that counts. It's what he is today. An' I'm twice as good as I was bad . . . an' I was plenny bad." As for his past dealings with women, he told one group of college students, "Prostitution is a *turrible* thing,

° Evers, *Evers.*
°° PLAYBOY Interview.

the worst thing I ever did in my life, and I regret it to this
day. I'd fight it with all my power if I became gov'nor. Because it shames a woman. . . ." Although he did not ex-
press his conversions clearly all the time, the distorted val-
ues of his old life were something he *was* ashamed of. At
worst, he was a chauvinist in the traditional male sense.

I suspect that the deep scar of his life prior to Medgar's
death was not his father's infidelity but his death. He died in
a freezing basement of a Mississippi hospital because black
patients were not allowed in the main wards. He discussed
it in his book:

> I raised all kinds of hell about it. . . . I tried to insist
> that they put him in a ward, but they refused. When
> he died they called me and I jumped in an ambulance
> to go after him. Being an undertaker I knew how bod-
> ies were handled, and I didn't want my Daddy han-
> dled that way. So I went and got him. And the white
> doctor said, "How in hell can you do something like
> that. If you can pick up your dead daddy and drive
> him back to Philadelphia, you ain't got no heart."
>
> And I replied: "You've got enough heart to put him
> down in a place like this and let him die. Sure I've got
> enough heart to carry him in my own ambulance. I'd
> rather do it than see some of you do it."
>
> Then I rolled Daddy on out and put him in the am-
> bulance. When I got back to Philadelphia I was going
> to embalm him, but those around me wouldn't let me
> do that. But I looked on while they embalmed him.
> And I dressed him myself. Then I went upstairs, and it
> was strange knowing that Daddy was downstairs,
> dead, and me upstairs trying to sleep. But I couldn't
> sleep.
>
> At church, for the funeral, I broke down and passed
> out. . . . I didn't know then that I would lose my

mother before too long . . . and Medgar would be shot.

He left Mississippi in 1956, shortly after his mother died. He had become modestly successful as an undertaker and hotel manager in Philadelphia, but whites systematically destroyed him financially when he began voter registration drives. He left with $26 in his pocket.

Medgar Evers' career took shape about the time Charles left for Chicago. At his brother's urging, Medgar became the first black applicant to Ole Miss in 1954. He was, predictably, turned down, but the very attempt made him a hero to Mississippi blacks. While Charles immersed himself in the Chicago underworld in his struggle for survival, Medgar was becoming a legend in Mississippi as field secretary of the NAACP. During the time they were apart, both Charles and Medgar knew the younger man's life might be in danger. Charles returned to Mississippi frequently for voter registration drives. Perhaps the psychological effect of his parents' death had made Charles hypersensitive about Medgar.

Medgar's death was the turning point. After the funeral the first thing he did was dream about revenge, about hiding in the bushes and killing whites as a sniper. "But something told me it was wrong. This battle was going on within myself. Everyday I'd go to the office and sit at Medgar's desk; it was like he was there with me, and something kept saying, 'Medgar wouldn't want it like that. That's not the way.'"

Picking up his brother's mantle was only one part of Charles Evers' period of traumatic change. In 1963 his life took on a new dimension both because of his work in Mississippi and in the growth of a sense of self. In his new career he was changing the Mississippi of his past, the land where love had so long been crippled by hate. Returning from Chicago, he saw that the only alternative to revenge was to attack racism as hard as he could with every element of him-self except hatred, for that had been inside him in Chicago, and hatred had killed Medgar. The civil rights movement was something through which he sought to resurrect the feeling he had had for Medgar by applying it universally through his work.

As with Medgar's spiritual presence in his ego, Evers' po-litical side had grown from his remarkable relationship with Robert Kennedy. "I loved that man like a brother," he told me on two different occasions. Kennedy had been more than a political cohort. The two had personal and emotional bonds. Each man shared in the other's loss of a brother, commitment to social change, and uncompromising attitude about politics and its place in society. Robert Kennedy was the second alter ego in Charles Evers' life.

Medgar and Charles had met JFK and his younger brother in 1960; they had campaigned for the Presidential candidate in Mississippi. Charles and the President could hardly have been said to share a friendship, but, as Charles later noted, at best it was "a sort of political alliance." When Medgar was assassinated, Charles sat with President Kennedy in the White House and was told by the Chief Ex-ecutive, "I will do anything that I can to keep something like this from happening again. We can't let your brother die in vain."

As suddenly as Medgar died, Bob Kennedy entered Charles Evers' life. The Attorney General stayed with him during Medgar's funeral and called him continuously in the following weeks. He gave Evers his private phone number and said to call any time. But the deep bond between the men grew when Kennedy lost his brother five months later. Evers was at his side immediately and remained with him throughout the ordeal. After the funeral, despite the dif-ference in geography, the two men saw each other fre-quently, and called at least once a week.

Commiseration alone did not propel the relationship. Kennedy and Evers saw in each other reflections of the same identity, dilemma, and hopes. Jack Newfield has written in *Robert Kennedy: A Memoir* that the two forces in Kennedy's life were "competition and religion." Kennedy's Irish Catholicism, like Evers' black southern Protestantism, was a cornerstone of his culture. Kennedy's competitiveness, which Newfield explains grew out of his zeal as a boy to prove himself his older brothers' equal, was only mildly analogous to Evers' growing pains in Decatur. But the force behind both men was molded in a similar spiritual growth.

Both men had brothers who were intellectual, revered, and murdered. Each took over many of their brothers' responsibilities after their deaths. And both men endured early criticism: Kennedy from the national press when he resigned as Attorney General to run for the Senate from New York, Evers from the NAACP and SNCC when he audaciously announced he was assuming his brother's job as field secretary.

To his critics and political foes, Kennedy was arrogant and ruthless. But Robert Kennedy began to take on an awareness about people and issues as he emerged from the dark of the President's death. His entire life, to that point, had hinged on his brother's. As he moved rapidly to the ideological left, his new concerns lay not with politics per se but with politics as a social force applied to the struggle of black people and grape-pickers, and to the terrible war in Vietnam. Evers was likewise arrogant to his foes, telling civil rights workers who disagreed with him that they had a choice: work with him or without him, but he was staying. He shrugged off the criticism that he was only Medgar Evers' brother and went ahead building the shopping complex, flouting capitalism in the face of the socialist-oriented activists of the movement.

Competition is perhaps too mild a term to describe the intense spirit Evers and Kennedy instilled in their followers. As Victor Navasky has suggested in *Kennedy Justice*, the Attorney General's determined pursuit of Jimmy Hoffa left no room to question the means involved in achieving the end. The wiretapping, constant surveillance, and huge financial outlay, and the fact that an entire force of men was created for the purpose of arresting one man, fit right into RFK's philosophy: he wanted Hoffa. Kennedy's reputation as a ruthless campaign manager for his brother and as a campaigner himself grew because he called his own shots, usually ignoring politicos and ward bosses who wanted him to seek their advice. Moreover, Kennedy always competed to *win*.

Evers' pugnacity and individualism—indeed, competitiveness—was of a similar grain. The decision to encourage votes for Swan, which caused nearly universal condemnation, was simply something he wanted and got. The Mayor's attitude about political banquets was also gut-level politics: he demanded half of the proceeds from paid-plate functions. The local candidates would get the rest. As he put it, "They wouldn' have anybody come to a banquet if they didn't have a speaker . . . so who they kiddin'? They'll get more than they could get with a fund-raising rally with jus' themselves givin' speeches." (He did, in fact, speak for free in the poorest areas; but in counties with solvent political organizations, he wanted them to split, and they did.)

Evers and Kennedy became close during the 1964 Senate race. Evers was keynote speaker at the NAACP's New York banquet that year. He fumed while the organization's officers attacked Kennedy and sang praises of Kenneth Keating, the guest of honor. Evers delivered the keynote address and attacked Keating for his lack of initiative in civil rights. He concluded the speech, to the chagrin of the NAACP, with a rousing endorsement of Kennedy. Evers campaigned for him tirelessly.

Martin Luther King moved into Evers' life around 1964. Their friendship grew quickly but they already had much in common from the fact that they shared the same race and its trials. Martin, the scholarly religious, was much like Medgar, and Charles "loved him like a brother." Bobby Kennedy became like a brother as well, especially since there were qualities of Medgar in the senator. He was younger than Evers, more intellectual, and had a rigid sense of ethics drawn from his religion during childhood.

Through civil rights work Evers became close with whites like Joe Rauh, Allard Lowenstein, and Gil Jonas. Kennedy's ongoing constituency included Rafer Johnson, Rosie Grier, and Cesar Chavez. Evers and Kennedy grew by expanding their lives through new work, with new goals and were better able to surmount tragedy because of it. Their friendship was underlined by a sense of discovery about their changing lives.

The effect of Robert Kennedy on The Mayor's life was visible. He had pictures and mementos of the senator hanging in his home and his office, and he would occasionally speak of him in relation to our campaign. Once he told Alec Berezin, who was always sensitive to the feelings of the people he dealt with, "advancin' ain't hard, Elix. When I advanced for Bobby all I did was walk into the hotel and make sure everything was set up. Then I'd go to where he was gonna speak and I'd tell 'em to git everybody there—or else!"

The time he mentioned Kennedy with the most striking pathos was in midsummer. We were alone in his office, where I had just read him a press release. This was during a period of great personality problems between Magnolia and me. The Mayor, who had never discussed the problem, looked at me with sad eyes and said softly, "Ya know, the thing about Bobby Kennedy I cherished the most was how he learnt to change. When I first got to know him, he was

Attorney General. He didn't know nothin'. He was the President's brother, he didn't care. But he changed. Lawd, he changed! He changed when Medgar died. He changed when John died. He kep' on changin', tryin', workin'. That was the thing about him, Jason. He never quit. He went out and saw racism and what it did to people, and he tried to change it. Changin's rough, Jason."

Evers had reached his decision to run for mayor of Fayette as a result of Robert Kennedy's death, although he had been thinking about it before that. In April, Dr. King was shot, and for a second time Kennedy had been at his side. At the end of the long Atlanta funeral procession, he had broken down and sobbed in Kennedy's arms. Three months later, after celebrating the senator's victory in the California primary, he had to see it happen all over again. He was five feet from Kennedy when he heard the sound he thought was balloons popping.

In *Robert Kennedy: A Memoir*, Jack Newfield recalls walking out of the hotel at dawn the next day, finding a red-eyed Charles Evers on the front steps, watching the dreary sky. Evers embraced him and cried, "They kill all our leaders, they kill all our friends."

When Charles Evers returned to Mississippi, Medgar and Martin and Bobby were gone. Evers was alone. He told many reporters during the campaign, "That was the day I decided to run for mayor of Fayette." I suspect it was also about this time he got an inkling to run for governor, if for no other reason than to prove to himself that the vision of the two men closest to him was painfully taking shape.

His gubernatorial campaign had a definite Kennedy flair. Remembering the diversity of the Kennedy political family —the various lawyers, political advisors, brothers, sisters, in-laws, journalists, and friends who came together whenever there was a campaign—The Mayor insisted we ride in motorcades. Our crowd could be counted on to include whites, blacks, women, occasionally a priest, by late summer two nuns, one or two of The Mayor's daughters and sometimes his wife, Dwight and the Evers 4, sometimes the Everettes (a dance troupe), a Fayette spiritual choir if Dwight couldn't make it, a visiting journalist or film crew, and usually a black minister. The camaraderie of these trips was always spirited. And there were always volunteers, and people who just showed up and came along. The sprawling heterogeneity of these trips made for great rapport with reporters in urban areas. A Gulf Coast television commentator remarked to me after covering a rally, "I never expected a whole parade. Jesus, we shoulda done our whole news show out here. You got ten stories in all those cars!" The Mayor's attitude about the press also had a Kennedy touch. He told me early in the race, "The press is our ally. You're doin' the right thing—make those guys know we like 'em as people. They gotta be a part of us."

The larger the campaign entourage, the more invigorated he became. He also romanticized his staff. At one rally he pointed at Alec Berezin, who had just finished his first year at Case Western Law School. "Amazing Grace" droned in the night, and The Mayor, in high spirits, said of his advance man, "Yeah, black folks, we got political help from all over. See this young man? He's *almost* a Harvard Law School graduate . . . come all the way down to help us run for governor!" And in Vicksburg one night he pointed at me and announced to four hundred black folks, "Jason here caught a steamboat up the Mississippi River, come all the way up from his sugar plantation in Loosiana to work for us!"

This spirit was always with us. No reporter captured the feeling of the campaign better than Walter Gordon of the Baltimore *Sun*. He accompanied us on a speaking tour of southern Mississippi. Mendenhall, perhaps the worst town in Mississippi for blacks, was last on the stop.

A Negro candidate for governor does not just sashay into Mendenhall. He plans a campaign that would have honored Ulysses S. Grant.

When Charles Evers, the first Negro candidate for Governor in Mississippi's history, drove into Mendenhall a few days ago, the residents could hardly have appeared more worried if he had been Grant and their town had been Vicksburg, which is only 60 miles to the northwest. . . . The fear was palpable. . . .

With voting in the November election expected to polarize around race, even Mr. Evers' most ardent supporters concede him no chance.

But he is proving something: that a black candidate for Governor can march into Mendenhall.

Once it was obvious that memories of the past were straining him. On a sweltering afternoon in Clarksdale, Allard Lowenstein gave a deeply emotional speech. His last words were, "And in Mississippi in 1971 you are showing that the dreams of John Kennedy, Medgar Evers, Martin Luther King, and Bobby Kennedy are still alive!" Introduced by his friend, Aaron Henry, Evers' eyes welled with tears and he said in a cracked voice, "I cain't talk . . . Aaron, you talk for me. Sometimes it jus' gets too much. . . ."

Medgar, Martin, and Bobby died of forces that had festered in Mississippi since before Charles Evers' birth. A certain piece of Evers died when Kennedy was buried. In 1971 people were not shooting; the campaign was moving. He was the first black mayor, the first black gubernatorial candidate in Mississippi's history. He was making history, changing history. The new force in his life, the campaign, was making him stronger than anyone had ever seen him. He ended one speech by saying, "Look out, Mississippi, you ain't never lookin' back!" His energy, ideals, hope for the future, and understanding about the importance of the task at hand were reflected in the faces of each member of his campaign.

What he had and what we lacked were the brutal and tender remembrances of the past. But those we learned about at every speech, in each church, whenever he talked to us individually. His ego was the heart of the campaign, and the campaign never stopped moving.

CHAPTER

8

The irony of the Democratic runoff was that Sullivan and Waller had been widely billed as moderates. Although both men had answered questionnaires from the NAACP and indicated they would not veto HEW grants, neither had promised to implement sweeping employment of blacks in state agencies. Nor had there been any other firm commitments made to blacks. To say that a man was a moderate revealed little about his philosophical approach to policies and projects that would affect blacks and poor whites. The joint conviction to employ blacks in state agencies was a decision Sullivan and Waller knew would have to be made eventually, lest it be handed over to a court of law.

Perhaps these men were moderates, as compared to Swan and Perry, but they were still Mississippi politicians. And behind Waller and Sullivan were the same county politicos and profane powers who had supported Ross Barnett, John Bell Williams, and the primitive James Eastland. While on TV and in the press Waller and Sullivan were part of the New South, in the backrooms and hotels of Mississippi, the men backing them, the old warhorses, once again joined the fray.

Sullivan had strong support from the Hedermans, white liberals, and, tacitly, the Republicans. He was also the choice of the John Bell Williams people, many of whom would rely on the governor for a four-year extension of employment. Waller, the underdog, would not have been a good bet for them.

But while Sullivan had his supporters, Waller had *his*: notably, Ross Barnett, Paul Johnson, and James Eastland. To win, Waller needed the Swan vote, the hard-core rednecks. Ross Barnett, the granddaddy of all bigots, was a definite plus. The financial sources Johnson and Barnett could tap were important. But the power and thrust behind Waller's campaign—that is to say, where he got his money—came from Eastland. This was apparent by the second week of the runoff. Though Waller denied it publicly, reporters around his campaign began to notice Eastland's county leaders, his old campaign contributors, and, as rumors went, even an occasional member of his staff in Waller's circle.

For if Sullivan won and—as many observers believed—defected to the Republicans, many old-line Democrats would go with him. For Eastland this would be a bad situation. The Democratic governor of Mississippi is titular head of the Democratic Party in the state. But the governor was a Republican and the officially sanctioned Democrats were the Loyalists, so Eastland's powerful chairmanship of the Senate Judiciary Committee was in jeopardy. Waller, promising he would lead Mississippi Democrats back into the fold of the national party, would fight for Eastland's qualification as a Senate Democrat. The dispute about the "official" sanction of the state party would be resolved at the Democratic National Convention in 1972. A widely circulated rumor said Eastland had met with Roy Adams, Waller, and Ed

Pittman in Washington prior to the summer primary and told each man he would back him if he got into the runoff against Sullivan. Sullivan and Eastland had hated each other over the years.

Eastland is a legend in Mississippi. Vardaman was more colorful, Bilbo more cynical, Ross Barnett more stupid; but Eastland is the most *powerful* demagogue. In 1971 no reporter could remember his ever having held a press conference. The Mayor asked a group of students how many of them had ever *seen* the man and only five of the 350 raised their hands. In the Delta, Eastland is the symbol of all evil. Fannie Lou Hamer sang an impassioned song at a rally one night, and concluded by saying, "Ah sang that song when ah was locked in the jail cell in Sunflower County. . . . Sen'tah Eastland's men was beatin' me . . . they was beatin' me and callin' me a 'dirty nigger' . . . but ah kep' prayin' and singin' . . . 'cause ah knew Gawd was on my side . . . ah knew that Sen'tah Eastland wouldn' win. . . ."

Eastland was appointed to the Senate in 1941 to serve the remainder of the term of deceased Senator Pat Harrison; the post was secured for him by his father, one of the wealthiest planters who ever lived in Mississippi. Eastland fought an attempt to put a ceiling on the price of cottonseed oil, and overnight he became a minor hero. He was elected to the Senate in 1942 and never looked back.

A floor leader for Bilbo in the Mississippi Legislature, Eastland took his cues from another man in Washington. Riding the crest of the Dixiecrat revolt° to reelection in 1948, Eastland found a new dimension to his own politics in Senator Joe McCarthy. McCarthy the witchhunter was the shaping influence of Eastland's career; he was a lesson in

° Dissident parties of Alabama, Mississippi, South Carolina, and Louisiana walked out of the 1948 convention in protest of the civil rights plank read into the party platform by a Minnesota mayor named Hubert Humphrey. Strom Thurmond ran for President, Mississippi Governor Fielding Wright for Vice President on the Dixiecrat Ticket. Truman won.

the mechanics of Washington. For the power that Washington gave Eastland was something that had been part of him all along. It was the same power Joe McCarthy held as he interrogated frightened innocents accused of communism. The palpable awareness of his own rule was never clearer to Eastland than when he sat on the porch of his Delta home gazing out into the draining twilight. The 5,800 acres of midnight alluvium before him lay flat, stretching clear to where the land kissed the sky, a sprawling cotton monarchy dotted with serfs who were black like his soil and who constituted a miniature city in themselves. (A city, as reported by journalists during the civil rights struggle, whose citizens were paid upwards of fifty cents an hour for field labor; a municipality of cesspool outhouses and liquid filth carrying insects along festered gully and lane where black-skinned babies learned how to walk.)° Washington gave Eastland power in bigger and better quantities.

The year that made Eastland was 1954. After the Supreme Court decision in *Brown* v. *Board of Education* he became a keynote speaker at countless Citizens' Council rallies. And by now he was a powerful subcommittee chairman of the Judiciary Committee. Eastland's career as a Democrat from then on was something of an unnatural act with history. He opposed all of the enlightened domestic policies of the Kennedy-Johnson Administrations and, because of seniority, his power grew. The theme of his rhetoric from the late fifties was that Communists were infiltrating the South. As Judiciary Chairman, he bottled up over 100 civil rights bills during the fifties and sixties; his committee was the civil rights graveyard. In Mississippi he told throngs, "I've got so many bills that I jus' stuff 'em deeper into my pockets. My wife sews the pockets deep!"

° A field study by a team of doctors, a Mississippian among them, unanimously concluded that black babies in the Delta died each winter because of starvation. Eastland claimed this was a Communist lie, though the deaths occurred within a hearty spit of his acreage.

The judges' opinions in the 1954 decision frequently referred to Gunnar Myrdal's classic study of race, *An American Dilemma*. Eastland lashed out at the book's documentation, saying that the scholars and social scientists who assisted in the study were "agitators who are part and parcel of the Communist conspiracy to destroy our country." He introduced sexual allusions into the 1954 decision when he said:

> Laws against *adultery, fornication, sodomy, incest,* and *bestiality* were known in the laws of Moses. They were in the Common Law of England. They were in the laws of the colonies when the Constitution was adopted. They have been brought forth in the laws of the forty-nine states. They inherit their efficacy from ethics and religion, and have been fed on spiritual meat. These laws are known wherever the spirit of decency flowers and men look up through the mist at God. In only one place are they held in low repute; that is the U.S. Supreme Court, where we find nine men dissenting against the judgment of mankind.

In 1961 he gave Attorney General Kennedy his "word as a gentleman" that Harold Cox, Eastland's old roommate at Ole Miss, would be a just federal judge. Cox was recommended to the President, who appointed him to the bench in Biloxi, where he has since established himself as an unabashed racist. He called a group of black lawyers "chimpanzees" and later threw out indictments against the seventeen Neshoba County men arrested for the murders of Schwerner, Goodman, and Chaney. (Eastland himself had labeled the search for the missing bodies "a hoax.") Robert Kennedy's recommendation of Cox is believed by many to have been a trade for Thurgood Marshall's nomination to the Supreme Court—held up by Eastland for a year. Eastland is said to have met RFK in the Senate halls one day and remarked, "Tell your brother when I get Cox, he gets the nigger." (Most civil rights historians suggest the "deal" was Cox for Marshall; however, Victor Navasky in *Kennedy Justice* has said that RFK probably assumed in his interrogations of Cox prior to recommendation that Cox was honest in answering the questions. This proved not to be the case.)

Eastland pointed a finger at civil rights workers and accused them, without evidence, of having venereal disease. He called them Communists, and, like McCarthy, never proved a word he said. The most horrible part of James Eastland's success is that the system is responsible. It has allowed him to survive, with all his powers intact. In 1971 he was still chairman of the Senate Judiciary Committee. He had a vast network of Mississippians in his debt. He had secured more jobs, done more favors, and had more owed to him than any man in the state.

One reporter told me of a friend who confided to him, "I don't know what to do. I wanna vote for Sullivan. I like him, like what he says. But Jim Eastland called me and put down the word. He said vote for Waller and I had to make a healthy contribution. Eastland got me a big loan when I first started out. He told me straight I owed him a favor. So I gave Waller the money and I guess I'm votin' for him. . . ." This was the way Eastland worked. He was the most influential man in Mississippi, both politically and financially, as the two realms often intervene. People listen to Jim Eastland. He's made Mississippi people rich. They owe him favors. Plenty of them.*

* Eastland's influence reached farther than Mississippi. In 1971 a rotund man from Texas was often seen with the Waller campaign. Though it took nearly a month before people knew who he was, it was later learned he was Bunker Hunt. His father, H. L. Hunt, was the Texas oilman who spearheaded the right-wing propaganda "Lifeline" radio series. Reports later circulated that young Hunt had underwritten most of Waller's $200,000 media campaign in the primary. The Hunts had recently acquired land in Mississippi and were friends of Eastland.

Mississippi had come of age in candidates Waller and Sullivan, moderates. The Mayor's position on the two was enunciated repeatedly between August 3 and August 24: "There ain't a dime's worth o' difference between 'em." Both candidates were clearly hesitant to make direct overtures to blacks. Sullivan had the support of a small group of blacks who worked for him secretly. Sullivan had solicited the tacit support of the NAACP in his race for lieutenant governor in 1967, and Reverend Allen Johnson of the NAA was now supporting him in the primary. Johnson sent out a flood of letters endorsing Sullivan. One Sullivan leaflet read, in part:

> You KNOW where Charles Sullivan Stands . . .
>   Here is what he said about EDUCATION: "*All* of the children must be educated."
>   . . . And Sullivan will take advantage of Federal funds and programs wherever they can benefit *all* Mississippians.
> VOTE SULLIVAN FOR GOVERNOR ON AUGUST 24th. (Sullivan is the *last* name on the ballot.)

Evers was upset about Reverend Johnson's support of Sullivan. "I can understand some low-down fella doin' this, but I cain't understand ole Allen. He and I worked together in civil rights. He's a burly man, jus' like me. Stood between me and three Klukkers one time in Natchez and said, 'Chollie, it's more important for you to keep goin'. If somebody's got to git killed, it's me. You're more important.' I cain't understand *him* doin' this. . . ."

Sullivan, with 38 percent of the first primary vote, had the clear lead as the race drew to a close. But The Mayor began attacking Sullivan hard: "I've received numerous reports o' Mr. Sullivan sneakin' around the back door, askin' for votes. If he wants black votes, he's gotta come out in the open." But then an ironic twist occurred. A. B. Albritton of *The Commercial Appeal* discovered that Jimmy Swan had thrown his support behind Sullivan. Waller, as everyone knew, could win only if he gleaned the Swan vote.

But the implication here was obvious. Imagine Swan, the wiry would-be populist, sitting on a bed in his hotel calling his backers around the state on a WATS line, urging them to vote for Sullivan. Evidently Sullivan was picking up his campaign debt. Ironically, though this was not written about in the press because Waller's people disclaimed it, Swan's publicity agent had allied himself with *Waller's* camp! Swan was purely paying off campaign debts with help from both men. It seemed that the critic of the fat cats was getting the best of both gravy trains.

Because of his fierce claims of independence, Swan working for Sullivan didn't sit too well with the rednecks who had voted for him in the first primary. His being in cahoots with Sullivan made both men look inconsistent: Swan to the rednecks for his hypocrisy, Sullivan to the blacks for accepting Swan. This development was not as significant as a second turn of events, however, which was the Hederman papers' support of Sullivan in the final weeks.

For while Waller hammered away at the ills of machine politics to which his opponent was tied, the machine was fighting back ruthlessly. One Hederman paper depicted a robot spewing nonsensical phrases, and the caption said that this was the machine-produced Bill Waller, product of an out-of-state candidate-maker. And on August 10 an incredible editorial appeared on page one of the *Ledger*:

CAMPAIGN REAL ISSUE IS STILL EXPERIENCE AGAINST INEXPERIENCE

The only real issues in this second primary gubernatorial campaign that has two weeks to run continue to be those of the first primary: experience in, and knowledge of state government, proven ability and loyal service to the people of Mississippi.

Charles Sullivan has twice asked the voters to elect him and twice the voters, in effect, sent him back for experience. Heeding this advice, he ran for Lt. Governor four years ago and was elected. Today he has the invaluable experience of loyal effective service through the four years.

Mr. Sullivan's second primary opponent four years ago asked the voters to elect him governor. In effect, they told him to get experience. But he decided against this plan, and chose instead to employ an out-of-state professional organization specializing in directing political campaigns.

Their speciality is a slick build-up of a candidate lacking in experience and knowledge of the job to which he aspires. . . .

One highly successful gimmick is the spreading of slanderous rumors. . . .

We have heard these rumors and so have you.

This editorial is being published for the purpose of branding them for what they are—lies—vicious and malicious lies.

Charles Sullivan has never been this desperate to win an election.

Charles Sullivan is the son of a Baptist minister. He was brought up in a Christian home. He taught Sunday school classes for adult men, and sang in the church choir, served as a deacon, chairman of the church day school committee which inaugurated a school that runs from kindergarten through junior high.

When in Jackson on state business, he frequently attends services at First Baptist Church. He is extremely active in Boy Scout work.

He is married to a lovely Christian woman, the former Mary Lester Rayner, product of a Baptist College, with major in art and home economics, Sunday school teacher of senior girls, Vacation Bible School leader, study course leader, Christian drama coach, and a church choir member.

Charles Sullivan has not appeared in person on live television on Sundays. But his opponent, Bill Waller, ran advertisements in the papers on Sunday, July 25, and again on August 1, *inviting people to stay at home from church on each of these nights*, and call in questions for him to answer on a live television show. These shows were held at 7:30 pm, the precise time when many people were going to worship services in their churches all over Mississippi. [Italics added]

Even more than this, Bill Waller ran an advertisement in the Gulf Coast Daily Herald inviting people to "Bill Waller Family Night" on Sunday night, June 20, for "Shrimp, Beer." . . .

These live programs and the shrimp and beer supper were advertised in advance especially to draw crowds. These are some of the tactics being used to advance the cause of the candidate with no experience in state government. . . .

And so we come back to the prime issue in the campaign—a qualified, experienced, and tested candidate against an ambitious novice who is trying to short-cut the process of training for the job to which he aspires. He is substituting a gimmick-laden drive which we believe will miss its mark.

The editorial did not mention the fact that Waller had twice been elected district attorney of Hinds County and that he was one of the most successful lawyers in the state. Nor did the editorial mention that the Hederman family worships at the First Baptist Church of Jackson . . . where Bill Waller is a deacon.

On Sunday, August 15, black leaders of the Loyalists met in Jackson to discuss a possible endorsement. The Mayor was totally opposed to an endorsement. Aaron Henry, by all indications, seemed to be pushing for one. The only endorsement thus far had come from the Hinds County FDP, an independent arm of the Loyalists. Al Rhodes, the group's president, told me, "We decided to endorse Waller. Sorta for the hell of it . . ." "Why?" I asked. "Just to make some noise. Let white folks know we planned to vote." "Didn't you know The Mayor's position against them both?" I asked. He shrugged his shoulders again and looked away imperviously. Aaron Henry rapped on the podium.

Aaron Henry had endured much. He was balding, and looked older than his fifty or so years. By late summer The Mayor had told different crowds, "Black folks, you gotta show your freedom by votin'. Look how much we paid for it. Y'all know Aaron Henry? Dr. Aaron Henry who used to be NAA president . . . you can look at him now and see how much the white folks done to him, how much they tore him up." In Clarksdale, where Aaron Henry was born and raised, he was periodically arrested on trumped-up charges for civil rights work until about five years ago. During the sixties his house was fire-bombed twice; he was shot at numerous times; city authorities tried to condemn his drugstore as a health hazard; he was once tied to a garbage truck and forced to walk the streets as an example of what blacks had to pay for their (civil rights) crimes.

But Aaron Henry was a fighter. He led marches, testified in Washington, and induced liberal senators and congressmen to come down and see for themselves what they were voting for. He embraced his friends—senators, black folks, white volunteers alike—with a huge bear hug. His eyes watered and crinkled when he smiled. About the best way anyone who knew him could describe Aaron Henry was to say he was something of a saint. (In June I asked him why he favored Sullivan. He grinned. "He's not such a bad guy, really." I countered, "But wasn't he the D.A. who threw all you folks in jail, fined folks, and all?" Aaron smiled. "Yeah, but he was only doin' his job . . . he's not such a bad guy, really.")

Bifocals midway down his nose, Henry said, "Now, for the business at hand—"

At which point The Mayor walked through the door, Woody hustling after him, and the room broke into applause and commotion. Aaron smiled. "Here come de judge!" The Mayor flashed the peace sign, strutted up to the front row, embraced Aaron, and sat down.

Henry said, "At the outset, I want to make it clear I haven't advocated an *endorsement*. I think we ought to consider both candidates, though, and see what they have to offer, if anything. I should correct you on one point, Charlie. It wasn't Sullivan who tied me to the garbage truck. He wasn't D.A. at *that* particular time. He's done some sordid things in his day, but there's no sense givin' him credit for somethin' he didn't do. . . ." Evers nodded.

Henry continued, "We invited both candidates to speak to us today. Neither of them are here. Two representatives are present, however, and we'll hear Mr. Sullivan's first."

Sullivan's man was about twenty-seven, an OEO worker. Many people in the audience knew him. His comments were brief and to the point. "I want to say first I'm not a Sullivan campaign worker. For one thing, I'm under the Hatch Act, and I guess I'm overstepping boundaries as it is. . . . I'm not getting paid to do this. I came because I know Charlie Sullivan personally. I can tell you he did everything he could to help us get OEO grants when he was lieutenant governor. He's assured me he's not going to veto anything like John Bell did. . . . I have every reason to think he'll make a good governor, and be a departure from the past." A few people smiled as he concluded. No one clapped.

The man speaking for Waller was about forty. Most people knew him. In his own words, "I know most o' you folks remember me from the last few years. Mayor Evers knows I was the first white man practicin' law in Mississippi who took on black clients. That was back when you had to pack a gun. . . . Now, it's socially acceptable.

"I'm not a campaign worker, either, but I am voting for Bill Waller . . . and I hope all of you do, too. I wish his politics were more like mine and yours, but they're not. I can tell you this much, though. I went into his Jackson law office frequently during the sixties. Sometimes I had black clients. He let me use his law library, and never once treated me— or my clients—with anything less than respect. I researched some cases that would prickle the neck hairs of folks who're gonna vote for him. He's a good lawyer, he's always dealt with me square and straight, and I think he'll act that way as governor."

At various intervals, folks craned their necks to see Evers. He stared at the floor, disinterested.

Aaron Henry spoke again: "I know y'all are waitin' to hear Chollie, but first Rev'nd Bowie has somethin' to say." Harry Bowie was forty-five, heavy-set for his five-ten frame. An Episcopal minister ordained in New Jersey, he had been in McComb since the movement's early days. The moment Harry spoke the atmosphere changed. His voice was an electrifying blend of politics and the Sunday pulpit. "Black folks, we gotta get somethin' cleared up and straightened out right now before this day goes another *hour*! We're not talkin' about choosin' a man to endorse on the twenty-fourth! We're talkin' about a strategy that goes all the way to November 2!"

"A-men, Rev'nd Bowie!"

"If we elect one of these two guys—if we announce some endorsement—we'll be jus' like black folks in Chicago! They elect Daley every time, and he goes to banquets they throw for black folks and he tells 'em nice things about how everything's fine—but it's *not* fine! They're livin' in neighborhoods the city lets go to hell, and they elect Daley because o' patronage—and that's all they get—a few black cronies who get good jobs!"

"Speak, Rev'nd"

Harry was beginning to sweat. "We gotta remember the story about the black man and the snake. Black man's walkin' down a cold road and he sees a snake half-frozen to death. Snake says, 'Mr. Black Man, please put me in your shirt and hold me next to your breast so's I can get warm.' And the black man says, 'Snake, if I do that you'll bite me!' Snake says, 'No, no. Please . . . help your ole brother Snake. I won't hurt you.' So, the black man takes him next to his breast under his shirt, and warms him.

"They walk along awhile and then the black man says, 'Well, Mist' Snake, how you comin' along? You warm now?' Snake says, 'Well, nigger, I guess so.' Black man says, 'Why you callin' me nigger, Mist' Snake? I been real kind to you.' And that ole snake, just before he sinks his teeth into the black man's chest, says, 'Nigger, *once* a snake means *always* a snake!' "

The crowd exploded: "Snakes! That's right! All snakes!" The lawyer and the OEO man shifted uncomfortably.

Harry closed defiantly: "If these two men are so *busy* that they can't come today, I want to know—how many *real* candidates can afford to be 'too busy' to talk about gettin' votes from 37 percent of the state's electorate?"

"Right on! Say it, brother!" The applause was volcanic.

The Mayor rose to speak, and first addressed himself to the white speakers. "I know you fellas mean well, but I jus' cain't digest what you're sayin'. Somehow, I got a bad taste."

He paused. "Because any man that comes here and *suggests* that a black man or a black woman should vote for either of those two scoun'rels . . . is sick! Plain sick!

"Chollie Sullivan is the SAME man . . . who got on TV the day after Jackson State and said it was justified. *Justified!*"

"Say it!"

"An' we supposed to think about votin' for the man who started the private school of Clarksdale? Chollie Sullivan, who sat aroun' and never said *nary* a word for four years while that racist scoun'rel, John Bell, vetoed *all* them federal grants! Fifty *million* dollars which woulda helped black folks, and poor white folks! This man we're gonna endorse? That ain't strategy, black folks. It's sickness!"

"Dat's de truf! Sickness!" the crowd was roaring. "Say it!"

The Mayor was dripping and his skin beneath the lights shone like slick black leather. He slammed his fist on the podium, CRACK! "And Waller? Who we kiddin'? C'mon, black folks. He got his kids in private, for-white-only schools. He ain't got a black man *near* his campaign office. An' him sayin' he's against busin'! How many times they bused us across town when we was kids?"

"Too many times!"

"Answer me that: how many times they bused us past some ole Rebel statue, past city hall, all the way into the woods where they had some ole beat-up shanty shack—"

"Amen! Amen! Amen!"

"—ole shack what had *no* heat in winter and was nothin' but hot hell whenever it got to be warm. An' they called that *school*? An' him sayin' he's against busin'! Who's Bill Waller for us to waste a vote on him!"

The crowd began to thump its feet, clapping, crying, "That's right!" The Mayor was pointing his finger at them. "Y'all are the Loyalist Democrats, Official Democratic party o' Mississippi. You axed me to run. Nominated me at a convention in this very hall! Now you're talkin' about an *endorsement*? All white folks got to do is smile a li'l bit, not holler nigger, and like that ole snake, we think they up an' changed! *That ain't so!*"

"NO! NO!"

"I'll debate 'em both on TV and pay for the time! I'll debate 'em to hell freezes over! But I'll tell y'all this—they're poison-in' your minds! You vote for them and you not only vote against me, you vote against every black soul in this *country*!

"But I don't care. 'Cuz y'all cain't hurt me. Bobby's gone and Medgar's gone. An' after that, I'm tellin' you, ain't nothin' can hurt me! 'Cuz I done been hurt. You can call me names, vote against me, it don't matter. But I'm tellin' you while I still got breath in my body—you vote for one of them two and you're pullin' the lever for Byron De la Beckwith! ° You're jus' as guilty as them white devils who killed Schwerner and Goodman and Chaney! An' I'm tellin' you, it gets to a point where you cain't go no further! You cain't hurt me, jus' you! When you vote for one o' them two, jus' remember that Medgar and Martin and Bobby and John and all of them ain't carryin' us no further cause they're all dead and we on our own and that's all I got to say!"

The vote was unanimous not to endorse either man.

A week before the primary runoff, the FBI and a squad-

° The man who was tried for the murder of Medgar Evers. His fingerprints were found on the murder weapon. He was acquitted by an all-white jury.

ron of Jackson cops surrounded a house on Lynch Street where members of the Republic of New Africa were living. At dawn the police, according to news reports, had shouted through a bullhorn at the residents, telling them to come out. They had a murder warrant for an RNA member from Michigan. What happened after that is not clear. The police (and press) on August 18 contended that the RNA returned the call with a fusillade. During the gunfire, policeman Louis Skinner was shot in the head. Two others were wounded. The blacks yielded to tear gas and were captured before 10 A.M.

Our office was like a powder keg. People were at one another's throats; nerves were tense; people were angry, depressed, distraught over the shootout. The only consolation was that no blacks were wounded, something of a miracle for Jackson. Magnolia went out to lunch early, very upset. Lois Williams' face became steadily bleaker as morning wore on. Ed and Alec were out of town. The Mayor was due in from Fayette after lunch. I wanted to clear out to collect my own thoughts.

As it happened, I had been invited to lunch that day by a Catholic priest, an aide to the bishop. He told me candidly as we ate, "You've got to get The Mayor to issue a statement condemning this. It's very clear—the RNA shot first. They shot Skinner. Remember, when Medgar died, the Church responded and went to the funeral."

I was in no mood to discuss the Catholic Church and what I saw as meager progress in the headway made among white Catholics. The bishop, himself no spokesman for racial progress, was a member of an old, conservative, and wealthy Mississippi family. But the RNA incident had me brooding and I kept thinking of the priest's comment. I was against the RNA's philosophy. And every reporter said the RNA shot first. I couldn't forget the way they had treated The Mayor, either. Later in the day it was announced that policeman Skinner had died. Eleven members of the RNA had been bound over to the Hinds County Jail.

I returned to the office at 2 P.M. and The Mayor was at his desk, listening to news reports on the radio. I knocked and entered. We listened for about five minutes. Then he said, "Well, I hate to see this happen, but Jackson is the worst place in the country to try and organize some separate nation. We've been strugglin' for independence I don't know how long, and look at the toll it's taken. . . ."

I thought for a while and then said, "What would you think about sending condolences to Skinner's wife?"

He frowned. "What for? I had nothin' to do with this. . . ."

"I was talking with Father ———," I said, "and he told me that the Church, Human Relations Council, and so forth are sending letters. Seeing as how no blacks were hurt, if you issued a brief statement to the effect that you condemn all violence, maybe it would ease some of the tension in the white community. . . ."

"Welll . . . okay. Write a statement and read it to me." I wrote a brief statement to the widow, saying that the sender of the telegram lost his brother through violence, but that one must look ahead and have faith. He okayed it. I sent it out over Western Union and then issued it to the press. The Mayor and Martin left about an hour later. Ed and Alec returned by 4:15; Squeaky, Ramberg, and the rest of the staff were in by five. Squeaky called me into a corner and said, "What the hell did you write that statement for?"

"I thought we ought to say something. I didn't think we should let the thing pass without some statement of moderation."

Everyone in the room had crowded around us. A voice said, "That telegram was a disgrace. You know how many black folks have been shot, without so much as a word from any white folks?"

"A lot of 'em," I said. "But a man died—aren't we supposed to set an example?"

Another voice: "not at the expense of the black community."

Another: "You're worried about the white folks' feelings and you're handlin' press for a *black* campaign. Man, how do you know those press reports were right?"

Suddenly I couldn't talk. After two months of frustration because of the Hedermans' biased press coverage, I had succumbed to a simple, white man's instinct. I assumed the blacks shot first, since it was reported that way. Someone rushed in and told us, "I was just over at the NAA office and the word there is that cops shelled the house before anyone knew what happened. It was a miracle none of the blacks didn't get shot."

Magnolia said, "Do you realize what kind of vibrations The Mayor's statement's gonna have in the black community?"

"I didn't think—Jesus, do you think people are going to get mad at him? He agreed to it. Wouldn't he have said no if he thought it would be politically damaging?"

She replied, "Probably not. You know The Mayor. He hates violence. He hates killing. He prob'ly thought like you—that maybe it wouldn't be too bad if he sent condolences. But it's gonna enrage a lot of blacks, especially the young folk we're trying to get."

The lump in my throat settled in the stomach. Ed beckoned me into his office and said sternly, "What I've heard, bein' in town only an hour, is that the RNA brothers had a tunnel under the house that they hid in while the cops blasted away. Only reason they didn't get shot to pieces is because of the tunnel. And why did the cops attack so early?—surrounding the house with guns and bullhorns. How come the press was tipped off?" He looked at me with a discouraged look. "Jason . . ." His voice trailed off.

I drove out to the Ross Barnett Reservoir that night. A furious rain thundered high and flooded half the state. The water pounded on the car and, despite a bright moon, only twenty yards of the sprawling lake could be seen. The rain pelted so thick that everything was black. I felt horrible.

The next morning Hinds County D.A. Jack Travis announced before all the news cameras, "The charges will be murder and treason against the state of Mississippi. Police and FBI are conducting a full-scale search for more members of the conspiracy." Later that day two RNA members were arrested by plainclothesmen for using profane language; however, they were later released for lack of evidence. The judge hearing the case was Russell Moore, who had a firm reputation as a racist among many people in Mississippi. The charge that there were eleven accomplices to a murder was unbelievable; few people felt that the treason charge would stand. But Jack Travis, who was up for reelection, stepped up his radio advertisements: "Criminals hate Jack Travis. Jack Travis means trouble for criminals. Vote for Jack Travis. He'll protect and defend *you*." The RNA case went from moves to countermoves. A long trial began. The eleven were transferred to Parchman penitentiary.

I was very unpopular in the office the rest of the week.

For the next two months black students persistently asked The Mayor why he was *against* the RNA, to which he replied that he was not against the RNA per se, but against the notion of separatism. He explained again his feelings about the farmland dispute, and he concluded by saying the RNA's attack by Jackson cops and the FBI was a terrible thing. The only positive note on the RNA battle was that neither Waller or Sullivan exploited it on the stump. Either man could have, and one can only surmise whether it would have helped them. The fact that they did nothing more than condemn the act was a vaguely positive indication that perhaps they sensed deeper, more tortuous problems might arise if they played on emotions.

But in the final week of the runoff the issue of race suddenly appeared in the campaign. It happened in the oddest way. Ed Cole and Alec Berezin were on the Gulf Coast and were told that Sullivan was to meet with a group of blacks in Pass Christian at the home of Father Philip McCloone, a white priest serving a black parish. Waller had been invited to speak the next night; neither meeting had been publicized in the press. Sullivan backed down at the last minute, but Waller came the next night as planned. Ed and Alec were among the people in the room when Waller spoke. Alec called the Jackson office that night and whispered into the phone, "He's not saying much. He's giving fairly forthright answers. Says he can't openly discuss the race issue because it's not politically economical."

"Does Waller know who you guys are?" I asked.

"He hasn't made any indication that he does. I doubt it."

"Why did Sullivan cancel the other meeting last night?"

"Somebody tipped him off. Sullivan's got a black guy working under the blankets for him here. I don't know who, though. . . ."

"What kind of impression is Waller making?"

"Not much. I imagine they'd vote for him over Sullivan just because he came. He's been fairly straightforward, given his politics. We're gonna talk up The Mayor's stand real heavy after Waller leaves. Well, I gotta go."

The Mayor's stand was enunciated in a five-minute broadcast on statewide TV the next night. "Cholly Sullivan and Bill Waller are nothin' but the same ole soup warmed over again. . . . Let's look at Mr. Sullivan—runnin' around the back door for black votes; has his children in that segregated academy of Clarksdale, which *he* founded; he's part o' the John Bell Administration, the worst we've ever had. He even ran for President in 1960 out o' Texas, and called for *re-peal* o' Social Security. . . .

"Bill Waller's no different. He's got his kids in private schools. He's got Barnett and Big Jim Eastland behind him. . . . He cain't do no good.

"I'm askin' all my supporters to vote for all the local candidates but don't vote for these two. They're the same old politicians we've always had. . . . Won't be any different. As God is my helper, if you vote for me on November 2, you'll never regret it. Thank you very much."

But on Saturday, August 21, with the election three scant days off, a news commentator in Jackson disclosed a "startling discovery." Bill Waller had met with a group of blacks in secret on the Coast! The announcer, Hank Downey, said on the late news:

> Several days ago, black candidate Charles Evers charged that Democratic candidate Charles Sullivan was meeting secretly—"sneaking through the back door" Evers called it—with black groups in order to court the black vote in Tuesday's Democratic runoff. Channel 16 News has learned now that Sullivan's opponent, Bill Waller, has met secretly with blacks, including representatives of Evers' own campaign organization, in an apparent effort to accomplish the same purpose. . . . We have obtained an affidavit sworn to by one person who attended the meeting, and that affidavit outlines some of the questions put to Waller and his answers.

The affidavit quoted Waller as saying few things that were different from what he had been saying throughout the campaign. He did, however, talk at length about the importance of hiring blacks to state jobs. The affidavit also quoted

Waller's statement about discussing race: "This campaign is economical, not social." The point was hard and clear: it was a backdoor meeting.

But anyone with an iota of political savvy could see what had happened. Bill Young was the man who had sworn out the affidavit. Young was black, and the affidavit made it obvious whom he supported:

> Mrs. [Olivette] Matson told me that the meeting would be held and that Mr. Bill Waller, candidate for Governor, state of Mississippi, would meet with Fr. McCloone and a group of other people at 11 o'clock at night. She also said, "if you guys decide to go, tell him that she had told us about the meeting."
>
> Mrs. Matson said she was not going because she felt that Father McCloone had not done right about Charles Sullivan. She informed me that a meeting had been planned that same morning with Father Mc-Cloone and Charles Sullivan. So she went to Father McCloone's house at 9 A.M. the same day, and Father McCloone told her that there was not going to be a meeting—that Charles Sullivan had cancelled. . . .
>
> Upon arriving at Father McCloone's house we found two other men—one black and one white (of the Jewish nationality) so we talked from about 11 to 11:40.
>
> •   •   •
>
> At the close of the meeting, Father McCloone and those who represented Mayor Evers said: "At first we thought we would encourage people not to go to the polls and vote in the governor's race, but now there seems that we have a candidate that we can vote for. . . ."

Young's concluding remark was, of course, a bare-faced lie. Evers himself was on statewide TV the very next night

telling his supporters to boycott a vote for either man. Ironically, we were on the Gulf Coast when the news broke. Ed
Cole called Mrs. Matson from the Buena Vista Hotel. She
said, "I kin tell you one thing. That Bill Young is one liar."
Ed tried to contact Young, who had mysteriously left town.
I called a statement in to the Gulfport *Daily Herald*: "Our
guys went to the meeting when they heard Waller was
going to be there. They listened to his answers which apparently were forthright. But no deal was made. Mayor Evers'
position has been made quite clear." °

The Jackson *Clarion-Ledger* ran a front-page headline on
August 21 proclaiming "Political Bombshell in Telecast
Queries." Waller's reply, filmed for TV as well, said that he
went to the meeting at the priest's invitation, spoke, and
asked for their votes, then left. He said he didn't know
Evers' workers were present, and was surprised to learn Ed
Cole was there. He said he would have expected him to
identify himself. Ed chuckled at that: "I wonder who he
thought those two cats in the back of the room were, askin'
him all those sticky questions." Alec was amused at being
identified as Jewish. "Young got *that* part right," he said.
Waller told a TV reporter that the affidavit was a last-ditch
attempt by Sullivan to damage his campaign, and that was
definitely true.

On August 23 the Jackson *Daily News* poured the last
can of kerosene on the flame. A full page opposite the editorials juxtaposed three Waller ads with three similar ads used
by Dale Bumpers in his Arkansas campaign. The wording

° That night my parents called from New Orleans. They had just returned from
Poplarville, where a neighbor had dropped by and had said, "I was readin' the
Gulfport *Herald* this mornin', and it seems they got a nigger named Jason Berry
workin' for Charles Evers." My father had grinned modestly and said it was his
son, who was white. "Was there any trouble?" I asked. He replied, "Naw. I don't
think they're too high on this, but we know all those people too well. One man told
me a father can't be held responsible for his son, and ———'s wife said the least
you coulda done was picked a guy who was gonna *win*. Don't worry, though." He
said to wish the candidate good luck.

and pictures were nearly identical, and the issues mentioned were the same. DeLoss Walker, of course, was the media consultant for both men. The similarity of the ads wasn't really dramatic, since ads and billboards are used and re-used all across the country in campaigns. But the Hederman press sought to exploit it:

MEMPHIS AD OUTFIT TAKES BILL WALLER FOR A RIDE

Is Bill Waller being played as a big, fat sucker by his Memphis-based propaganda machine, or is he knowingly permitting himself to be depicted as something that he isn't in a deliberate attempt to seduce Mississippi voters?

You may draw your own conclusions after seeing the deep similarities in his hotty-totty advertisement blitz as laid out by his Memphis publicity machine for Dale Bumpers . . . and that of Bill Waller of Mississippi.

Please look at the next page for the rare comparison. . . .

It's such a patent re-run of ideas that it borders on the absurd and a man who aspires to the high office of Governor of Mississippi has no business being taken for a costly ride. Counting the 15 percent ad placement fee by his out-of-state advertising agency, one can only imagine the amount of Waller money that will leave Mississippi after midnight Tuesday. . . .

To tell the truth, to study the ads on the next page, one can easily see that a part-time college student could have edited the Bumpers propaganda in about 15 minutes to make Bill Waller look like the synthesized, manipulated, non-original candidate that he is in this campaign. . . .

If Bill Waller can be bilked so slickly by his own

plugged-in pals of Memphis as a candidate, think of what a real sharpie could do to him on a $10,000,000 building program for the people if he would be Governor. Whee!

It seems Bill Waller has been played for a sucker by his Memphis advisors. What do you think?

The difference between the "fat sucker's" media campaign and Sullivan's was well illustrated by the last night before the election. Both candidates had half-hour slots of statewide TV time; Sullivan spoke first. Half of the film showed him on the stump; he spoke another ten minutes in front of a desk piled high with law books and with bills enacted during his term as lieutenant governor. Sullivan almost dropped one book, and grinned boyishly. Then there was a thirty-second film cut of his eighty-year-old father, smiling from his farm in southern Mississippi. "The old gentleman wanted to appear live tonight," Sullivan said, "but he just wasn't feeling up to it." The last five minutes showed Sullivan, his wife, and their kids. Sullivan earnestly solicited every Mississippian's vote.

Then came Waller. His TV advertising the last month had been of a different ilk altogether. Every time Sullivan had countered the charge that he was backed by a machine, the lieutenant governor had spoken from a studio. The blue wall behind him showed up drab-gray on a black and white screen. Waller, on the other hand, had always talked in front of a pond, discussing the problems of Mississippi in an almost off-hand way. "Let's beat the machine," he had repeated. Swans had touched down lightly on the pond behind him.

Now, on Primary eve, music played softly in the background as four film cuts stressed issues of the race. Waller was in every film cut that was narrated, always seen talking to voters. He appeared between the film cuts, talking about highways, drug problems, tourism, etc. The last five minutes showed Bill and Carroll Waller and the five little Wallers. Waller introduced them all, and slapped one tyke on the chest, saying, "This is Eddie, folks. He's in the fifth grade. He plays Little League ball and he's a real good campaigner!" Carroll thanked everyone who had helped them in the campaign, and said she was thrilled at having met so many good people across the state.

The next morning, August 24, Mississippians chose the man who would run against Charles Evers in November. By 8 P.M. with 70 percent of the vote in, to the astonishment of nearly everyone in the state, Bill Waller had won. He had crushed Sullivan; the percentage was 54.7 to 45.3. Of the 650,000 votes cast, Waller had 60,000 more than Sullivan. Not only had Waller won the Swan vote, but he had also cut deeply into Sullivan's first primary stronghold, the populous Gulf Coast.

The TV coverage of the two men who had conducted million dollar campaigns was a marvelous contrast. Sullivan, clad in white suit, tears streaming down his cheeks, told supporters, "I look into your eyes and I must admit I am sad. . . . But we must get behind Bill Waller, as he is the next governor of Mississippi. That is the way this American system works . . ." he croaked, "and it is the greatest system there is."

And on Capitol Street, in front of the Waller headquarters, a swarming mass of backers hoisted the chunky attorney onto a makeshift stage. Rebel yells pierced the night. Standing next to Mrs. Waller was a smiling Ross Barnett. Bill, grinning through his freckles, yelled, "Whaih's zat ole Capitol Street gang? Thaiy didn' do it, but thaiy said thaiy would! . . . It's not mah vict'ry, but a vict'ry for the payple of the grait stait of Meesiseepi!" Waller then asked the crowd for silence so a great Mississippian could lead them in prayer. The humble man, Ross Barnett, led a brief devotion, and then everyone began yelling. Amid it all a reporter managed to ask Mrs. Waller how she felt. She smiled and said daintily, "Oh, this is certainly a thrill, but to all our friends we're still just plain old Bill and Carroll."

The Evers campaign was as surprised as the rest of the state. We had had no preference, but Waller's victory was encouraging. Waller had run a campaign without using racial issues. And despite the support of Barnett and Eastland, Waller's victory had daunted the John Bell Williams machine.

Three factors contributed to Waller's victory. His underdog status and the beat-the-machine theme appealed to Mississippi voters, many of whom hated John Bell Williams. Lieutenant Governor Sullivan was unable to shed the Williams image. Waller's superb media campaign accentuated the point. When the Governor's Mansion was condemned, the people's reaction cost Sullivan dearly. Sullivan's strategic error was in not making a clean break by denouncing Williams early in the primary.

The second reason was the machine itself. The Hederman support was simply too tasteless and vicious for people to stomach. The "Shrimp and Beer" editorial had been a mountain of asininity. Not even a Baptist preacher believed such a dinner on Sunday night was keeping folks away from church. The attempt to make Sullivan seem a fervent Christian and Waller a heathen was not only callous but plain dumb. (A reporter later told me that Sullivan had privately confessed he was most embarrassed by the piece.) And the Bill Young affidavit was a clear attempt to inject race into the campaign. The fallacious statement was an attempt by Sullivan aides to give the Hederman papers something they could really sink their teeth into. As one reporter later mused, "That was a pretty dumb-shit thing to do. Any fool could see a black man swearin' out an affidavit for Charlie Sullivan wasn't doin' it for love of the candidate. He's in it for somethin' more—try the hip pocket." The caustic *Daily News* editorial calling Waller a "big, fat sucker" had been too much for the majority of voters to bear. It seemed to me that Waller's strong and startling vote on the Gulf Coast was, in part, a protest against the smear attempt by the affidavit. Waller's victory was a significant step forward in that he proved that someone could beat the Hedermans. This will be of lasting importance in Mississippi politics.

The last reason Sullivan lost may not be the most vital, but it likewise will serve as an indicator in years to come. The Evers speech denouncing both Waller and Sullivan on the Thursday night before the election undoubtedly cost Sullivan thousands of votes. His campaign tactics, furtive as they were among blacks, were nevertheless wider and more concentrated than Waller's. The vast majority of blacks voting in the runoff did as Evers asked: they voted only for local candidates, and didn't vote for either gubernatorial candidate. Those who did vote for the top slot split their votes roughly equally. Had Evers not gone on TV, Sullivan would have taken his share of the black vote his aides worked so hard to get. He might have won.

On August 25, Tom Ethridge, racist sage of the *Clarion-Ledger*, cheerfully noted in his column: "Jesus was rejected when he was on earth, and Robert E. Lee, the greatest general of all time, suffered crushing defeat. So no losing candidate in Mississippi should feel this is the end of the world."

Two days later, Ethridge disclosed his analysis of the Waller upset victory:

> Bill Waller's qualities as a successful campaigner are too well known to need detailing here, but we have heard many admirers say that one of his strongest assets is the friendly smile which obviously wins friends and influences people.

A Waller booster has phoned us to suggest that our new leader will be the first "smiling governor" since the late Theodore Bilbo. . . .

Thinking back over the political past, we agree that Waller was about the nearest thing to a "smiling governor" since the late Theodore Bilbo.

Bilbo's successors had real virtues and sterling qualities, but were generally straight-faced and matter-of-fact, none famous for any great sense of humor or a magnetic smile as a distinguished quality. . . .

Bill Waller did a super job of selling himself and projecting personal warmth to maximum effect. *Observers generally agree that there were no great issues in the run-off*, so it seems logical to credit the victor's smile as one of the influential factors in the Waller triumph. [Italics added]

The general election campaign had begun.

CHAPTER

9

As Philip Carter of the Washington *Post* noted, the events of the Waller-Evers race were much like a movie script. In 1963 a black leader had been murdered. A young white D.A. risked his reputation with a vigorous but unsuccessful prosecution of the accused killer. The brother of the civil rights leader left a gangster's life and returned to Mississippi to pick up the fallen standard. Now, in 1971, the reformed brother and the white lawyer faced each other in a campaign. Perhaps Evers and Waller had foreseen this. Evers recalled sitting in Waller's law office in the winter of 1967, after Waller's unsuccessful first run for governor. Waller had grinned. "Someday, Charlie, it might just be you and me runnin' against each other." Evers had smiled back.

Evers' appeal lay in his positive campaign rather than a critical approach to his opponent. Waller's post-victory invitation to all Sullivan supporters to come into his corner seemed to make little headway. Much enmity lingered between the two camps. Our challenge now was to reach whites who had supported Sullivan for his moderate stands —and to reach Waller voters who had cast protest ballots against the Hedermans. Evers' fragile hopes for victory—and the success of the candidates on the Loyalist slate—depended on a massive black vote and, according to the usual pattern, a low white turnout.

We also felt The Mayor would have solid appeal among young whites. Although a state college association ruling banned political speakers on campuses during an election, white students from across the state were phoning to invite The Mayor to address student bodies. The largely amiable atmosphere in towns where he had spoken during the summer apparently impressed college presidents, most of whom ignored the rule and granted the student requests.

To reach the rest of the voters we needed media exposure. Joe Huttie was working feverishly contacting political film-makers; the price had to be low. My efforts at getting coverage for The Mayor were more successful when Waller announced he was not campaigning in September. The primary had been long and costly; he decided to rest. Thus, Evers came to center stage alone for the first time. Waller also said that Evers' campaign was an attempt to "polarize the races." This, coming from a "moderate," was hard to stomach. Evers retorted, "I'm a Mississippian runnin' for governor who *happens* to be black. I'm the only candidate in Mississippi who's got a biracial staff. Waller talks about his concern for *all* Mississippians, but he only hires whites to work for him. . . ."

Our major news vehicle was still the press conference. We adopted a new strategy here, deciding to make them as exciting as we could. The Mayor began calling political friends up north asking them to campaign for him. Black Caucus members committed themselves; Mayor Richard Hatcher of Gary, Al Lowenstein, and Senator Muskie also made arrangements.° Joe Huttie advised us to try to sepa-

---

° Muskie scheduled a visit for September but later canceled to have lunch with South Carolina Governor John West, a potential supporter of Muskie's pre-Presi-

rate each visit of a prominent figure by a week or so. "If we drop the hint to the press," he said wisely, "that the arrival of a news figure will come about once a week—in other words, if we let them know that they'll have a big *story* when Evers calls a news briefing, then we'll get better press coverage." To intensify the excited atmosphere, I called reporters and said, "He's got an announcement to make tomorrow morning. . . . I can't say what it's about. We're still ironing out some details."

The Mayor announced a list of luminaries who would rally to his cause. An AP reporter was jumping up and down: "Dates! Dates! You got any dates, Mayor Evers?" The Mayor smiled. "You'll have to check with my P.R. man on that." I made it a practice to release the date of a visit less than three days before the arrival, and never gave the time. The night before the guest was due, the phones rang continually. "What time's he comin'? What time?" This was perhaps an inconsiderate and unprofessional method, but the reporters were excited when The Mayor, never on time, barreled into the office with someone famous right behind.

But the problem about such politicking was that Mississippi whites hated the notion of "outside interference." They had seen the civil rights movement as the product of northern infiltration. Northern politicians campaigning with Evers wouldn't sit well, perhaps even with white college students, whose votes we were working hard to get. But Evers said, "My job is to change all the old misunderstandin'. What Mississippi folks need to learn is that in politics you get politicians to campaign for you. I did it for Bobby in California, with Rockefeller in New York. Just cause Mississippi ain't never done it before doesn't make it right. Mississippi got to learn a *new* tradition."

dential campaign. Muskie was, however, one of Evers' largest donors, to the tune of $4,500. Evers was nevertheless furious over the cancelation. He told a Muskie aide trying to reschedule a visit, "He comes when I want him or he doesn't come at all." Muskie never came.

John Conyers (D—Michigan), chairman of the Black Caucus, arrived on Friday, September 2. After a news conference and luncheon with The Mayor, he departed for Madison County with Representative Clark and local candidates. The Mayor left for two rallies in Natchez. He was in Jackson again the next morning to welcome Mayor Richard Hatcher of Gary, Indiana. The Mayor was on all of Jackson's news shows, Waller noticeably was not, and the AP, UPI, and Mississippi Radio News did long stories that ran statewide. I spent two hours Saturday feeding cuts of the two mayors' speeches to twenty radio stations.

The *Clarion-Ledger* did not print a word about any of the campaigning that weekend. Furious, I demanded of editor Purser Hewitt why they had refused to run the wire service stories. He told me that, since it was football season, politics had to take a back seat. To which I exploded, "Everybody in *Mississippi* wants to know what Evers is up to! I'll bet even *Ole Ross* wants to know! We've had reporters from Germany who came all the way down here to write stories about a campaign *you* won't cover. It's news, whether you like it or not!"

He was about to speak when for good measure I snarled, "You know, *some* southern papers tried to write biased stories during the Civil War, and look where it got us. We got our asses whipped!" He said curtly, "We thank you for your opinion, sir." Perhaps Hewitt wanted to save a little face; Charlie Hills called the next afternoon to inquire if we had any late news. He did not, however, commence attending our press conferences.[*]

But the Hederman press coverage became less and less important. Evers was campaigning five full days a week, re-

[*] I tried to induce one good reporter from a Jackson bureau to do a story on the unfair press coverage by the family's papers. He refused, saying, "Our circulation's going up and we're closing in on the Hedermans. I don't want to rock the boat by startin' a fight with them. . . ."

serving Thursdays for Fayette and one other day for fundraising up north. And the reporters from other papers were turning out, too. Even in small towns the editor of a weekly or a reporter on a nearby daily would lurk in the rear of the crowd, jotting down notes and then briefly interviewing Evers after the speech.

Evers *was* making news. He was speaking about issues with more candor than any politician in the state had done. He was also probably making more *sense* than any politician in the state's history. His issues were geared to the common man, black and white.

He irritated Catholics on the supposedly progressive Gulf Coast by saying, "Everybody knows y'all got gamblin' down here. I say do one of two things—either cut it all out and enforce the law or legalize it and make money off it. I'd like to see our Gulf Coast become our Gold Coast. Legalize that gamblin' and let's get the tax revenue. Why should Mississippi folks go down to New Orleans to watch the ponies run when we can do it right here? And keep the tax money instate!"

On more important issues his platform was well researched and by late summer he knew it inside and out. Had he been a white man with any measure of appeal, I have no doubt his tax proposal alone would have elected him. (It's questionable whether a white espousing such a program would get the money raised to present it in a campaign, since his supporters would have been of a different political and economic philosophy.) He said, "Everybody knows that the county tax assessor *fixes* taxes. A plantation owner in the Delta slips that ole assessor a hunnerd bucks and gets his land evaluated at nowhere near what it's worth! ° The farmer in Forrest County pays the same property tax as the Delta man. That's jus' plain cheatin'." He proposed 100 percent homestead exemption for people over sixty-five.

° This is alarmingly true. In some counties plantations worth $200,000 are assessed at under $5,000 to qualify for homestead exemption.

Because of the sham property tax system, education in Mississippi suffers terribly. This is because property taxes go directly to a county's schools. The Legislature then doles out 57 percent of the state budget to education. The person paying for the school is, in effect, the less endowed land-owner—who pays, proportionately, far more than the wealthy landowner—and he also bears the brunt of taxation at all levels. Unlike rich men, many of whom are legislators, the poorer landowners can't afford to send their kids to private schools. Evers proposed that the position of assessor be abolished, and that the state hire impartial assessor-collectors. He also espoused legislation to enforce equalization of tax assessments on property.

Seventy-five percent of Mississippi's revenue comes from consumer taxes. Here again, the lower- and middle-income resident pays more than he can afford. Mississippi's sales tax is abnormally high. Evers proposed a graduated tax scale for both corporate and individual income. He also advocated tax rebates for the impoverished consumer because "the only folks in Mississippi who can afford sales tax are folks who got a lot of money."

Further, one might add that the reason 50 percent of the college graduates leave Mississippi every year is because there are insufficient job opportunities. On the question of employment, Evers pointed to Fayette's success. "We've brought in jobs, factories, and federal programs. I'll be Mississippi's most aggressive lobbyist. I'll go after all the programs John Bell turned down. Besides, if I'm elected governor, everybody in the U.S. will bend over backwards to send somethin' down here—Nixon, the Democrats, General Motors; Mississippi'll be the country's 'cause' with her black governor!"

Waller's approach to taxes and jobs was less involved. His campaign literature printed speech excerpts:

Mississippi has one of the highest tax structures based on per capita income of any state. Such a tax burden demands strict and careful management of tax dollars. The state payroll has doubled the last four years without material benefit to the people. Waste in government must be stopped. I will propose fair and equitable tax reforms and plug up unfair loopholes. We can save substantial dollars by enforcing and perhaps strengthening our laws that require competitive bids for products and services sold to the state.

JOBS: the per capita income of our people must be raised. With our ideal climate, water supply, clean air, natural resources, and rivers, industrialization must be actively and progressively promoted. Therein lie more and better paying jobs.

Waller's rhetoric was progressive, and he was one of the first gubernatorial candidates to admit that there were gross inequities in the state's financial and tax mechanisms. But just as his predecessors had done, he either had no alternative plan or was remarkably opaque about proposed solutions.

On education, Evers wanted more money from the Legislature for public schools before anything else, with less money from the Legislature only after the equalized property taxes were collected. His staff found that certain federal programs had been passed up for lack of matching funds. As an example, The Mayor frequently cited the National School Lunch Act: "Last year, all the Legislature had to do was appropriate $30,000 extra and we coulda received more than $700,000 in HEW money. But no, they didn' do that. Instead they gave raises to all the judges in the state. An' who suffers? Undernourished Mississippi kids!"

He also attacked the inequities of the university and junior college appropriations: Ole Miss, State, and Southern

Mississippi receive more than the entire junior college system although they service half as many students. Jackson State and the black colleges receive incredibly low subsidies per student as compared with white schools, regardless of size.

The Mayor was the only candidate to call for a compulsory school attendance law. Fayette had one but Mississippi did not. Waller's stand on schools—public and private—had of course already been clearly indicated. Waller never discussed the intrinsic relationship between underfinanced schools and the sham property taxes. Unlike Evers, Waller did not speak of the importance of getting impoverished whites into Head Start programs.

Perhaps the only issue on which Evers and Waller expressed similar views was that of highways. Both men deplored the terrible condition of the highways; both called for lowering of license-plate fees, and neither had a firm plan for getting the money together to build sorely needed four-lane highways. Both men promised that highways would be a top legislative priority.

People were beginning to listen to Charles Evers. A white saleswoman selling me a tie noticed my campaign button and said, without a note of sarcasm, "I saw him on the news last night. He may be a nigger, but he's right about taxes. My husband's gonna vote for Waller. Myself, I'm not sure."

When The Mayor dominated three minutes of a news broadcast people saw he was talking plain sense and hard, cold facts. Rallies grew larger and more whites came, edging in closer to the fringe of the courthouse lawns. In Philadelphia 1,500 people jammed the town square in the light of a fading August sun that colored the sky gold and red. A full squadron of police stood around the crowd and courthouse. Thirty whites were interspersed throughout the audience and twice that number stood under the stores opposite the lawn. Remembering the early publicity over the Neshoba County Fair, The Mayor said, "We all know our white brothers and sisters ain't all bad. The past is past!" He was heavily cheered.

In every speech he stressed his desire to see the races live together in peace and harmony—"as we're doin' in Fayette"—and then he hit home with issues and supporting statistics. Alec Berezin prepared fact sheets on each county for him. More community people got involved in the campaign. A half-dozen whites from a Jackson high school came into the office after Labor Day to get campaign literature. A Gulf Coast TV station wanted him for a thirty-minute news-talk show. Father McCloone called from Pass Christian to arrange a meeting with a dozen white women who had worked as volunteers for Charles Sullivan on the Coast. In Tupelo a local white boy and girl were working with the get-out-the-vote committee.

In Collins, in the very same courthouse where one of the most famous photographs of Bilbo was taken, rain beat down outside, and The Mayor, standing beneath the judge's bench, said, "Black folks, we got some singin' to do. This ole courthouse has seen some mighty *ba-add* days. We gotta sing 'Amazin' Grace,' that ole spiritual what keeps us re-memberin' who we are. Play now, Dwight. Real loud, m'folks. Sing up *through* that rain! We gotta *sanctify* this ole courthouse!" Dwight played the organ and everybody sang. The white sheriff who needed black votes for reelection was grinning and waving to folks in the crowd. His deputies held open the doors so the draft would cool the crowded room.

In Starkville the mayor of the town, Travis Palmer, greeted Evers at the speaker's podium, which was set up in the center of a football field. Of the 1,500 spectators, about fifty were white. Mayor Palmer said to the candidate,

"Mayor Evers, before you sit some of the finest citizens of Oktibbeha County. Many of them supported me in my election last year. They're good people to have on your team."

Even in front of such a large crowd, The Mayor felt sufficiently at ease to introduce a new and unresearched issue in his speech. "I drive down the highways and roads of Mississippi, an' I like to use the washroom now and then. I'm an ole man, y'know. Now I've noticed we ain't got no roadside washrooms where you can go relieve yourself. So when I become governor, I'm gonna take all the able men off welfare I can find, and send 'em around the state buildin' and then takin' care of roadside washstands. This'll keep some men employed, and help the state's hygiene out, besides."

That night we glided down the Natchez Trace, the old road of immense beauty etched out of the wilderness where greens and reds suffuse the landscape at dawn and dusk, and where, as for centuries, the nights are as serene and soundless as smoke. Fifty miles out, the taillights of The Mayor's car blurred and the cars following pulled off behind it to the shoulder of the road. The six men in the cars got out and stood on a grassy knoll leading down to the thick woodland. And in perhaps the same spot used by the Tishomingo Indians or Spanish explorers of half a millennium ago, they urinated. The candidate turned to his press secretary and said, "Y'see, Jason, I'm talkin' plain truth when I say we need those ole roadside washstands. Cain't no one say Evers' issues ain't for real!"

His issues were very much for real and soon people were recognizing his candidacy as viable. The campaign itself was taking on a new shape. By Labor Day we had been graced by the addition of two idealistic, gutsy Catholic nuns who were quick to make inroads with moderate white groups. Sister JoAnn and Sister Margaret were in between church-appointed jobs and thus came on as full-time staff aides. They received small salaries and were worth every penny,

for they were lining The Mayor up before whites. Neither
woman wore a habit, and The Mayor noted, "That's all
right, Sisters. I'm for any kinda freedom the chu'ch is for!
When we go on road trips and white folks see y'all husslin'
around with us, sellin' books and buttons and all, they ain't
gonna know y'all are nuns. They'll think ole Evers won himself two more converts."

As The Mayor began to dominate political news coverage,
our campaign motorcades added two statewide candidates.
Freddie Washington, twenty-six, a former schoolteacher
from Moss Point, was the Loyalist nominee for secretary of
state. His opponent was incumbent Heber Ladner, an old
man who smoked long green cigars and had been secretary
as long as nearly everyone could remember. No Democrat
had run against him in the primary.

The Loyalist candidate for state superintendent of education was a man of impressive credentials. C. J. Duckworth
had, in fact, been drafted by the party to run in late summer. Duckworth was in his mid-forties and was former president of the all-black Mississippi Teachers Association. A
fearless pioneer for integration, the National Education Association had thought enough of him to elect him their president.* Duckworth was director of a program designed to
ensure that black teachers and administrators would not be
demoted or ousted in the transition from segregated to integrated schools. Discrimination within desegregated schools
was a bad problem for blacks in Mississippi schools. Duckworth's office was conveniently located two blocks from the
Lawyers Committee for Civil Rights; he frequently conferred with them regarding abuses in desegregation practices.

Shortly after Duckworth announced his candidacy in late

---

* The MTA and all-white Mississippi Education Association had, despite dili-
gent efforts by the blacks, not merged. The NEA then expelled the MEA, and
sanctioned the all-black MTA.

August, the public schools opened. The mood of change was apparent; there were few incidents. In Jackson a biracial organization of parents had been formed to ensure that busing of some 60,000 kids would be smooth. The Chamber of Commerce ran an advertising campaign encouraging citizens to support public schools. The Jackson school system was now 60 percent black, but prominent educators were predicting that within five years whites would return in ever-growing numbers.

On September 10, shortly after 1 P.M., The Mayor formally qualified for the governor's race. A candidate's presentation of qualifying petitions usually is not a spectacular ceremony. The Mississippi secretary of state's office is on the third floor of the Capitol, just around the corner from the governor's chambers. Reporters followed The Mayor as he walked past Governor Williams' office; he waved at an old secretary, who scowled back. Then he presented his 7,000 signatures to the secretary of state's office; he had needed only 2,000.

The qualifying done, Mayor Evers emerged from the office to an enthusiastic press. I whispered to him, "Let's go down to the main floor. I think it would make a great story."

And so for fifteen minutes Charles Evers stood in front of the statue of Bilbo and fielded questions from Mississippi reporters. He flashed a splendid grin, the story ran statewide, and he even got his picture in the *Clarion-Ledger.*

With the campaign now accelerating, an immediate concern to everyone in the office was the relationship between Magnolia and me. Our differences had grown worse since June; they stemmed from an intense psychological dilemma within our campaign.

The problem was that no black male worked in the outer office. Martin, Woody, and Squeaky were always with The Mayor; McBride was advancing or with the band. Ed was confined inside his office. Thus the elemental duties of the outer office were divided between white men and black women. Had there been a black male with us he might have eased the subtle tensions that arose when a man criticized a woman, or vice versa. Indeed, his mediation would have served as a psychological catalyst, illustrating that the criticism did not reflect sex or color bias, but rather focused on the way one's job was being done. But there was no black man in the main office and by September some of the women were acutely sensitive to criticism, seeing it as implicitly racist or chauvinistic. The men, on the other hand, began to feel that criticism of them was a form of revenge. The arguments Magnolia and I had were by no means the only ones that arose between a black and a white. But they were the most frequent and, I would venture to say, the most basic.

Like the other women in the office, Magnolia wanted to take orders only from Ed or The Mayor; she was a willing co-worker, but she resented being told what to do by anyone else. As the office manager, she had to account for all materials. Additionally, she and Lois were in charge of phone reception and messages. They were also supposed to see that the office was kept clean.

The two major obstacles between Magnolia and me stemmed from her last two tasks, telephones and office cleaning. The telephone problem was awful for everyone, really. We had only two phone lines and a WATS. Everyone was supposed to keep conversations to the barest minimum; this was, however, often impossible. Announcing a press conference required that I make at least a dozen calls; often reporters would take up an hour with questions about itinerary, rumors to be confirmed or denied, and so forth. For

Magnolia, ordering a week's supplies necessitated a lot of phoning, too. To aggravate matters, her desk was ten feet across the floor from mine and frequently we would pick up the free line simultaneously, glare menacingly, and one would finally hang up and wait for the other to finish. After one particularly testy encounter (which saw me win the phone), she remarked, "Sometimes I think you think I'm your slave when it comes to that telephone. . . ." I lay awake until two in the morning thinking about that, wondering if she had said it spontaneously or after premeditation. I decided that it made little difference, for the meaning was crystal clear.

(The Mayor, despite repeated pleas by Ed and the staff, was against more phones. "I'm already payin' too much money. Anyway, y'all don't need phones that much. If everybody's doin' their job, you're not supposed to be on the phone. *Take turns* talkin' . . ." Later, after the situation had become so acute that Evers himself had to wait an hour trying to call Ramberg from Fayette, he had three new lines installed. That night, he proudly told a crowd in Sardis, "And in our campaign office we got *five* telephone lines, black folks. Sho' 'nuf goin' professional!")

The Mayor felt that keeping the office clean was a responsibility we all should share. This was the cause of much disgruntlement. The gut issue was mopping, which each of us vehemently hated. By late August, Magnolia had made a list that assigned every aide an evening to sweep and mop the floor. The task was actually rather complicated. The only time one could work without interruption was at night, when reporters, visitors, and repairmen weren't tramping in and out of the office. Thus, between 6 and 9 P.M. people threw themselves into important projects. To clean the floor, then, meant that one had to start sweeping at about 8 P.M., and then splash out the mop a few minutes later. After a ten-hour day and with work left to do, mopping was a most disagreeable chore. Each of us tried to avoid it, but the office managed to get cleaned about three times a week. Magnolia did more than her share.

Since I traveled with The Mayor to every rally, I managed to miss every mopping assignment. By mid-September that wasn't sitting well with Magnolia. Moreover, my handling of the RNA situation had cast a dark shadow over me for most of August. But gradually friction lessened. I was working hard and soon the mistake was accepted as part of the past. Nevertheless, I was still a white boy, and still learning. Reporters marveled at the energy and camaraderie of our office; I wracked my brain at night about why I was having such vicious exchanges with Magnolia over phones and mops.

Quite by accident we fell into a long and congenial conversation one afternoon just as the national news concluded a TV report on air pollution. She told me about the smog in L.A., where she had lived for six years, and compared it with Jackson. I talked about the problem as I had observed it in Washington and New Orleans. As she left for dinner, she smiled and said shyly, "That's the first time we've ever really *talked* about anything." After three months in Mississippi, I realized it really *was*.

The next afternoon found The Mayor in New York and the heat abnormally strong. I looked up from my desk around four to find an old black man seated under the air conditioner. I walked across the room, shook hands, and his eyes lit up as he said, "I'm so glad you have a little time here today. I took the train in from Brookhaven. I been wantin' to see how y'all are doin' in the great race for gubbernor. . . ."

I gave him a brief tour of the office and explained the duties of each aide. When we were back in the front office, he gently but persistently lectured me for thirty minutes about the spiritual problems of the young. "We got to teach them the Way of Jesus. The young folks don't know that. Too many of 'em don't listen to the ministers. The ministers tells us Jesus' life! They shines for us. They shows us the way. You tell Mist' Ebbers that. Please . . . I took the train in from Brookhaven today."

"Yessir, I'll be sure to tell him. . . ."

The old man departed and I returned to my desk, touched as always by the old black folks' sincerity. Magnolia deflated my enthusiasm by handing me a mop and broom. "The Mayor doesn't have a speech tonight and it's your turn to clean."

Trying to salvage some optimism, I said, "Did you see that old guy? He was really concerned about the young kids. He came all the way in from Brookhaven."

She snickered. "Didn't you know? He's been in here four times. He sells Bibles."

I took the mop, dismissed the old man from my thoughts, and spread water on the floor. The mood between us was suddenly rotten.

"Jason," she said, "you've got to sweep first. You can't mop without sweeping."

"All right. I'll sweep."

Ten minutes later I was about to start mopping when she said, "You can't jus' run the broom over the floor. Lookit all this dirt. C'mon now, sweep."

So I swept again. Then I put the mop into the bucket, cursed under my breath, and began to mop.

By 7:30 the floor was wet, muddy, and very obviously far from clean. I was exhausted, angry, and doing a lousy job. Magnolia, now impatient, wanted to leave for supper. "That looks awful. C'mon, mop it right."

"Magnolia, I don't need your advice."

"It looks like you need something."

"I don't need you standing over me."

Furious, she said evenly, "Your whole problem is that you've never mopped a floor before."

"Maybe I never saw any point in doing it. Look, I'm cleaning the floor now, so just keep your comments to yourself."

"This isn't like New Orleans. You ain't gonna have a black maid come in to mop your floor for you. An' you sure are doin' a bad job!"

I kicked the bucket across the room. It hit on the base of the white wall, overturning with a crash, and black water spilled across the floor. Magnolia gasped and I stalked out of the office.

"This," I told myself speeding through Jackson, *"is when I ask myself if I am wrong because I am white."* I drove toward the Interstate, the radio blasting empty messages, until the Jackson zoo suddenly appeared on the right side of the street. I parked the car, crossed the street, and found a trail sloping gently down a wooded hill to a large pond next to the animal cages. My head throbbed from the argument.

On the one hand, I remembered Ramberg's words: "You gotta understand it'll take time for you to get used to black folks. Remember, *you're* the one who has to change, not them." But then there was also *me.* How do you approach a woman you just don't like? Magnolia and I grimaced each time our eyes met. I told myself that she had absolutely no sympathy for my predicament as a white.

The path from the bridge led away from the pond. It wove through tall unkempt grass and gave way to a bank of dry mud. I stopped and sat on crusty dead grass. Ten feet in front of me was a picket fence. Inside it was a huge swimming pool: empty, cracked, overridden with bottles and weeds; even without water in it the smell was stagnant.

I lay back on the dead grass, with the hideous stench flooding my nostrils, and asked myself why I ever went to

Mississippi. It was hard to recall that I had gone to Mississippi because I believed in human dignity and wanted to help change the white system. The swimming pool loomed in front of me, and after my temper cooled I realized that it was white folks who had closed the pool, and it was white folks who had run the South for a hundred years. I thought about what Magnolia and I had said to each other. Finally, in the privacy of the Jackson zoo, I admitted that I had never mopped a floor before—or at least never done it well enough to remember. I walked back to the car, resolved that I was going to like Magnolia if it killed me . . . and clean the damned floor. The office was locked when I got back. The floor had been cleaned the next day—by Magnolia, I later found out.

The next morning we had a staff meeting and Ed remonstrated with both of us, saying, "Can't you two learn to accept each other as *people*?" The Mayor was in the office in the afternoon but he didn't mention the incident. That weekend, as the motorcade prepared to leave, I volunteered to drive the books-and-buttons car, which always carried at least four women. Lois and the nuns sat in the back; Magnolia sat next to me in the front. We talked all the way from Jackson to the Gulf Coast. We didn't talk about politics or our differences. I don't remember what we talked about. We just talked. . . . The following week I managed to clean the floor.

Our relationship began to solidify shortly after the Jackson County Fair opened. I wandered into the place and won a stuffed doll from a woman in a booth who boasted she could tell a person's age within a year; she made the mistake of guessing four more than I had. I gave the doll to Magnolia, she blushed, and that was the end of our stormy impasse.

The Mayor, of course, knew about the bucket incident. Had I been a volunteer—or perhaps, even, a northerner— he probably would have ordered me to leave. But as Ed later said, "He knew it was somethin' real important . . . somethin' y'all had to work out between you. It had a deep meaning to the whole campaign, to everyone in it."

The only time Evers even hinted about it was in, of all places, New Orleans. He delivered the keynote address to a banquet for the Inter-racial Council for Business Opportunity. My parents, now enthusiastically interested in the campaign, were dazzled when they met The Mayor in his hotel suite prior to the dinner.° He kissed my mother, shook my father's hand, and said, "I can't thank you enough for givin' us your . . . *flamboyant* son! He's added so much to our campaign."

My mother said cheerfully, "Oh, he certainly is flamboyant."

The Mayor was grinning. "Yeah, those ole girls in the office give him problems now and then, but he comes out on top. He stays right in there. Don't let nothin' keep him down. . . ." I kept envisioning the bucket and muddy floor.

The Mayor caught a late plane out after the dinner. The next morning as I got up early to drive back to Jackson, my father said, "Ya know somethin'? He kissed your mother last night. First time he ever met her. He walked right up, and *boom*, kissed her right on the cheek!"

I nodded, not knowing really what to say.

He paused and then smiled. "You know, I like that. That's got style. He doesn't mess around. That fella sure knows what he's doin'."

Driving back to Jackson, thinking about Magnolia and myself, I could not help but agree.

° Mother eventually sent part of her grocery money as a campaign contribution.

CHAPTER

10

Squeaky stood in front of the campaign manager's office, craning to see the incredible proceedings inside. Alec Berezin, Joe Huttie, Charles Ramberg, and I sat on the floor around The Mayor. Ed smoked his pipe behind the desk. Three white men who had driven up from Laurel sat near the opposite wall.

The presence of fifty-year-old James Simmons was remarkable in itself. A balding man from Forest Home, Alabama, Simmons had been a chicken farmer most of his life until he started sawing and hauling pulpwood to a large paper mill near his farm in the early sixties. In 1967 he had organized the Alabama Pulpwood Producers' Association, a group through which impoverished pulpwood haulers could voice demands for better treatment and wages from the mills. By 1971 he had begun organizing wood haulers in Mississippi. The makeup of both groups was unique; there were black as well as white wood haulers.

Tonny Allgood was Simmons' assistant. Tonny was a wiry man who had grown up in Louisville, a tiny town north of Neshoba County. During college years at Millsaps he had undergone a series of changes. In his own words, "Growin' up in the poorest state in the country, you saw how it stayed that way. People only knew poverty and ignorance . . . that's all they ever had to look forward to." The easy drawl shrouded his intense feeling that Mississippi would never change until the masses came together. Graduated from Millsaps in May of 1971, he started canvassing in Mississippi for the Voter Education Project, headed by John Lewis (formerly of SNCC) in Atlanta. In midsummer he left VEP to join Simmons in organizing the pulpwood haulers in southeast Mississippi in mounting a strike against Masonite Corporation of Laurel. He had cut his hair short, followed Simmons around, listening carefully to the instructions of the shy, nearly illiterate man from Alabama. Despite his youth, Tonny had gradually been accepted by the men and their families. He felt a personal accomplishment when Simmons said to him, "You went to college but you don't show it like some. . . . You care, and that's good." Tonny had not emphasized politics or race when he spoke, but rather the strike and its importance to the men's survival.

The third man was Bob Zellner. He had first come to Mississippi a decade ago as a civil rights worker. Zellner was SNCC's first white field secretary. He was born in Alabama; his father was a country preacher who was an early outspoken advocate of black rights. Reverend Zellner's influence on his son was strong, and in 1960 Bob created a stir at Huntingdon College in Alabama. School and state officials were threatening him with expulsion because of his growing involvement with blacks. He became friends with Reverend Ralph Abernathy and attended nonviolent workshops.

Zellner had first joined SNCC with a grant from the Southern Conference Education Fund, one of the oldest and most vital organizations working for integration and the economic equality of blacks and poor whites. SCEF was run

by another white man, Carl Braden, whose original bout
with the repressive elements of the South had come in 1954.
He was arrested after selling his Kentucky home to a black
man. The home was burned and Braden was jailed. He was
convicted of sedition, but the Supreme Court eventually exonerated him after an exhaustive appeals case. Braden and
SCEF had to run the gamut during civil rights years: members were forced to testify before congressional committees
chaired by irate southerners; SCEF's New Orleans offices
were sacked by Eastland people, by racist New Orleans
cops, by people working for Leander Perez, the crude
leader of the Louisiana Citizens' Council. Braden and SCEF
weathered the assaults and by the late sixties it was still an
active organization for social change.

The unique parity of former civil rights worker Zellner
and the Alabama redneck Simmons stemmed from the goal
Simmons had when he moved in to organize in Mississippi.
Simmons wanted people like himself to have some means of
recourse when exploitation by the paper mills became intol-
erable. Zellner knew the organization would of necessity be
biracial. The strike was working toward an ideological goal
of the civil rights struggle, racial unity leading to class unity
leading to self-improvement. Since the denouement of the
movement Zellner had seen the departure of the activists
with whom he had once worked and suffered in the southern sun. In the winter of 1968 he had heard about the Alabama wood haulers and sought out Simmons. SCEF sent
Zellner to work with the effort, and the organization contributed a monthly newsletter to the cutters' group.

Money was the gut issue in the Laurel strike. The average
wood hauler, be he black or white, earns $4,000 a year, if he
is lucky. The pulpwood hauler is paid in terms of the quan-
tity of wood he cuts and delivers to the paper company; he
has no hourly wage. He owns his own dilapidated truck, and
his annual earnings must not only pay for repairs and parts

but also provide for the lives of his family. Many wood haulers use food stamps.

Seated in Evers' office, Simmons was gesturing with his hand, concluding an involved discussion of wood-measuring standards. Next to him sat Zellner, his unshaven jaw bulging to one side. I wondered if he chewed tobacco for the same reason Tonny Allgood had cut his hair: to create a rapport with the wood haulers. Simmons had a deep voice with a direct clarity strengthened by his simple choice of words. He was speaking to Evers, whose face expressed no particular emotion. "Ah'll level with yuh. Ah contacted Eastland firs'. Man in his office said ah had Commonists workin' for me. . . ." He gestured at Tonny and Bob. "So ah wrote Sparkman o' mah state, Allu*bum*ma. He said about the same thing. Then Sulluvun and Wallah wouldn' touch us. So ah come to you."

Evers rocked forward. "Lemme make sure I got this straight. Masonite's done changed from a volume measure to a weight measure. . . ."

Zellner shifted the tobacco wad. "Yeah, and under the old volume measure system, a man brought in so many *inches* of wood, and it averaged out to about 5,200 pounds. A cord of wood averaged about that much."

The Mayor said, "An' now that they changed to weighin', y'all have to bring in more wood."

Simmons drawled, "Raht. Now a man brings in wood and it *has* to weigh 7,200 pounds. In dollars, what it means is the man who cuts pu'pwood for a livin' is losin' $20 to $35 each load he hauls in."

The Mayor said quickly, "That's a violation of wage-price freeze, ain't it?"

Zellner: "Yeah, we thought about that, but it's hard as hell to prove. You got make noise and set folks thinkin' first. What we need first is to get noticed. Which is why we came to you. . . ."

Simmons continued, "The other thing is that they're cuttin' off food stamps for our people goin' on strahk. The woman in charge at the food stamp office is tellin' 'em they get nothin' till they get back to work."

"She's lyin'," Evers said. "She don't have that right. . . ."

"Ah know that," Simmons replied, "and mebbe you know that. But that don't mean she's gonna quit. . . . Wull, you're runnin' for gov'nor. You're sayin' you for black and white together. You kin help us. We need it."

The Mayor said, "Sure I'll help. When's your big meetin'?"

"Thursday. An' bring reporters. We need publicity. We meetin' in the Laurel courthouse."

The Mayor smiled. "Laurel, huh? I know Laurel. . . ."

Then he turned to me. "Call the networks, *The New York Times*, the *Post*—git 'em all." He turned back to Simmons. "We'll git this thing covered."

Simmons' mouth was a slight, twisted curve. "You know who ah voted for in '68?"

"Unh-unh. Who?"

"Gawge Wallace."

The striking drama of the approaching meeting between Evers and the wood haulers was that these were the populous classes severed after Reconstruction and pitted against each other by the Bilbos, Vardamans, Eastlands, and Wallaces. Now, they suddenly stared each other in the face, united in the simple struggle for survival. The alliance between the Gulf Coast Pulpwood Association and Charles Evers was likewise purely economic. As Tonny Allgood later told me, "In the process of gettin' involved, you could see them lookin' at each other as men, knowing what they had in common and not worryin' about what made 'em different." There was something sadly expectable about the fact that Simmons had first contacted white politicians. But after being spurned, his choice was to get *anyone* or no one. He needed a figure, black if not white, to stir up the men and to draw publicity.

For Evers, it was politically expedient to speak before the wood haulers. It would be a dramatic news story, a boost to his campaign. The wood haulers needed him, but *he* wanted them. Like Zellner, he saw the struggle from a personal perspective; it had been his way since the day his brother died.

I alerted the networks, but only ABC sent a camera team. Roy Reed of *The New York Times* and Philip Carter of the *Post* (Hodding III's younger brother) made arrangements to cover it. More than any other journalists covering the campaign, Reed and Carter consistently wrote the most penetrating stories. Both men were white Southerners.

The impact of Evers' support would not be felt until the meeting actually came off. Unfortunately, a second development overshadowed the wood haulers' story, which showed me the deeper myopia of the best reporters in Mississippi. Less than a week before the Laurel rally two black lawyers brought a law to the candidate's attention, the 1935 Corrupt Practices Act, which said that no candidate could spend more than $50,000 per party primary. Typically, this was a law Mississippi had not enforced. By the fifties political campaigns were costing more than the law allowed, yet legislators didn't bother to repeal it. With passage of the 1965 Voting Rights Act, Mississippi and other southern states were forced to submit any and all changes in election law to the Justice Department for approval. In 1971 the Legislature voted for repeal; however, the new law that would replace it was not submitted to the Justice Department until September—after the costly primaries. The Justice Department affirmed the repeal, but Evers and his lawyers felt that the law had, in effect, been repealed retroactively. If this could be borne out in a lawsuit, it meant that Waller would face disqualification! The Mayor told a press conference, "If

Bill is guilty, he's got to go to jail. An' I'll become governor." Waller immediately emerged from his campaign inter-
mission to announce that he had broken no law and that the
case would not stand up in court.

The stellar Mississippi reporters, even those who admired
Evers and covered him honestly, were incensed over the
possibility of the suit. I did not mind the subsequent denunciations these men wrote in their columns; indeed, the suit
was a long shot and I thought it had no chance at all. In politics you play to win, and a long shot is at least a shot. But in
the process of writing detailed analyses of the legal move,
the reporters simply ignored the Laurel strike. I spent two
days talking up the meeting with reporters, but all said, in
effect, "Yeah, that strike's something nobody expected, but
what about this lawsuit? You can't throw a man out on some
outmoded law that's already been repealed by the State
Legislature back in April." Much legal research was involved in the lawsuit; it would not be filed before early October.

In Laurel, meanwhile, the people with vested interests
were getting upset. On September 20, the Laurel *Leader-
Call* printed a statement on page one issued by E. A.
McGrummond, manager of Southern Woodlands Division
of Masonite.

> The controversy over the price paid for pulpwood at
> the Laurel plant appears to be a deliberate attempt to
> confuse the public and those who supply us with pulp-
> wood. . . . The amount of money which the suppliers
> received for a load of wood delivered to our yard was
> not changed. . . .
> There are 1.3125 cords per a unit of 7100 lbs. We
> have always used "Units" as the basis for payment.
> Since Sept. 1 we pay the same for a unit of wood as we

did prior to that time. We can see no conflict with the wage-price freeze.

Since there has been no change in price we can only assume that those who would harass and confuse must have some motive for their action other than the interest of the pulpwood suppliers.

A Gulf Coast Pulpwood Association strike bulletin told it differently:

> The action against Masonite began September 1 when the company changed the weight factor. It had been using a scaled stick to measure wood by the cubic foot. On September 1 it began using weight scales to measure the wood.
>
> Under the stick system, Masonite called 168 cubic feet of wood a unit. It paid $20 for each unit put in Masonite's yard at Laurel. Under the weight system, the company calls 7100 lbs. a unit. It pays the same price $20, for each unit, as it paid before. The haulers find that under the weight system they have to deliver 20 to 25 per cent more wood in order to have a unit.
>
> For example, one cutter with a steel rack on his truck found that he was getting 21½% less for a load of 14,750 lbs. Under the stick system, he was paid $52.30 for a load of that size. Under the weight system, he got $41.10 for the same-sized load. Under the old system he was getting $20 for 5700 lbs. Under the new system he got $20 for 7,100. He had to deliver 1,400 more pounds for each unit in order to get the same amount of money as before.
>
> The cutters say that a unit of wood should be the same as a cord of wood, which averages 5200 lbs. This would get away from the confusion by Masonite when

it uses a different system of measuring—and then changes the system.

The cutters say that Masonite is trying to beat the price freeze by cutting their pay. A cut of 20 to 25 per cent in the amount paid for raw material, the wood, is the same as Masonite raising the price for hardboard by that amount. It increases Masonite's profits.

The pulpwood haulers' strike was a direct challenge to the feudal labor practices that have flourished in many parts of the South since paper mills were first built. The mills originally set up shop in an ideal location: myriad rivers and creeks, astonishingly low corporate tax rates, no pollution laws, the sprawling rich woodland, legislators of wealth with no qualms about passing tax moratoriums. But most important, they found poor people who knew little save how to live and work off the land. The race factor conveniently separated groups who might have gone on strike.

Another newsletter of the GCPA shed more light on the cord-unit dispute:

Mississippi is the only state in the US where wood is bought by the "unit." Unlike the cord, the unit *is not standardized by the Federal or state governments.* Therefore, a wood dealer or paper company has full authority to determine what a "unit" means, how much it weighs, and how it scales with a stick. As long as the companies are allowed to buy the "unit," they know they can make extra profits off the woodcutters' backs. For instance, if a paper company gets involved in a costly lawsuit, which might cut their net profit from $400 million to $399 million, they can make up for the loss by requiring more wood per unit, but paying the same price as before.

The weight factor for a unit in West Mississippi is

8100 lbs, in Southern Mississippi it's 7600 lbs, on the
Eastern state line it's 6800 lbs. Just the difference between regions is proof that the unit is not standardized. . . .

The day before the meeting, a Laurel radio station manager in sympathy with our campaign called to say that the
TV station was going to air an editorial attacking the woodcutters' support from Braden and SCEF. "I was at Rotary
Club today," the man said, "and a lotta people are upset
about that Communist background business. . . ."

I told him that the strike was economically and not politically motivated. "Besides," I said, "anyone who's ever done
civil rights work or organizing of this kind has been called a
Communist."

"Yeah," the man said glumly, "and we got people here
who still think the Kennedys and Dr. King were
Reds. . . ." I assured him for a last time that no plot was involved. We said cordial goodbyes and I cursed the Laurel
Rotary Club to myself. Philosophically, Braden and Zellner
were socialists, but the literature and speeches of SCEF
workers in the dispute strictly avoided anti-Americanism.
The approach was the traditional "radical" thrust of the
labor movement throughout the twentieth century. The
SCEF newspaper, the *Southern Patriot*, and the strike bulle-
tins dealt with movements and battles that involved laborers
and their employers, the fight for equitable balance.

The TV feature placed SCEF in a different light. It did
not discuss the humanist enterprises of the organization or
its laudable victories in the southern struggles of the past.
The report accused Braden of being a Communist and
quoted a *Time* magazine article that probed into his background and listed titles of subversive reading material in his
home. *Time* wrote about a jail term Braden served in 1954
for violation of a Kentucky sedition law. Braden had pur-

chased a house in an all-white neighborhood and sold it to a black. The house was subsequently fired on and a bomb was set off. The TV editorial bafflingly implied that Communists had started the violence—but why would Communists burn down Braden's house if he himself were a Communist? The report concluded:

> Today, Television Seven investigated the origin of SCEF. In 1947, the House Committee on Un-American Activities, issued House Resolution 952, in which a group known as the Southern Conference on Human Welfare Organization was named as a Communist-Front. . . . SCEF was identified as the Educational wing of the Red Front. Moreover, a newspaper, the *Southern Patriot*, was identified as the Front's propaganda organ. Braden's wife, Ann, is presently the paper's editor.
>
> This afternoon several woodhaulers told Television Seven News that they not only didn't know Braden, but that they didn't know the purpose or background of SCEF . . . or why Braden and SCEF are involved in the Laurel dispute. The woodhaulers say they'd like to have the answers to these questions, however one of them said he was ready to quit if Communists are involved.

The editorial explained only one side of the story, and most of the purported "facts" from *Time* were actually allegations. The editorial also implied that communism was behind the Klan's terrorism of Braden in Louisville. Nor did the station reveal what Braden had said of his jail term. He told journalist Pat Watters that he spent the time "going over my life, trying to decide whether it was worth it to do the kind of work I had been doing. I finally decided that I was not going to live under a system where a man could be put in prison for selling his house to a Negro. I decided I would spend my life trying to change the system." His conviction was overturned by the Supreme Court, and Braden pressed on—which was not mentioned in the editorial. But the persecution against him did not cease, and eventually he went to jail.

Watters later elaborated on Braden's "Communist ties." In *Down to Now: Reflections of the Civil Rights Movement*, he wrote of Braden's testimony in 1958 before the notorious House Un-American Activities Committee:

> . . . to questions about whether he or various associates were Communists, he replied: "Gentlemen, my beliefs and my associates are none of the business of this committee." Asked if he were pleading the Fifth Amendment (against self-incrimination), he replied: "No sir, I am standing on the First Amendment to the United States Constitution which guarantees my right to associate with whom I please, to write what I want, to say what I please." He was cited for contempt and sentenced to a year in Federal Prison. And he lost an appeal to the Supreme Court.

After the TV editorial, Simmons, Zellner, and Allgood visited wood haulers and told them to go to the meeting with Evers; Evers and the SCEF workers were not Communists. Nor was wanting better wages and food for one's family tantamount to believing in communism.

Tonny Allgood had recently begun having difficulties. He was followed by various cars. He was almost hit by a truck as he stood talking to woodcutters in a picket line. Twice he was stopped by Laurel police on "routine checks"—his first in Laurel. His landlady was threatening eviction because blacks had visited his apartment.

Thus, on September 23, four cars left the Evers office for

the meeting anticipating a tense atmosphere. Two black food stamp workers from Jackson accompanied the campaign aides. We met at Tonny's apartment for a brief meeting prior to the speech. Woody and Squeaky checked the bushes, then the driveway, and then ushered in The Mayor's car. The candidate hopped out quickly and bounded into the house; we crowded in behind him. Squeaky stood in the doorway and eyed the street. He said to Tonny, "Who's the cat in the car drivin' back and forth outside?"

"He's a security guard from Masonite," Tonny said. "He's been drivin' around for two hours. I don't think he's gonna do anything. He knows y'all have guns. I doubt if he has one, anyway."

Zellner was talking quickly. "We don't have much time. Let's get a few things understood, Mayor. There ought to be a hundred and fifty folks, about half black and half white. But black folks have been scared to walk in the picket lines." Then Simmons recounted the TV editorial.

Evers said, "Your folks scared o' Red-baitin'?"

Simmons didn't bat an eye. "Yeah, they sure are. So, talk about hungah and money. That's what the strahk's about. They need a fahr lit under 'em."

The Mayor was getting impatient. "Okay. Let's roll!"

A gold September moon hung in the night above the Laurel courthouse. A cadre of nervous policemen stood by the front steps, clearly self-conscious, apprehensive should any trouble occur with the northern reporters inside. As we parked, I thought back to the visit to Laurel on the hot kickoff day in June. Black folks had had a hard time warming up to Dwight's music; they were scared stiff. But a hearty group of supporters led by The Mayor's sister had since organized a local campaign office. We had come to Laurel in late August to a crowd twice the size of the first one. Now Laurel, hotbed of the Ku Klux Klan, was the meeting place for white and black pulpwood haulers. They sat in the county courthouse restless and unsure of themselves.

Squeaky and Martin on either side of him, The Mayor entered the court. About 250 people began clapping; blacks and whites were seated in racial clusters. The blacks clapped louder. The whites were peering at Evers when the applause died. Simmons and Zellner waited at the front of the room. The whites were as much in awe of the solemn bodyguards as of the candidate himself.

Simmons pushed through a crowd of whites and greeted The Mayor. "Mayuh, ah want yuh to meet some membuhs o' the Gulf Coast Pulpwood Association. . . . This is Fred Walters."

Fred Walters was a tall, thin man in his mid-forties; his hair was damply matted and his skin was rough. His eyes were wide and white and his jaw hung open, showing few teeth. The Mayor boomed, "I may be black, but I ain't gonna bite you. We' all in this boat together." Walters grabbed his hand and shook it vigorously.

Evers walked into a crowd of Mississippi white men; a group of black men stood farther to the rear of the room. White men carefully stood back as he passed, eying him, nodding politely if deferentially. To The Mayor's right sat his sister and a few dozen old supporters.

He approached a white man in dark stained khakis with a blue thermal undershirt cut off jaggedly above the elbows. The man's jaw had taken on the shape of a wad of tobacco and he had only a few teeth. His hands were calloused and the hair on his forearms was the color of rust. The Mayor said, "Well, don't you be afraid of me! You got Masonite to conten' with!" The man guffawed and shakily extended a hand, which Evers shook.

A brawny, wind-burned man in his late twenties, black hair prematurely receding on a damp forehead, moved to make room. Evers gave him a playful thump on the stomach and said, "You ain't scared o' me, are you?"

The man shook his head. "Naw."

"I hope not. We need plenny folks if we gonna beat Masonite."

"That's true," the man replied.

Next in line stood a sixteen-year-old boy with red hair. He stood next to a barrel-chested man who obviously was his father. Both wore muddy coveralls. The Mayor said to the young man, "You ain't afraid to help your daddy out, are you?"

The boy shook his hand and looked at the Negro with wide eyes. His father extended a raw hand, saying, "He ain't afraid. How you doin'?"

Their forearms locked momentarily and Evers said, "They givin' y'all food stamp trouble?"

"Yeah. Ah reckon so."

Simmons ushered him to the front. The Mayor stopped and shook hands with a half-dozen black men in faded clothes, then moved in and took a seat. ABC had sent a film crew, now set up beneath the judge's chair next to the crew from the Laurel station. Reed and Carter sat with an A.P. reporter and the Laurel reporter. My radio announcer friend from the Rotary Club sat beneath the mantel, enthralled by the proceedings. The previously quiet courtroom was now abuzz; the excitement was palpable. Everyone was shaking hands with Evers, moving out of Evers' path, watching the black folks wave at Evers, watching the white woodcutters gape at Evers and then shake his hand, watching Evers accept the situation with verve but steady cool.

Zellner stepped through camera wires and started talking. "We all know why we're here. Reason's simple. Money, right?"

The crowd answered loudly, "Right!"

"Now I'm like y'all, I git scared when someone says I'm a Communist. No one likes to be called that. But I sure haven't met any Communists in this crowd. . . ."

Zellner introduced Simmons, and the big man kept looking down; the lights irritated his eyes. His hands stuck deep in his pockets, he rocked back and forth on his heels. "Ah was raised on a old cotton farm in Allu*bum*ma. Worked all m'life, don't have much education. Ah started cuttin' wood a few years ago because ah needed income. Ah didn' find much money, and that's how we got this association started . . . 'cuz we're workin' for more money!"

He discussed the strike, reiterating the woodcutters' demands. Then he talked about Braden and the Communist rumors. "Ah've known Carl Braden a long time, but I never met him 'til he came . . . he came, spent some time with us, gave some good ideas. He's an old union organizer from way back." He explained the sedition conviction being overturned and then said, "Carl says, 'My whole life is in behalf of workin' people.' It didn't make any difference who they were, where they came from—that's who he works with. Carl hadn't never made no money. He's gettin' a salary of $70 a week plus expenses. And most anybody that's doin' anything is makin' more than that. In the five days Carl Braden was here, we enjoyed him bein' with us, enjoyed all the talks he gave us. Sometimes he talked to us pretty rough and the last thing he told me this mornin' before leavin' was we wasn't workin' hard enough. . . . Ah think we might need more Carl Bradens."

Simmons then introduced Evers, and by now the crowd was clapping hard. "The first thing I wanna say is I'm glad we all got *together*!"

"A-men!"

"Here we black an' white folks been livin' in Mississippi all these years, doin' nothin' but mindin' our own business, and that ole Masonite won't give you the pay what you deserve! I always knew that poor black folks and poor white folks *some*how would come together. . . . Thank God it's beginnin' to happen here in Jones County. We been tole too long to kill each other all our lives. Now we're beginnin' to see the right way . . . because whichever way *one* of us go, we *all* go!"

"Tha-at's right."

He pointed to some black men. "Now you black folks who ain't been out on the picket lines, lemme tell you somethin' real quick. It's a shame—and I don't mind tellin' you this before all our white brothers—for you to sit here and let one man and all these whites do your work. You *git up* and *git out* there tomorrow! It just don't make no *kinda* sense— we ain't gettin' nothin' unless we *fight* for it! And it's time out for bein' *afraid*! You ain't got nothin', anyway!"

He swept his hand over the room, pointing particularly to a group of whites in the front. "I know what it is to be poor. Reason's that I've been born and reared in Miss'ssippi. I've been subjected to the same that all you have. See, lotta folks been confused, thinkin' only black folks been denied. That ain't true! There are jus' as many white sisters and brothers in this state as there are blacks who've been denied. But no one *speaks* for 'em. No one *fights* for 'em!"

He paused for air, then spoke softly, "Our poor white brothers and sisters, and I do mean *poor,* lookit us all—we all live off $1.65 an hour, *or less.* We all live in shacks, *or no shacks.* We all live on farms, *or no farms.* We all wear blue jeans, *or no jeans half the time.* So what we got to get upset about? We got to work together!"

He turned around and pointed at the reporters. "Now, press, don't y'all come down here and go hidin' out. Git out and let 'em know these folks need help!" The reporters laughed, nodded.

Then he pointed to Simmons and Zellner. "I heard about this communism charge. Here we all born here in Laurel,

Hattiesburg, Newton County—call us *Communists*? Who are *they*? They must be outa their minds! I mean, what are they? What've they done done to us all this time? Here we black an' white folks in Mississippi, livin' all these years, and ain't done nothin' wrong and all of a sudden we're Communists! Don't make no kinda sense!"

He waved a hand across the room. "White folks, black folks, and any other folks—two things in this country those that got power respect, and that's *political* power and *economic* power. If you're poor and broke, ain't nobody gonna care about you.

"Now we got to get down to business—talkin' big is a joke. Action what counts. We need money. Don't need no prayers. Most families are poor. We gotta get this strike movin'. I want all black folks to come up here and sign this list of folks for picket lines. Y'all gotta be strong, now."

About a dozen black men signed the list. Then Simmons borrowed the microphone briefly and exhorted the whites; thirty white men came forth, amid much applause.

Evers scowled. He bellowed into the microphone, "Black people, we been cryin' all these years about how much the white folks kep us down, and lookit us—they gone and signed *three* times as many as us! *Black folks, y'all sign this list!*" Twenty new blacks emerged from the seats and signed.

Evers then called for a donation. "You gotta compensate folk for stuff they need when they ain't workin'." He took a crisp bill from his pocket and gave it to a white woman holding a hat. She looked at the bill, held it high, and yelled, "Look! He gave a *hunnerd* dollar bill!" That set off a charge among the whites; they slapped each other on the backs.

The Mayor continued, "I always say it ain't *what* you know in this country that counts, but *who* you know. An' I know the right folks. I'm flyin' to Washington nex' week and I'm takin' three o' you wood haulers wi' me. I got friends up

there. We'll see Teddy Kennedy, Muskie, McGovern—
what's his committee?"

Ed piped quickly, "Senate Committee on Nutrition and
Human Needs."

The Mayor concluded to spontaneous applause. Black
and white wood haulers swarmed around him, cameras
whirred, the meeting ended on a high note. An AP reporter
—a man who had recently been transferred from Detroit to
Jackson—pushed into a mass of gnarled white men and
asked one of them, "What do you think about a black man
doing all this?"

"It don't matter if he's a nigra as long as he helps us win."

"Would you rather have Senator Eastland helping you?"

"Naw, ah think Eastland's a son-of-a-bitch. Always have."

An intense man was leaning over the newspaperman's
shoulder, saying, "John Bell Williams and all them others
ain't nothin' but a bunch o' bastards."

The reporter scribbled hurriedly on his pad, then nudged
me. "This meeting was absolutely amazing. Incredible. I've
never seen anything like it."

I hurried through the crowd to a phone booth, as I had to
call the story into the UPI desk in Jackson. Woody yelled at
me, "Hurry up, we wanna roll in five." Driving back in Ed's
car, we were all ecstatic. Alec was ebullient: "If this thing
spreads, there's no tellin' *how* many whites'll vote for The
Mayor!" Ed whooped, "You saw the way the white folk *took*
to him?"

The night was warm and the moon made the sky fluores-
cent. Ahead, we could see The Mayor silhouetted in Ed's
headlights. He was gesturing excitedly; Woody was nodding, nodding, nodding. Fifty miles out from Laurel, the
caravan stopped at a roadside gasoline station-grocery store.
All twelve of us got out while an aged man serviced the
cars. We filtered into the store, buying ice cream, cigarettes,
and Cokes. Two old men sat near the counter, unable to be-

lieve the crowd moving in. The name of the grocery store was Sullivan's Hollow. The man behind the cash register asked The Mayor, "You're Charlie Evers, ain't you."

The Mayor grinned. "Yeah, this here's my campaign staff."

The old man said, "Y'know, I'm Charlie Sullivan's uncle. This store's been in our family for a long time. You're in Sullivan Country." He explained that his part of the clan had remained, while the lieutenant governor had long ago moved north into the Delta, where he had been living, practicing law, and politicking for twenty years. Sullivan's father still lived in south Mississippi. The Mayor told the man about the wood haulers' rally. Mr. Sullivan was interested. He said he had a late cousin who had worked at Masonite. Mr. Sullivan was soon in great spirits. He was realizing a sizable revenue from our hungry, thirsty crowd.

Unwrapping an ice-cream cone, I walked to a corner to throw the paper in a can. Another old man, puffing a pipe and swatting occasional mosquitoes, sat on a barrel. He had watched everything in silence. He motioned me over. "You work for Charles Evers?"

I said yes, quickly adding that I thought Charles Sullivan a fine man who had run a hell of a race.

The man nodded to himself. Then he said, "Well, I guess I'll vote for Evers." He looked at me to see if I was surprised. I was.

"We sure appreciate that," I said. "The Mayor needs every vote."

He looked at me and said in a low, stern voice, "I'm votin' for the ne-gra because of the lawsuit." He scratched a stubble of whiskers and observed, "When young Charles Sullivan lost, I knew that Waller fella *must* have done somethin' corrupt! *Throw* that lawsuit against the sombitch! He *had* to pull a string to win!"

The wood haulers' meeting had to share billing with a story of related importance. On the afternoon of September 23, Mississippi Supreme Court Justice Tom Brady submitted his qualifying papers for the governor's race shortly before the deadline. Brady, *Black Monday* author and an unmitigated segregationist, was an old crony of Eastland's. We were in high spirits when the old bastard announced. The lawsuit had scared him, and now with three candidates in the race, Evers stood a better chance. Brady said that he was running to ensure that the rights of the people of the great state of Mississippi would be protected. A Waller supporter, Brady had jumped in at Eastland's bidding, or so thought The Mayor. But soon it became obvious that Brady was not going to campaign. There was no way the lawsuit could be heard before the election; it was yet to be filed.

The Evers campaign rolled on. After basketball star Bill Russell concluded a three-day tour, Jimmy Ward pounded an angry note in the Jackson *Daily News* on September 27:

> One can hardly view or hear an electronic "news" program without a large segment of the program being devoted to Candidate Charles Evers who is receiving more enduring free campaign propaganda time than any white candidate could dream to obtain. As Evers brings in professional athletes, the Evers political cause has infiltrated the sports segment of these programs. As far as can be determined, Evers hasn't invaded the weather segment of these programs, but he may be credited for the sunshine the next clear day.

Ward's column went on to list a joke the editor had "overheard" of the young boy asking his mother why Charles Evers' skin shined so brightly. Because, she answered, his skin is under the lights so much.

In Laurel, however, Masonite had issued another statement on the strike. On September 24 it ran on page one of the *Leader-Call*:

> Masonite has always paid good prices for pulpwood. We have loaned responsible men money, interest free, to help them buy trucks, and wood hauling equipment, without restrictions on who they would sell their wood to, and without regard to race.
>
> The present furor, we believe, is a deliberate attempt on the part of a few out-of-state activists of questionable affiliation to divide the people of Laurel and Mississippi.
>
> Those who are involved feed upon dissension and conflict. Where there isn't conflict they create one.
>
> They claim they are working for equality and unity. In fact, they seek to divide and to return to the strike-ridden days of 1967. . . .

But the wood haulers were not that independent. Many owed binding debts to the company. Despite the "interest-free" loans, the wood hauler was like the sharecropper whose crop must provide money for the materials he used to grow the crop. The cutter borrows money to buy equipment, and when he has been paid subsistence wages for the wood cut, he is barely able to provide for his family. His debt may be as little as $100, but often that can't be paid for a year—another year in which he is indebted to the company. He has little choice but to haul his wood to the dealer to whom he owes money.

The "strike-ridden days of 1967" had indeed been plagued by conflict. When production workers in the plant went on strike, Masonite employed "scabs" (strike-breakers) to do the work. The striking men were infuriated, and violence ensued. Bob Zellner had been involved in organizing the strike. He had worked for the Committee for Better

Union Leadership. The strike had been successful, though it took nine difficult months for the men to get the wage increase they demanded.

The Jackson *Daily News* was not about to let this strike pass unnoticed. True to form, the paper attacked the strike and attempted to show the "Communist plot" involved. It also implied that the key issue had been resolved.

> Actually, Masonite has instituted weight standards that the pulpwood haulers association sought at the last session of the Legislature, making the weight factor a straw man as far as the legitimate issue is concerned.

It was a lie, of course. A bill had been presented in the 1971 Legislature by Representative Bob Donald of Clark County. Simmons and the woodcutters asked him to introduce the measure that would have eliminated converting pounds to cords, or cords to units. The bill went before the Forest Committee of the Legislature, chaired by a Port Gibson man who was backed by woodmill owners. The committee was stacked with wood dealers, and the bill was voted down.

The editorial concluded, "We wonder if Moscow is pleased with such a turn of events at Laurel."

The editorial was reprinted in the Laurel *Leader-Call* and in the Hattiesburg *American*. Hattiesburg is thirty-five miles from Laurel, and it is also a region of plants, mills, and cutters. The *American* is owned by the Hedermans.

The only newspaper in Mississippi that dealt with the wood haulers' strike honestly was Hodding Carter's *Delta-Democrat Times*:

> Without dealing with the issues involved in the strike at all, the Hedermans' afternoon organ has tried to

make it appear that strategy shots are being called by "outside agitators" and crypto-Communists.

Such attacks, coupled with "nigger baiting," have succeeded in the past in tearing apart fragile interracial alliances. Today, however, they may not be as effective. The pulpwood men know what they are striking about, and it is a bread and butter matter, not an ideological one. They also know that Charles Evers is the only person with stature enough to help them nationally who has done so. That consideration is viewed by them as more important than his skin color. . . .

. . . Evers' hopes have been buoyed accordingly. Whether they are dashed, as is most likely, or not, he is raising a banner to which an electoral army far larger than many Mississippians expect may be rallied in the coming decade.

The Hederman press news play did *not* daunt our campaign spirits; if anything, it made people more determined. Joe Huttie spent a long afternoon on the phone, setting up conferences for the group with McGovern's Senate Committee on Nutrition and Human Needs, and with senators Muskie and Kennedy. Jackson food stamp workers immediately filed reports on the Laurel office and two days later a wood hauler phoned to say the woman "with sort of a forced smile on her face, has been givin' 'em out to folks proper-like."

Evers spoke at Millsaps College that week, and the predominantly white crowd of five hundred students and faculty gave him a generous ovation when he said, "Sure you'll read those funny newspaper stories, but jus' remember, these are the *same* men who been livin' and workin' in Mississippi all their lives. . . . My goin' there was because they was po' and needed help. You young folks o' Mississippi are the products o' change. Y'all got to show the older folks who are still blind how to see." A half-dozen white volunteers from Millsaps became a part of the Jackson office from that afternoon until the end of the campaign.

On the evening of The Mayor's flight to Washington with the wood haulers we still had no media program. The press was now keyed in on Evers. In McLuhan's terms, he was the "hot" candidate. But the vast majority of Mississippians saw him only on news shows in their parts of the state when we traveled, or in the morning papers, which of course were not dependable. The campaign desperately needed professional film spots to show as TV ads. Waller had spent upward of $400,000 on media in the last month of his race. The Mayor as of September had run the campaign on $80,000, nearly half of which had been his own money.

Huttie had meanwhile been contacting leading political film-makers around the country. All offered lower-than-normal rates, but none would come to Mississippi for less than $80,000—which was about our entire budget for film production and purchasing the TV time. The Mayor was interested only in short spots dealing with issues. Anything over five minutes could be filmed in a Mississippi studio, since it would involve only Evers and his remarks. Finally, through friends up north, Huttie came upon a lead: Edward Frost Productions of Washington.

"Who's Ed Frost?" The Mayor asked.

"He's not like David Garth or Guggenheim or Bob Squire," Huttie said.

"They're the best."

"Yeah, Mayor, and they're also the most expensive. Frost and his guys don't do political stuff. They're young, a sensitive group of artists. They deal with issues. They did the Urban Coalition film—'Let the Sunshine In,' the back pan shot of Johnny Carson and all those famous people singing."

"Yeah, I've seen that on TV. It's good."

"Like I said, they've never done political work, but they're willing to shoot for you. They don't consider this ordinary politics. They made a cut-rate offer, too—only because they believe in it."

But the Mayor refused to commit himself. He was impressed with the bid, but said he would decide when he arrived in Washington with the woodcutters—where Ed Frost would be waiting with reporters in the Senate Chambers. Huttie emerged from Ed's office that night and had a tired look on his face. "I told Frost The Mayor agreed to it," he said. "I just got off the phone."

"Has he?" I asked.

"Hell no," Huttie said. "Frost has bent over backwards for us, and I couldn't tell the guy that The Mayor's still undecided. When they walk in for the meeting with Senator Kennedy tomorrow, Ed Frost will be fighting his way through the national media to try and *introduce* himself to The Mayor! If The Mayor decides he doesn't want him . . . I'm going the hell back to Minnesota."

That night The Mayor spoke to striking wood haulers in McLain, a town near the Alabama line (population less than 3,000) in southeastern Mississippi. The wondrous confrontation of Laurel repeated itself. After the meeting a weather-beaten man said to me, "I ain't never shook hands with a nigger, sure never voted for one. But if he takes those boys to Washington, he's got my vote!"

They left for Washington at 8:15 the next morning. Evers, Simmons, Zellner, Fred Walters, and a black man named John Padue stood among bleary-eyed Jackson reporters who could not believe their eyes. Charles Gordon stood on the edge of the crowd, peering at the group. He tried to mutter a question, which couldn't be heard above the din. Ramberg growled at him, "I hope *you're* not planning to write a Red-baiting story!" Gordon didn't. Perhaps he was too stunned at the sight of Fred Walters, his arm around The Mayor, grinning at Tonny Allgood and saying, "This is the first time I ever been on an airplane!"

Evers then announced that the Medgar Evers Foundation was going to give the wood haulers financial help. Shortly thereafter, the NAACP began distributing emergency relief money to the impoverished men, black and white.

The one disappointing aspect of the departure was that the wire services and a major Jackson TV station didn't cover it. I raced back to the office and wrote a long release for the AP and UPI, since they hadn't bothered to send men. I called a TV reporter and asked him why he hadn't attended. "I'm all for Chollie," he said, "but when he goes crusadin', I got better things to do." By now I was beginning to realize that, worse than not comprehending what was and wasn't news, many of the key reporters were simply lazy. I had covered a most important news story for them, feeding releases to the wire services. They apparently couldn't get men out before breakfast.

The Mayor's plane took off with the hopes of the populist coalition *and* our media program, about which he hadn't yet made up his mind.

We received progress reports through contacts in Washington: by 12:15 they had met with the McGovern Committee, by 1:30 with Kennedy, by 3:15 with Muskie. And at shortly after four, Huttie pulled a chair next to my desk and breathed a sigh of relief. "The Mayor and Frost hit it off."

"Great. The Mayor likes him?"

"Not only that, at The Mayor's suggestion they took the wood haulers to Frost's studio and in between a meeting at the Senate they shot an hour's worth of film. Frost said he's already got material for five spots."

"This is tremendous." I thought about Huttie's anxiety prior to Evers' departure, at which time it was uncertain what he would decide. "Well, isn't he a sly bastard?" I said.

Huttie was elated. "Not only that, Frost and his crew sat in on the Kennedy meeting, which was closed to the press, and they shot all of that. The Mayor talked with 'em for fifteen minutes and then they signed the contract. It was love at first sight. They'll be down to shoot some in Mississippi next week."

Huttie smiled. "Y'know, I have a feeling The Mayor knew damned well what he wanted to do before he left. He just didn't want to be tied down to any decision. He wanted to wait until the last minute. He had to be alone to make the decision. . . ."

Later, one of Frost's assistants told me, "We got him in the studio and I said, 'Mayor Evers, we've been looking at your campaign flier, "6 Points for a Better Mississippi." You want to talk about these points on film?' He looked at me and said real innocently, 'Y'know, I bet that's some name my staff has for all our issues. I don't know no six points, but I can tell you all about Mississippi and what she needs.'" The spots were priceless.

Suddenly the campaign was moving at a terrific pace. Ed Frost and Company came and left, shooting two days' worth of film. The candidate spoke at eleven towns in eight hours on a swing through the Delta one Saturday. The wood haulers' strike was spreading through southern Mississippi; Simmons campaigned with Evers twice. Martin and Squeaky, feeling the effects of the accelerating pace, would roll into the office at 11 A.M. weary after getting half the sleep they needed. I left the office one evening to do some long-awaited laundry and made the mistake of lying down on the bed in my apartment, only to be awakened at 8:30 A.M. by a New York volunteer saying, "You ought to take off your clothes before you go to sleep."

Community leaders were filing in and out of the office; reporters were flying into Jackson for two-day stints, securing reservations for November. Security was tightened. Charlie

Ramberg and Ed Cole worked with Gil Jonas via long-distance phone in organizing 250 lawyers to come into the state to serve as poll watchers and legal aides on Election Day. Howard University pledged eighty-five pollwatchers. Ramberg and I lined up a speaking engagement for The Mayor at Georgetown and two days later the student body president called to say a busload of students would be coming to help at the polls. Roly-poly, effervescent Reverend John Hunter roared into the office "all the way in from the heart o' Macon, Mississippi, and I sure hope all the young folks workin' in this here office are doin' so with gusto, since I'm very much lookin' forward to eating' bar-b-cue at the Governor's Mansion come January!"

October came. The heat was still oppressive, but by now we were oblivious to it. The Mayor flew to New York for four days of speaking engagements and private fund-raisers. He paid a courtesy call to John Lindsay, who endorsed him at a press conference and then said he would try to campaign with the candidate in Mississippi. Ed said The Mayor was thrilled to be able to tell his campaign manager that Lindsay, like other northern politicians, was serious. He *wanted* to come. His appointments secretary called the next day to plan dates.

The wife of a rabbi began coming to headquarters each afternoon, donating daily two boxes of doughnuts. Her son became a volunteer. A black artist volunteered an afternoon and painted a colorful sign on the storefront side. It read "Evers for Everybody." Cars slowed down each day to look at it. The assistant to the archbishop of Mississippi called to ask if The Mayor could deliver the keynote address to the Mississippi Priests Senate.

Finally, since The Mayor was in New York, I managed to get to a laundromat. I settled into a chair and began to read Faulkner. A few minutes later a fellow my own age came in, and we recognized each other. He was a volunteer from

Millsaps who had come into the office to stuff envelopes in the past week. I put the book down and we began to talk as we waited for our laundry. He told me about the difficulties he had undergone in deciding to work two afternoons a week in the office. For not only was he married and carrying an eighteen-hour class load, but his uncle was Bill Waller's campaign chairman in his home county.

I asked why he had decided against working for Waller. He grinned and said, "My uncle's a lot older than I am . . . and he went to high school way before integration."

I didn't say anything for a while, intrigued by a college senior from the heart of an old Klan county who was spending two afternoons a week for Evers without his family's knowledge. "You think anyone else in your family will vote for Evers?" I asked.

"Just my wife. I have a brother twenty-eight. He graduated from Ole Miss before Meredith. He hates blacks. My parents are for Waller."

He lit a cigarette and reflected. "You have to understand, integration's changed a lot of kids. You don't see it all the time . . . I mean, you won't find too many interracial couples or things like that, but the changes are there. They really mean something. I had to change—a lot. It happened when I was in high school.

"I was a sophomore when our school back home integrated. I wasn't any different from a fifteen-year-old white —hated blacks socially, didn't mind playin' ball with 'em in the fields and all. I wanted them to keep to their own. But I started lookin' at things differently when they came to our school. It was a real transformation for me. I guess it happened in several stages.

"The first stage was gettin' up the guts to go over and *talk* to one of 'em. That may not sound like much to you, but that took guts. It took six months before any o' us would even *talk* to 'em. We were afraid. We hated 'em. We didn't know 'em. In the middle o' January I finally walked over and talked to this one ole boy. We were standin' next to each other in lunch line and I figured what the hell, so I sat down and ate lunch with him. That was hard, believe me. Just sittin' and there and talkin', I could feel the differences. We were *both* scared stiff. But one thing, not one white said anything bad to me. I think—I *know*—they were all watching, and wondering.

"Well, the next step was understanding that they were really human, that they had emotions and feelings just like us. Of course, the races have always lived close to each other down here, but white kids never compared their lives to blacks' until a few years ago. I think that's when the real change came. The more I talked to 'em, the more I realized they had a completely different version of Mississippi . . . they lived in a different world. Learnin' about that was amazing.

"The third step was becoming friends. You couldn't do that at home, of course. School was really the place where you became closer and closer. By the end of junior year I had a brand new perspective about the state. I really began to like blacks, to see them as a whole new world of people. There were two fellas who became real good friends, and still are. Of course, we didn't go into each other's houses. The town was still tied down by the old attitudes.

"The fourth step," he continued, "is what we're in now—changing the system for our kids. I love Mississippi, I really do. My wife and I want to stay. After I graduate in May, I'm going to graduate school, probably the University of Texas. But we're comin' back. Mississippi's got great potential, no doubt about it. Look at the environment, the woods, and our waters. It's the kind of place I'd like my kids to grow up in. But it'll need a lot more changing between now and then. I'm not a big Evers fan, but I respect him a lot. I read his book—about Chicago and all—and I have to say *that* part of it turned me off. But I understood that plenty of things happened because of Bilbo, Barnett, and their ilk. I guess if blacks can forgive whites, I can forgive Evers.

"So now we're up to the next step, living according to our convictions, accepting blacks as I do now, sharing things with them, having them as friends—all so your kids won't grow up afraid of playing with them or bringing black friends home to Mom and Dad."

He stepped on the cigarette and lit another one. "I'm damn glad I went through the changes I went through, but I don't want my kids to have to do it. Society will have God-knows-what kinda demands on them when they get old. I don't want *race* to be one of 'em. Maybe they can make Mississippi into a real paradise, a model for the rest of the country."

He looked at me and grinned. "It'll take us at least a generation before we get a black governor. So, we gotta start now!"

He slapped me on the knee and got up to change his wash. I fumbled for my place in the Faulkner book. After I found the place, it was hard to read.

CHAPTER

11

It was nine years to the month since James Meredith had registered on the frightful October morning that saw a campus scarred by the tread marks of jeeps and the Oxford coroner examined two dead bodies. It was nine and a quarter years since the town's famous resident William Faulkner had died. Died, according to a good friend, while perplexed over the volatile explosion of emotions and violence throughout Mississippi. He had been living in Virginia for several years prior to his death.

Evers stood at the podium in the auditorium of the Ole Miss Law School. The three hundred students jammed into the small room could have been sitting at Harvard or Berkeley: blacks, whites with long hair, women in blue jeans, the traditional skirts and sport coats.

As was his practice before white groups or on television, he dispensed with his usual colloquialisms and spoke directly, professionally. "I'll tell you why I'm runnin' for governor. It's very simple—because I want to see this state move. I want to see it grow and change. I'm tired of being on the bottom. I'm tired of being scorned. I'm tired of being laughed at all over the world because of poor leadership in our state. That's why I'm runnin' for governor. That's why I'm going to be elected."

The students stared at him earnestly, but there was little enthusiasm. He explained the Corrupt Practices suit, as he saw it, and observed, "Now I'm told he spent $900,000. Now why would anyone spend that kind of money to become head of *anything*? The job only pays $35,000 a year . . . who's he gonna owe all that money to? And it's Mississippi folks who're gonna suffer."

The argument did not impress them. He moved on to a different point. "We got to change this state. That's why Mississippi has been so far behind. Because you've had nonprogressive men and—an' I bite no bones about it—the same men who led Miss'ssippi a few years ago are behind my opponent. If you don't believe me, look who prayed for Bill the night he was elected . . . good ole, tobacco-chewin' Ross: Ross Barnett!" The audience roared, and the first burst of applause came forth. The Mayor smiled.

Some students were leaning forward. They were beginning to enjoy the speech. He reviewed his campaign platform, and then said Mississippi needed "men who understand the difference between good and evil, men who'll do good. Lookit that scoun'rel Eastland."

He changed the tone of his voice and effected a nasal sound, and he spoke in a bawdy imitation of a redneck: "An aaah'm the grea-att Sinitawr from Meeseseepee . . ." The crowd roared. "An aah'm against all this and ah'm against all that . . ." He finished with a plea for support, and then answered questions. Most dealt with the Corrupt Practices suit and whether or not the law had been in effect during the campaign. Few students seemed impressed with his conclusion, but the applause was lengthy and he shook students' hands for ten minutes.

His speech to the undergraduates was better. He was

warmed up and let loose with a full-scale attack on Waller, the private schools, corruption, Eastland, the county supervisory system, prisons—and the kids loved it. There was explosive clapping and foot-thumping when he said, "An' I ain't gonna appoint *nary* a Hederman to any o' them boards—and I mean *not nary*!" He received a standing ovation, and for thirty minutes after the speech stood in the cool October evening talking with Ole Miss students, most of them white. We ate dinner at the Holiday Inn in Oxford and The Mayor was jubilant. "Ain't that somethin'? Ole Miss! Did you see those kids?—they stood up and clapped. Couldn' a been more'n ten percent of 'em black, either. You *know* Mississippi's changin'!"

It seemed he was right. The people of Jackson were jolted when The Mayor received his first newspaper endorsement —from the St. Joseph High School *Rebel Yell.* The Catholic school was 90 percent white. The boy who wrote the editorial, Bruce Nelson, spent an hour interviewing The Mayor. The October 15 article was entitled "*Man* vs. *Machine.*" Reviewing the wood haulers' dispute, he said:

> . . . the mayor is appealing to the common people. The common white man, the redneck who five years ago would have put a bullet through his head, is now taking a stand with Mr. Evers. . . . Although the incident received little publicity from Mississippi newspapers, it attracted nationwide attention as a human interest story.
>
> It really doesn't do justice to Mr. Evers to label him a "politician." This word has become a derogatory term because of the low integrity of our Mississippi statesmen, in this writer's opinion. However, as a Mississippi "politician," Charles Evers breaks all the rules of a candidate's etiquette. He is honest, surprisingly straightforward, and his frankness and refreshing can-

dor have left his opponents stunned with open mouths
and only their feet to place in their obsolete cavities.
He spares no deserving victim his full verbal wrath.
The Hedermans, the present state administration, Mississippi Power and Light Company, his opponents and
other political institutions, both state and federal, received all due acknowledgment for their contribution
to the state's miscegenist image. Evers' blunt honesty
is surpassed only by his confidence that Mississippians
are ready to welcome a new era of progress and cooperation. Popularity is not his goal; trust is the key
word of his campaign. "You don't have to love me, and
whether you love me—that isn't important. What's important is that you trust me, that's all."

A perfect contrast, for example, is his major opponent, Bill Waller. Mr. Waller's campaigns have been
based on his attacks of his alledged [sic] "political machine." But his spineless vacillating in politics and his
reluctance to specifically define the members of his alledged [sic] enemy, the "machine," indicates to this
writer that he is a hypocritical member of that sover-
eign institution. Waller stands as a typical example of a
Mississippi "politician."

. . . A campaign poster expresses my convictions in
the best way I have yet seen: "Don't vote for a black
man. Don't vote for a white man. Vote for the best
man. EVERS for Governor."

The cover of the paper was a large photograph of The
Mayor, his face intent as he spoke on a phone. Superimposed on the picture were the words:

> southern man, better keep your head,
> don't forget what your good book said,
> southern change gonna come at last,

Now your crosses are burning fast,
                         southern man
                      Neil Young°

Nelson himself then became a news story. He was interviewed by two Jackson stations, and a brief story ran on the
wire services. An anonymous caller also told the Evers office
that the Catholic Church had sold itself down the river with
the endorsement. Nelson, who became a volunteer, glibly
recounted an evening spent with the enraged father of a fellow student. The man had stormed up and down his living
room, talking about responsibility. He had become doubly
incensed when Bruce told him he felt it was his responsibility to endorse Evers.

By the second week in October, cadres of white high
school students were coming into the office to see The
Mayor. His schedule was packed. The office volunteer
corps, nearly half white, now stood at about twenty.

Ed Frost's TV spots were aired on October 15. The quality and color of the film were flawless, and The Mayor came
across beautifully. The woodcutters spot showed the Laurel
contingent, Evers, and Ted Kennedy seated around a table.
Zellner and Fred Walters explained the lot of the wood
hauler. Evers said Masonite was exploiting them. Then Kennedy said, "Well I think now that the situation has been
made clear there's no reason why we can't get some action
taken." "Evers for Governor" was superimposed on the picture, and a voice said, "The woodcutters of Laurel had a
problem. They went to Charles Evers for results. And they
got them. This is the kind of commitment he brings to all
the people of Mississippi."

Perhaps the most effective clip was a minute's footage of

black and white babies rolling around in different cribs. The voice said, "I am the future of Mississippi. I've known the past—the mistakes, the hatreds, the shame. And I am tomorrow's father, tomorrow's mother. I want a life with love and freedom for everyone." After a pause, the voice said, "Tomorrow is in your hands. On November the second, vote for Charles Evers."

As our media campaign began, Waller came out of seclusion. He spoke to selected groups in various parts of the state—Jaycees, Rotary Clubs, and the like. His TV spots showed the candidate shaking hands with people, and a silly jingle vaunted Bill Waller. We had a limited budget for TV time but Joe Huttie, spending six hours on the phone daily for a week, managed to secure prime times. The ads appeared as commercials on the morning and evening news shows, and the midday coffee hours, as well as selected prime-time TV shows. Ed Cole, returning to the office one afternoon from the Buena Vista Hotel, told of a trio of elderly white matrons watching the TV in the lobby: "The spot with the babies came on. They looked at it, looked at each other, then looked back at the TV again. None of 'em knew what to say. You could tell it sure set 'em thinkin', though."

Buoyantly, The Mayor sat next to Howard Lett, news director for WJDX radio in Jackson, and fielded questions on a phone-in show. Before the show began, one of the technicians said, "Seven years ago our TV affiliate was the first station to run a paid political spot of a black man. It was a minister runnin' for Congress, a symbol, you know. We had bomb threats and rednecks cruising by cursin' out the windows all night long!"

But the callers on this show, nearly all of whom were white, were remarkably courteous. Some complimented the candidate, others said outright they planned to vote for him. One irate man asked him about busing:

. . . If a child is taken out of a school with his friends, you know, where he can walk to school two blocks away, to be bused all the way across town, or all the way across the county, just to maintain racial balance—now is that right?

EVERS: Well, I don't know whether it's right or not. I'm not going to question what's right or not. It does sound hard. But then, let's have open occupancy, where a man can buy a house anywhere he pleases. And let's have all our communities together, then we can have our neighborhood schools. But until that happens, we've got no choice. . . . And I think if we just be fair—if our white brothers and sisters can realize, you know, how *wrong* we've been all these years to deny people, because of the color of their skins . . . Because b'lieve me when I tell you: black folks are the only really true friends that white people have in this country. We've proven that over the years. And I think *you* know that. If you do . . . it really boils down to this: you've trusted us with your money, with your automobiles, with your cows; with whatever you've had, you trusted us. And even your lives. And all we're askin' for now is a chance to be a part of . . . and involved in . . . together . . . that's all we're askin' . . .

CALLER: As governor, you *will* be for busin'?

EVERS: . . . I'm for gettin' our people together. I'm for integration, yessir. I'm for whatever it takes to get us integrated . . . Let's understand each other. I'm for that.

CALLER: Well. (Pause, breath) Thank you very much.

He answered another question in his customary robust style.

CALLER: Mayor Evers, are you a Christian?

EVERS: I think I am.

CALLER: That's what we need. A fine Christian Governor.

EVERS: That's me. I don't drink, don't gamble, don't dip *nor* chew. Check some of the rest of 'em.

CALLER (Chuckling): Okay. Thank you.

One of the last callers was less friendly.

CALLER: You say you're a friend of Mr. Waller's . . .

EVERS: Well, I like Bill. I don't know if he likes me or not. I think he does. How's that? As a human being . . . We're not hugging and kissing cousins.

CALLER: You would like to have him as an advisor [if you're elected], is that right?

EVERS: I certainly would.

CALLER: You also made some reference that he and Sullivan were just old coats with new lining.

EVERS: They are. He is. You know who's supportin' him? Jim Eastland . . . Ole Ross.

CALLER: Barnett! I think Ross Barnett did plenty!

EVERS: You *do*?

CALLER: I do!

EVERS: Well, bless your heart.

The Mayor's campaign was given a wealth of free, if not as usual, provocative, publicity when the October issue of *Playboy* reached the stands. His was the feature interview. A reporter had spent three days following him in midsummer. The interview reiterated everything his book had dealt with, in less depth, of course, and had an interesting effect on whites in the state. His reflections on women continually resurfaced in questions. In one of the major TV appearances of the campaign in the waning days of October he faced five reporters on a half-hour meet-the-press show. The campaign paid for the time but the reporters could ask anything they wanted. Charles Gordon represented the Hederman press; however, his questions were about government and were respectfully submitted. (I had thought about asking Hills, but figured he might lie or slander The Mayor in some way.)

Jack Hobbs, news director of WJTV in Jackson, knew Evers and had covered him for four years. But toward the end, he shot a hard question at him: "Mayor Evers, I want you to clear up something for me. I read that *Playboy* interview and I know a number of ladies who feel you hate women. I read that interview, and it seems you have some pretty rough feelings. Can you tell me why a woman should vote for you?"

I nearly swallowed my tongue, and Joe Huttie, who had put the program together, cursed under his breath. The Mayor had a pained look on his face, which the camera caught. He raised his eyebrows and said, "I dunno about that interview . . . I don't *hate* women. I cain't say I've always done 'em right. I cain't—I *did* everything I said in my book. And about that interview, it goes the same. I'm sorry, but I did do it. But I asked God to forgive me. I believe in forgiveness."

He stammered momentarily, "I . . . all I can say is that my campaign staff is more than half female, my Fayette staff's the same. I love the women workin' for me. I love my wife . . . my daughters. I want every woman in Mississippi to vote for me. . . . I don't know what else to say. I'm sorry about the past. I hope those who are watchin' will understand that all men make mistakes, and I wish I never made mine. But the Bible says forgive him who sins seventy times seven times if necessary. And I'm only askin' for once. . . ."

The questioning went to another reporter, and when

Hobbs' turn came again he asked forcefully, "I understand you got a gun-control law in Fayette, saying a man can't carry a gun in public, including the back of his truck. Now there's no Mississippi law to that effect. How do you justify it?"

Evers looked at Hobbs, then looked at the camera. "I had a brother killed by a sniper. My best friend, Bob Kennedy, was killed that way. Martin King died that way, too. I know plenty of people, black and white, who've been killed because of guns and violence. Everybody in Mississippi knows somebody who been killed because of a gun accident, some accident, like when two hunters get too much whiskey. Mississippi's had too much death and violence. When people walk in my town, I want the streets safe."

Hobbs interjected, "Yeah, but there's no Mississippi *law* that says you can't carry a gun!"

Evers pointed his finger at Hobbs and retorted hotly, "Well, if Mississippi wants to change my law, they can come on down and try to change it! Until then, people ain't gonna get shot and the law's gonna stay!"

After the broadcast The Mayor slapped Jack Hobbs on the back and said, "You, Jack Hobbs! Whatcha tryin' to do, askin' me all them mean questions?"

Hobbs grinned. "Charlie, if somebody hadn't asked you, people would've called it a fixed show. And I wasn't gonna let anyone make that charge against me."

Hobbs was flooded with calls after we left. He was complimented for "stickin' it to him." But there was a tone running through all the calls, typified by an old white woman who said, "Mr. Hobbs, I want to compliment you on standin' up as a white man should. But you know somethin'? That man told the truth. There's no gettin' around it. He didn't back down one inch." Another woman identified herself as "a true southern lady," but observed, "I'll tell you what—that nigger told the truth. He said every word honestly. I'm gonna vote for him!"

Although The Mayor was making headway with whites, problems now arose with blacks. The most publicized trouble was with James Meredith. He had returned to Mississippi from New York in early June, commenting to newsmen that "the racial atmosphere in northern cities is becoming extremely tense. And it's going to increase. The gap between white and black in the cities is so wide . . . there is just no relationship between white and black." He cited a more peaceful South as his major reason for coming back. Reporters had been quick to point out that his New York years had not been untroubled: he had been found guilty of failing to provide hot water and other services for an apartment building he owned, and he had reportedly harassed white tenants. Why he had returned to Mississippi, in my opinion, was anybody's guess.

In October, Meredith announced he was organizing a voter canvass on Election Day for certain black precincts in Jackson. Quizzed by newsmen as to whether he supported Evers, Meredith enigmatically said that his service was "nonpartisan." The reporters quickly picked up on the indirect slap in Evers' face. The Mayor was asked to comment on the day Mrs. Martin Luther King came to campaign with us, of all days. The widow of the Nobel winner had spoken in a smooth, clear voice, telling reporters, "I think most people have a great deal of admiration for any black man who would run for governor of Mississippi. My good friend, Charles Evers, is showing the way toward a new understanding between blacks and whites. I think Mississippi could be an example of what the South can become."

As soon as she had finished, Evers was asked about Meredith's project. He pointed a finger at a TV camera and said, "What he said don't mean a thing. James Meredith can't even vote in Mississippi because he just came back. Besides, where was he when all the civil rights struggle was going on? He got his Ole Miss degree and then he took off for New York and lef' the rest of us down here to keep up. Now he comes back and figures he's something big. He ran off when it was dangerous. I don't need his support."

The motorcade was greeted by huge crowds in Port Gibson, Fayette, Natchez, and Woodville. Mrs. King spoke eloquently. People flocked to her and her face became excited and sparkled as she spoke. She was such a tender woman, but with a beautiful strength. "I know that my husband, were he alive and with us, would say that he feels as you do," she said. "I'm so happy to be here with you, to share your joy in this great campaign to change Mississippi." But that night Mrs. King flew back to Atlanta and the Meredith problem remained.

A few days later someone threw a rock through James Meredith's window. In a statement to reporters he said it might have been the doings of Evers supporters, retaliating! The charge enraged everyone in the office and I immediately released a statement for the campaign saying, "We bear no malice whatsoever toward Mr. Meredith, and we condemn the action taken against him."

Meredith then purchased fifteen hours of radio time on WOKJ, Jackson's AM soul station. His speech was pathetic. Meredith's statement read, in part:

> I say to you, good people, if James Meredith can be bulldogged and muzzled, then what black in this state can feel free to stand up and speak his mind and his convictions upon the issues, little and big, which affect our lives and the lives of our children. . . .
>
> These people also made a vicious attack upon the deeds I have done over the past several years. I was called a "coward" and advised to leave the state of my

birth because "no one wants him here." . . .My present goal is to identify the factors that will be decisive in determining the success or failure of our present efforts to make freedom and equality a reality for black peoples.

Meredith went on to endorse "each and every black candidate," which presumably included The Mayor. Evers and the rest of us in the office viewed the speech as an attempt by Meredith to save face, so The Mayor let the matter drop. Looking back on the situation, I wondered why Meredith had been nonpartisan to begin with. It was truly a fiasco, for who else besides blacks (Evers included, since he was the head of the slate) *could* Meredith endorse?

But James Meredith was only a passing problem. Certain leaders in the counties were angry that Evers was not giving them money for their local campaigns. Although the Voter Education Project in Atlanta gave some assistance, as did Sargent Shriver through a fund-raising party in Maryland, some county leaders felt the gubernatorial effort had snowballed and lost control of itself. We were spending money on media advertising and little in the counties. There was validity to the charge.

The only monies the counties got from Evers were a split in books-and-buttons collections and from banquets in the certain counties. Counties had to raise the rest of the campaign funds on their own. By October some counties hadn't raised the money needed for placards, bumper stickers, gasoline and travel expenses to various areas of the electoral district, and so forth. In retrospect, I believe that The Mayor's approach was probably wrong. More money should have gone to the counties. The poorer counties, especially in the Delta, had little economic independence from whites and it was extremely difficult to raise funds.

Evers' own attitude about distributing money was in large

measure influenced by the successful campaigns our strong counties had put together. He felt if Coahoma and Madison could do it, the others should be able to also. By October five black-majority counties appeared likely to elect their slates of candidates. We were anticipating at least eighty-five blacks elected in November. The Mayor, now campaigning thirteen hours a day in these concluding weeks, felt that the more visibility his candidacy received, the more black voters would be impelled to turn out on November 2. By mid-October it looked as if The Mayor might receive a whopping vote, what with the huge black crowds, overwhelming reception by white students, and the media program, which was producing positive response from circles of older whites. And, of course, we also had the wood haulers. Although the Laurel story never received the newsplay in the other southern states where it would have great effect, the strike was spreading. A few Jones County whites displayed red "Evers for Everybody" stickers on the back of their beat-up pick-up trucks. Waller was nowhere to be found, save selected speaking engagements. Evers dominated the media coverage of the race.

But slowly, a new black spirit was emerging. John Conyers' words to Madison County candidates spelled out the terms of the general election to *all* voters: "Your organization and activity tells the white man he has to reckon with you. We proved that in my city, Detroit. Black people can change things if they vote together. That's how I was elected to Congress. You can do it here, too." The effect of The Mayor's summer stumping was beginning to show. For now, in areas where political survival demanded it, white politicians were speaking before black groups. For blacks, the fact that one of their race was competing for the highest office gave credence and dignity to the rallies.

Of the five strong counties, Coahoma seemed the best organized. The seat of the Delta county was Aaron Henry's

Clarksdale. The fourteen-candidate slate had a central storefront in Clarksdale. Each candidate had posters with a picture and the slate's slogan: "He Can Do More for You!" The posters, bumper stickers, buttons, and so forth had been paid for through a well-oiled community machinery, numerous rallies, and contributions from northern friends of Aaron Henry. He had organized the slate, urging folks who never thought of themselves as possible politicians to run for public office.

Aaron Henry's race for the Legislature was one of the most important county races in the state. Black registration in the county now stood at 55 percent. His opponent was Kenneth Williams, forty-seven-year-old three-term incumbent, a founder of the private academy of Clarksdale, leader of the local White Citizens' Council chapter during its inception. His family owned a 3,000-acre plantation. In 1968 he had lost his spot as a delegate to Chicago because of the Loyalist challenge which Aaron Henry helped organize.

Williams had told Ed Williams of the *Delta-Democrat Times* that "Aaron's slogan—'He Can Do More for You'—is easy to promise, but to deliver is a different deal. . . . It takes time to learn about the legislature, to establish contacts in state government that enable you to get things done." Williams said he felt most blacks weren't qualified. Moreover, "a lot of blacks don't care much for Aaron. For some of them he's caused nothing but travail. Some of the preachers feel he's pushed them around. No blacks will oppose him openly, but I'll get some votes."

Aaron Henry didn't doubt Williams would get black votes. Like Williams, he rated the race a tossup. "He represents more of what I don't support than any legislator we have. I feel that in terms of family prestige, longevity in the House, I'm taking on the strongest candidate. He's been derelict in his duty to work for improvements in Coahoma County—the poor and black especially. Maybe some of us don't know much about parliamentary procedure or the law. We can learn that. But the legislators we have now don't seem able to learn what it is to be hungry, or live in a house that's falling down, or be sick and too poor to have a doctor."

The candidates had different views about the election. Said Williams, "I hear they're trying to get that same bunch down that helped in voter registration. I hear some of them were telling black folks that if they didn't register they might lose their food stamps and welfare." Henry said, "I think I'll win if it's a fair election. But a lot of black folks work on plantations, and the boss man tells 'em 'I'll know how you vote.' Some of them get worried about losing their welfare or their food stamps. . . ." (*Daily Herald*, October 31)

Madison County was unlike Coahoma. Nestled in the center of the state just north of Jackson, it was not plantation country. The relationship between whites and blacks did not rest on the feudal ties that existed in the Delta. Madison had three strong leaders and a sound NAACP chapter in Canton, the seat. The county slate had thirty candidates. The dominant leader was Flonzie Goodloe of the NAACP. A voter registration organizer and community spokesman for many years, Mrs. Goodloe had been elected an election commissioner from her supervisory district in 1968. Prior to that year the commissioners were appointed by the supervisors. Thus, a black was at last an influential part of the county system. The Election Commission oversees elections and trains clerks and poll managers. Mrs. Goodloe was nevertheless subordinate to the election commissioner, a white man named Shed Weeks.

A beefy man named Amzie Cotton was the second strong Canton leader. He had grown up in Mississippi, then moved away, and was just returned from Chicago. He owned a bar, and many of the younger men in the community accepted him as a tough and uncompromising leader. With the two aggressive leaders in the community, Madison was fortunate in having Father Luke Miscel, a white priest who had been active in civil rights for a decade in Canton. He was accepted by both groups. Often his mere presence averted potential ego clashes and united everyone in the common effort.

Claiborne County, adjacent to Jefferson, had the first black chancery clerk, Mrs. Geneva Collins, who was seeking reelection. A slate of twenty blacks was filed, but there were rumors of dissension. Mrs. Collins apparently had some fences to mend among blacks. The campaign manager for the slate was twenty-three-year-old Jimmy Smith, who had just lost a bid for mayor of Port Gibson in 1969. But Smith was unpopular with some of the older folks. Like Coahoma and Madison, Claiborne County had the votes on paper, but whether they would materialize in November was questionable.

In Wilkinson, the southernmost county along the Mississippi, a hefty black incumbent supervisor named James Jolliff had organized a slate; however he was worried about blacks being bought off by whites in this extremely poor area; he also feared white intimidation on election day. Wilkinson was high on our priority list for poll watchers.

In Jefferson County the slate was composed mainly of Evers' political allies. Even in his home county, Evers knew there was a small number of blacks who didn't care for him. The whites in Jefferson, most of whom hated The Mayor, knew which Uncle Toms were susceptible for election day. Ed Cole felt the Loyalist slate would carry.

In other counties, though, the situation was dismal. The factionalism in black communities was depressing. In New York there are dozens of political organizations in the Democratic Party that have fought each other for the last dozen years and have successfully managed to give the Republi-

cans the governorship and major elected offices. In Mississippi one would assume that the spiritual stake is so deep
that blacks would naturally be united. Unfortunately, this is
not the case. In a land where no one has great power, a person who suddenly obtains some of it, no matter how little,
becomes the subject of envy. Evers, no exemplar of humility, had thus enraged some Jefferson County blacks. Aaron
Henry, probably a better-liked man, nevertheless had a
small number of foes. But in a place like Sunflower County
in the Delta, the situation was desperate. Mrs. Fannie Lou
Hamer, the historic, heroic leader of the movement in the
sixties, was running for the State Senate. A brave woman,
Mrs. Hamer was respected in enlightened circles across the
land. In Mississippi she was something of a legend. Even her
influence could not settle the difficult problems of her community, however. Sunflower County was involved in a bitter
dispute over Head Start funds, and a splinter group had broken off. The order of our campaign—both from The Mayor
and Sunflower folks—was to stay clear of the situation. Let
Sunflower County handle it. But it was doubtful that they
could straighten things out by November 2.

Perhaps the greatest cause of factionalism was the one
Evers worked hardest to abolish. Black folks often felt black
candidates were not qualified. Comparing a black candidate
for supervisor with a white incumbent, some folks thought,
in the words of The Mayor, "Ohhh, I don't know about *you*,
but *I* sure ain't gonna vote for that ole so-and-so. I like him,
but he cain't do for me what the white man supervisor did
—that white man gave me a chicken last week!" This pathetic psychology stemmed from the black man's primordial
ties with the white man. If the white man gave him something, the black man felt obligated to return the favor, and
that could easily mean a vote. Moreover, white supervisors
in certain heavily black beats had foreseen the election

turnout and hired blacks, for the first time, on the road-building crews. This made an indelible impression.

Evers always identified black candidates and promoted their candidacies at rallies. "Black folks, what about this Mr. Washin'ton runnin' for circuit clerk? Here is a big, *brown*-skinned man who's been teachin' in our public schools. A man with education and background! Who says he ain't qualified to be circuit clerk? Sho' 'nuf he qualified! Nobody's a born circuit clerk! You gotta *learn* that job. I waddn't no born mayor!"

The most natural black politician in Mississippi was Bob Clark, the incumbent Representative from Holmes County. I saw him late in the race when he came into the office to pick up a box of fliers. We talked for a while and he mopped his brow. "I'm afraid a lotta black folks in my county aren't gonna win. I been travelin' my district since May, visiting every farm, every house, seein' everybody at least once a month. Haven't missed anybody. That's what our folks got to understand about politics. I been tellin' 'em—'If you want to win, you got to go out and *go after* the votes! Just 'cause some folks hear you talk at a rally don't mean they're gonna vote for you. You got to go campaign, talk to 'em, make 'em know you want *each* vote!' "

Clark chuckled and told how he had eliminated a potential black opponent. "Had this fella plannin' to run against me: I'll call him 'Henry.' Well, I heard ole Henry was gonna challenge me. A lady told me after church one day, 'Rep-'sentative Clark, I heard him sayin' a lotta bad things about you, him sayin' you don't care about us, and all. *I* don't believe him, but I think some folks might.'

"Well now, I coulda done a lot of things. But you know how I handled ole Henry? I saw him at a church picnic the next weekend. I went over and put my arm around him and asked how his family was. Told his wife I thought she had a *fine*-lookin' dress on. An' *she* liked that! Told him if I could help him out in any way, to come see me. Plenty folks saw that, too.

"Next thing I did, I brought him a pig. Went over to his house and gave him a fully cooked pig! Said, 'Here you go, ole Henry, m'friend. You always been a buddy o' mine, an' I thought your family might like a li'l extra pork. My wife an' I got plenny left over.'

"Well, after doin' all that, there wasn't any way ole Henry could say those mean things about me. Everybody knew what I'd done, been so nice to him. And what do you know? Ole Henry quit talkin' . . . and now he's out *campaignin'* for me!"

But Representative Clark said very frankly he doubted other black candidates were going to the effort he was in campaigning. He wanted that seat back in the Legislature. I had to admit I knew of no one expending the energy Clark was, save The Mayor.

It was about this time, the final two weeks, that I began to feel melancholy; not only because the end was in sight, but also because I realized that these people were *right*. They *could* do more for Mississippi; they did have the knowledge, but more important, the *compassion* to lead and legislate. I wondered if they would get a public mandate to use those talents.

CHAPTER

12

The last ten days of the race moved swiftly. Judge Brady announced that he wanted all Democrats to disregard his candidacy. "I would hate to be the instrument whereby the will of the people who spoke in the Democratic primaries would be thwarted." Clearly, the Regulars felt the corrupt practices suit was no longer a threat. The suit was filed in the last week of the campaign; by that time few people thought it would have any effect on the outcome. It would not be heard until long after the election. Filing the suit after Brady's announcement, however, The Mayor hoped some voters would vote for Brady as insurance. Brady's name had to remain on the ballot under the law. We were more concerned now with last-minute campaign tactics, such as getting the Lindsay trip organized.

Mayor Lindsay arrived on October 24, a Sunday. He had sent an advance team down a week ahead, and they all came with preconceived notions about Mississippi. They were relieved that there was such spirit in our office, and they blended easily into it. They were admirers of Evers to a man, and so we got along famously.

Josh Mazes was in charge of the first speech in Jackson. A veteran of Robert Kennedy's Senate campaigns and Arthur Goldberg's gubernatorial attempt, the first thing he did was confer with ministers. "Why ministers?" I asked. In a beautiful Brooklyn accent, he explained, "If the apathy in Jackson is as bad as you all say—and since I *have* to get a crowd —I'm going to get some choirs. Choirs sing, then they can fill up seats in the auditorium. Ministers know who sings in the choirs." He got the choirs. Evenings, Josh and volunteers disseminated fliers in shopping centers. The movie *Shaft* opened that week, and we hit every line every night.

Evers was aware that the Lindsay trip might have repercussions among the Mississippians who hated outside agitation. He explained to a reporter, "Mississippi's always sayin' we're against outside agitation. Well, 'outsiders' in the federal government give us the money to keep our state operatin' . . . and that's more money than we give 'em back in taxes! When a man becomes governor he needs all the help he can get. Mayor of New York is an important man. He's a good friend to have as an ally. If I get elected he'll do everything he can to help me. I campaigned for him when he ran for mayor in 1969. I'm glad he's comin' to help me." I think The Mayor also felt that Mississippi would just have to learn to swallow.

The Mississippi press was anxious to cover Lindsay. A Jackson TV commentator told me, "Waller's got Eastland speakin' at his first rally next week, Stennis at his second." He chuckled. "I got to hand it to Charlie, he's forcin' Waller to bring those old bastards home from Washington. Everyone in the state's scared stiff about that election, I think. I don't know anyone who can remember either Eastland or Stennis ever campaigning for a gubernatorial candidate. I wonder if Waller got jealous because of Lindsay."

The Hederman press was not about to take John Lindsay lying down. Tom Ethridge wrote a predictable attack in the

Clarion-Ledger on the mayor of "Fun City," calling him a carpetbagger. But shortly after that he penned one of the most vulgar articles I have ever read:

National Magazine Airs Possibility of Court-appointed Governor

. . . We received a copy of the nationally circulated "Review of the News" magazine. . . .

The article, headlined "Charles Evers—Master Hustler," is by Medford Evans of Jackson, a leading Southern spokesman. He holds a Ph.D. from Yale University and has been an executive for the Atomic Energy Commission, is a Citizens' Council leader and author of several books as well as numerous magazine articles [This article stated:]

"Evers is an instrument of men (probably all white) who intend to take over Mississippi from the outside. (They qualify as Insiders but they are outside of Mississippi.) Not only do they not expect him to win a majority of the votes in the state, it would endanger their whole project if he did, for then he would have a source of power independent of them. They intend to put him in the Governor's seat through federal court orders disqualifying that majority of Mississippi voters who are unquestionably opposed to Evers. . . .

"Evers has profited so much from his brother's death that the question has been asked (he says it has been raised with him by the F. B. I.) whether he could possibly have been in any way involved. He says he threw the F. B. I. agents who asked him out of his office. . . .

"The quickest way to complete Federal control of Mississippi might well be: (1) Get Evers elected Governor, (2) have him killed, (3) accuse the white population of the state in general, and some hapless redneck in particular, of having done the deed, (4) because of the apparently incorrigible racism of the majority of Mississippians, impose martial law on the whole state. There was a rehearsal of this sort of thing at the University of Mississippi in the fall of 1962, when General Creighton Abrams was responsible for military planning. General Abrams might get back from Vietnam just in time to return to Mississippi, where after all, he was much more successful."

The Mayor and his staff were furious. In one of the few moments I heard him curse, he called Ethridge a "rotten bastard," which was a more elegant term than the one I used. I was literally beside myself and by midafternoon had revised a third draft of a scathing retaliation to be given to the press later in the day. The Lindsay people, who had come apprehensive of hostility, were astounded. They called New York immediately, and read the article to two of the mayor's aides. Joe Huttie calmed everyone down and suggested that our office not reply to Ethridge in print. "Instead," he said, "let's Xerox the article and give it to all the New York and national media reporters when they arrive Sunday. Let the national press take it and run with it. We're sure to get good copy."

Two hundred Mississippians crowded into the portal at the Jackson airport as the New York plane touched down. Huttie and I distributed Evers press brochures as the reporters filed out of the plane; the Ethridge column was stapled to each brochure. The New York reporters were buzzing and talking, very busy, pulling at coats, pencils, lights, and cameras securely tied to them, looking enormously uncomfortable. Then Lindsay emerged to a huge cheer. He and Evers were led through the crowd into a side room off the airport lounge where the news conference was held.

The reporters herded into the lounge. They swarmed into

chairs, grabbing coats and notebooks, lighting cigarettes, snarling and grinning at one another. Technicians dove into corners and stabbed plugs into the walls. They were all talking, causing a din. By contrast, the Mississippi reporters were in complete awe of the situation. One Jackson reporter was sitting next to a strikingly attractive Jewish woman, a reporter for a large New York daily. She was tugging at her stocking, mumbling to herself. The Mississippi man's mouth hung open and he looked as though he was trying to decide whether to look up her dress or just concentrate on watching the phenomenon of a woman reporter from New York.

Evers and Lindsay emerged. The first question was to Lindsay, whose hazel eyes gleamed. He *looked* like he was going to run for President. "Mayor Lindsay, why are you campaigning for Charles Evers?"

"Because I believe in him," he replied tersely. "He stands for black and white together. That's what we're trying to do in New York. That's what his campaign is all about. Charles Evers is my friend, a fellow mayor. And we mayors have to stick together."

"Won't some people here in Miss'ssippi take this as an insult, campaigning against Mr. Waller?"

"I'm not campaigning *against* anybody," Lindsay said. "I'm campaigning *for* Charles Evers."

Then came the question I'd been waiting for. "Apparently there are some people in Mississippi who feel it's dangerous for Mayor Evers to be running. This article—"

Evers at that point took over the conference. "Yeah," he said, holding up the article. "There still some sick people left in Mississippi. He's writin' about a day that's gone." He turned to Lindsay. "This campaign, Mr. Mayor, is changin' all that."

The reporters burst into chatter among themselves, writing hurriedly. Lindsay was then asked about his plans for the Presidency, to which he replied that he was not a candidate but the mayor of New York. Then the assemblage piled into buses, the mayors into waiting cars, and we drove to the Jackson city auditorium.

The crowd, spiritual choirs included, numbered about 1,200. Some forty white students from Millsaps sat interspersed throughout the seats. All told, there were probably 150 whites. Lindsay's speech was excellent. "We knew about Philadelphia and Neshoba County, and we knew about the road to Jackson—just as we knew about Watts and Newark and Detroit. In the 1960s, places like these became symbols of America's oldest tragedy—the brutal legacy of poverty and race.

"But we never heard of Fayette until Charles Evers became its mayor. His victory was and is a sign of hope, a major step forward in the new direction we must take. But let no one think that is the end of it. Battles are not decided by single victories. It takes a great many of them and we have a long way to go.

"Charles Evers knows that better than most men. Mayors learn it the hard way. That's why we stick together. No matter the size of the towns and cities we govern—whether eight million people in New York or two thousand in Fayette—we face the same problems—jobs, day care centers, education, crime, and pollution. . . ."

Lindsay paused momentarily. He looked at the crowd, and said, "Some people don't like the idea that I'm here. They call me a carpetbagger. They say I'm an outside agitator. Well, I am an outsider. And that is precisely why I am here. And I'm proud to be here. Let's face the truth—most of us are outsiders. And that is why we are joining together here. There are too many outsiders in Mississippi, too many outsiders in America." People started clapping.

"Outsiders are all the people who this country has closed the door on—people without power . . . the poor . . . the people who are shut in . . . And there are the people who live in America's cities and towns—and so, their mayors are outsiders. They are outsiders because our national government has slammed the door on them, too. Black or white, city or country, Fayette, Jackson, and New York.

"That is why Charles Evers is running for office this year —because it is time to open the doors of our society for all those Americans on the outside. . . .

"So I'm here to join the struggle to work with men like Charles Evers to change this country. I think hard political action can make New York better and Mississippi better. It can make America better . . .

"And that is why I am in Mississippi."

The crowd accorded Lindsay a tumultuous standing ovation. Evers, having sat out five days of campaigning because of flu, was in rare form. He thanked Lindsay for his remarks, and swept his arm over the crowd. "These are Mississippians, Mayor Lindsay, not white folks, not black folks, just *Mississippians.* And we're gonna be elected November 2. Goin' right into the Governor's Mansion. . . . We ain't gonna carry no hate, ain't gonna carry no racism. We're gonna carry love. . . . So, Tom Ethridge, you and those who write mean articles in the *Clarion-Ledger*, you cain't stop us. . . . We're not gonna stop now." The crowd roared.

After a post-rally chicken dinner at Steven's Kitchen, the mayors, staffs, and New York press boarded the charter flight to Laurel. I was last on the plane; Joe Huttie beckoned me to the rear, where he, Ed, and the two mayors sat. I heard the reporters as I passed down the aisle: ". . . never had fried chicken in a place like that before, but it was *good*, real *good* ! . . . Haven't seen a crowd take to Lindsay like that in months. . . . Evers got a bunch o' kids runnin' his campaign. . . . Now I can tell my kids I been to Mississippi. . . . Hey, watch your hand! . . . Who's got a cigarette?"

I looked at the two mayors. Lindsay was leaning slightly

into the aisle. His press secretary, Tom Morgan, was whispering in his ear, occasionally gesturing to the front of the plane. Lindsay digested every word, nodding slowly and intently, occasionally glancing to the front of the plane to see when we would take off. Mayor Evers, on the other hand, was looking intently out of the window. He must have sensed me watching him, for he looked at me. Then he grinned boyishly and pointed out the window. "Look, Jason, you can see the stars."

We touched down in Laurel thirty minutes later. A crowd of fifty people—police, the deputy mayor of Laurel, local Evers coordinators, and curious onlookers—stood around the plane. As we descended the stairs, Lindsay's chief of security looked worried. The reporters meanwhile flocked to the Laurel onlookers like flies to carrion. The woman from the large daily captured a startled white boy and began scribbling on her pad. "I'm from New York City. I'm a reporter. Whyd'ja come?"

The boy gawked and said, "I never seen anyone from New York before, and I wanted to see what the mayor looked like."

She recorded the remark and turned to the man next to the boy, who was about twenty-five and clad in dusty jeans. He was eying her bemusedly. She said, "How come you came?"

He chuckled. "I'm his brother. He don't have a driver's license so I gave him a ride."

As the reporters surrounded the Laurel people to gather their reactions, Ed called me aside. "They've had a bomb threat. We can't have it at the auditorium, we're movin' to a church." When we reached the church, the press rushed out of the bus into the crowd of three thousand loud, exuberant supporters. They had crowded into the street in front of the church; the front door was locked. I could see Simmons and other wood haulers in the crowd. The New York reporters'

excitement was justified: this *was* a story. No Mississippi reporters had made the plane trip.

I ran around to the back entrance, where Squeaky
guarded the door. He grabbed my arm and pulled me
through a crowd of reporters. As I lurched through a voice
cried, "Hey, I'm from the New York—" And the door was
shut.

In a small room behind the hall leading to the altar,
Mayor Lindsay and Tom Morgan talked with Ed. Beyond
the room was a tiny anteroom; Ed disappeared into it, closing the door behind. The deputy mayor of Laurel was talking nervously with Lindsay. "I'm really sorry this happened.
Really, we didn't want anything to happen. There was
nothing we could do, though. We had two calls sayin' a
bomb—"

Lindsay said soothingly, "Well, things like this happen.
It's not your fault. You can never take chances with a bomb
threat. You did the right thing. We appreciate your help."

The deputy mayor said, "Our mayor is in Paris. He went
with a group of POW wives to talk to North Vietnamese
and American negotiators. It's an important mission, an
honor he was chosen."

Lindsay nodded soberly. I kept wondering where Ed and
The Mayor were, at which point the anteroom door opened.
Ed Cole emerged, followed by The Mayor, who had his arm
draped over the shoulder of a tiny, bald, quivering black
man. Ed was grinning. The Mayor was saying, "Now I know
Reverend wouldn' mind us usin' the chu'ch. . . ."

The old man spoke nervously. "Yeah, but Mist' Evuhs,
I'm a deacon an' I don't have responsibility or permission—"

"C'mon and meet the mayor of New York City, John
Lindsay." Evers introduced the little man to Lindsay, who
graciously shook hands and said he was glad to be in Laurel.
Then he introduced the deacon to the rest of the crowd.
"This is Tom Morgan, Mayor Lindsay's P.R. man. You know

Ed, here. And this is Jason, my P.R. man. Now we got three-thousand folks outside who in the hot air and they come to hear some speeches!"

The little man was shaking, nodding his head back and forth. "But I cain't—I got no authority—"

"An' we got all those rascals from the New Yawk press, come all the way down here to *Laurel*, Miss'ssippi, to cover our political rally. . . ." The deputy mayor's mouth hung open.

But at that moment Squeaky stuck his head in to say that, somehow or another, the front door of the church had been opened, and people were piling in. The old man shrugged his shoulders—his expression showed reluctance and relief —and we all went into the church.

The heat was overbearing, especially with the cameras' bright lights. Lindsay security men scurried everywhere, checking windows, nervously eying the enormous crowd that in less than five minutes had filled the church to twice its capacity of a thousand. The deacon hustled to the microphone, told everyone to please be careful and not damage anything, and then led us in a short prayer. Ed spoke, and introduced the woodcutters. Lindsay was eloquent and impassioned. The reporters were visibly moved. The Mayor restated the themes of his candidacy, and the crowd began surging out. A reporter grasped my arm—"That's a helluva man you work for." I said, yes, I knew; and I wondered to myself what sort of story Mississippi reporters might have written had they been there. (A Jackson TV team and the local Laurel reporters numbered less than a half dozen; Lindsay had been accompanied by some thirty-five reporters.)

It took nearly half an hour for the mayors, security forces, and reporters to board buses and cars. When the last New Yorker had been extracted from the lingering crowd, Evers and Lindsay shook hands and parted. By midnight the New

York forces had departed for the airport. As we began the long drive back to Jackson, Ed Cole lit his pipe and said, "I wouldn't mind seeing that guy President, I sure wouldn't mind." I said I wouldn't, either.

On Wednesday, October 27, The Mayor toured the Governor's Mansion. Waller had been taken on a personal visit by John Bell in late summer. We waited until the last week of the race to demand equal time. The Mayor's tour was yet another good news story. I had called the lady in charge of tours at the old home, a Mrs. Seely, and she had agreed to his coming. She said, however, that reporters could not enter the building.

The Mayor, Mrs. Evers and a friend, the staff, and the press paused at the gate of the Mansion, where a state trooper stood. I stepped forward, and he said, "Press can't come in." There was an embarrassing silence; no one moved. I introduced myself to the man. He reluctantly shook hands, noticing the cameras and reporters. He repeated, "Press can't come through the gate."

Jack Hobbs, news director of WJTV, Jackson, leveled his camera at the man and began shooting. The trooper scowled. I stepped up right next to the man so the film would catch us both. I said, "Sir, as I understand the law, no reporters can go in the *Mansion.* All we want is to let them film the grounds. Now these gentlemen of the media . . ."

Hobbs edged closer; reporters scribbled. The man was getting angry. "These reporters," I said, "have stories to file. There is no law as I know it that says they can't come in." A reporter gave me the peace sign. The trooper was furious. "Press cain't come in!" The Mayor had a smile etched across his face and Hobbs was edging closer with his camera. Dennis Smith, who worked as an anchorman with Jack Hobbs, held a microphone through the car window and asked the candidate what he thought. The Mayor said, "Well, we don't wanna cause no trouble. But I jus' cain't understand why reporters can't go into the Mansion grounds. It's our Mansion. We pay taxes on it. We the ones who had to suffer because it was condemned. I think every individual has a right to go in . . . at least go into the grounds. But we want to abide by the rules, don't wanna cause any trouble."

The patrolman turned away from the camera and snarled, "Let's check with Mrs. Seely!" I leaned into The Mayor's car and said, "I'm going to check about the rule."

The Mayor grinned. "That's right, Jason, we don't wanna break no laws. We come too far now to break the rules."

Of course, I had no idea what the "law" was—and doubted if there was one at all—but it seemed preposterous to block the press from coming onto the lawn of the building. Mrs. Seely met me at the door, very flustered, and stated, "I said no reporters!"

I smiled and said politely, "Yes'm, I know that. But the law, as I understand it, is that these men aren't to enter the *building*, which I am not about to let them do. But they're waiting at the gate. They want to film the grounds, of course—"

"No!"

"Well, perhaps if you called Governor Williams . . ."

She replied curtly, "All right. I *will* call the governor."

She disappeared into a back room and was gone for several minutes. No one moved. At last Mrs. Seely emerged. "The governor was in a meeting and he got mad. He said you either come in now without the press or go home. He's busy and can't take time to come over here and *deliberate*!"

"Of course," I said.

I strode out the door quickly. The Mayor and Mrs. Evers were standing in the gateway now, Squeaky parking the car, and the press was huddled about them. I walked down the stairs of the Mansion. The state trooper stood fifteen feet from me, midway between the gate and the Mansion. I called to him loudly, "Officer, the governor said the press can only come up to the stair of the Mansion—and *not one step more!*"

The reporters flooded into the driveway onto the lawn like the Mississippi roaring over her levees. The state trooper raced up the driveway toward me. His mouth was wide open and there was a fierce look upon his face. He was about to speak to me when I said quickly, "The governor wants you to stand at the bottom of the stairs and make sure no one gets up." His face was now red and moving toward a purple fury. He took a flying step and stood firm on the marble stairs, hand on holster. Mrs. Seely was obviously disturbed, so I said, "Don't worry, they're not going to break your rule. I guarantee you they won't try to come in." She nodded uncomfortably.

The reporters gathered at the base of the stairs and The Mayor gestured toward the lawn. "When we move in on inauguration day, we'll set up the bar-b-cue pits over there . . . have fried chicken and pork chops. We'll put B. B. King under that ole magnolia tree!" He grinned mischievously and bounded up the stairs behind the two women.

I introduced The Mayor to Mrs. Seely and he in turn introduced his wife and her friend, whom he said, for the benefit of both Mrs. Seely and the press, was "my *interior decorator!*"

Mrs. Seely showed us around the Mansion and she was a picture of politeness. She traced the history of the beautiful house, showing the portraits, which were over a half century old, and some of the furniture, which dated back before 1900. As we concluded the tour of the downstairs, The Mayor pointed at the stairway and said, "Can we go up?"

"No," she said, "that's the part that's condemned . . ."

"That's where all the holes are?" The Mayor said.

"Yes," she said, uncomfortably.

Mrs. Evers said cheerily, "Why, this is a beautiful house. I can't believe it's condemned."

Mrs. Seely smiled and replied, "Well, you know that was the same thing I thought when they told me. I've been showing it for twelve years and I never thought a thing was wrong with it!"

The Mayor asked if the gold doorknobs and bathtub faucets that Governors Barnett and Johnson had installed were still intact, and Mrs. Seely said yes, but they were upstairs. Joe Huttie had turned away from the dialogue, trying to conceal the broad grin on his face.

We exchanged pleasantries. I thanked Mrs. Seely again, and she nodded and smiled nervously, and we walked out the front door. The reporters stood around the base of the steps, the sultry state trooper on the porch. A journalist called, "What'd you think, Mayor?"

The Mayor paused and rested his hand on a grimy white pillar. "Well, my wife fell in love with the place, and my interior decorator thinks it has great possibilities." He grinned and ran his index finger down a wooden pillar, collecting a fingerprint of dirt. "It's just a little dirty, that's all. Just needs a li'l soap and water and we'll be ready to move in!"

The next morning Jack Hobbs called to say that he had received a number of phone calls over the news strip of my altercation with the state trooper. "They were all mad," he said. "All kinds of folks . . . everybody saying that Charlie was right—the Mansion ought to be open for *everybody*." All of the callers had been white.

Not to be outdone, Bill Waller had himself a Democratic unity dinner in Tupelo on October 25. Before the speeches a news commentator asked the candidate what he thought the vote count would be, and Waller predicted he would receive 65 percent of the vote.

Eastland was the keynote speaker. He praised the Democratic Party, which had elected him, Barnett, and Bilbo: "It has served our people faithfully and well through the years. . . . [As for Bill Waller] his name will be written on the honor roll of the party!

"I have boundless confidence in our party. The source of that firm faith is proven performance. Both the party and the nominee have been tried—and have been found fit to govern a great and independent people. I assert that the Mississippi Democratic Party, as the pages of time were turned, has fought all the good fights on behalf of our citizens—has finished every course charted for it by Mississippi's men and women—has kept the political faith of our fathers sound and strong."

Of Evers, he observed, "A two-year-old child, with a teaspoon, would have a better chance to dig the Tennessee-Tombigee Waterway than our opponent has to defeat Bill Waller!"

The Mississippi Democratic Party "Political Extravaganza" was held on October 28 in the Jackson civic auditorium. The crowd, according to Peter Schrag, a visiting journalist, numbered about one thousand, but "I didn't see very many people under forty." It was what Charles Hills, Jr., of the *Clarion-Ledger*, deemed "an impressive show of unity . . . a list of speakers resembling a Who's Who list in Mississippi politics."

His face creased, Senator Stennis, with his deep fatherly drawl, told the crowd of wealthy, middle-aged whites, "This election is nothing in the world but a forum to attract national attention and an opportunity for the Independent candidate for governor and some of his followers to get some money to spend. This candidate has spent a large part of his time in Washington soliciting campaign funds and attending fund-raising garden parties arranged for him by some of his rich, liberal friends who are using this situation for their own selfish political purposes. In fact, this election in Mississippi has become a national stage for certain Presidential candidates to appeal for the black vote, not in Mississippi, but in Chicago, New York, Detroit, Philadelphia, and other large metropolitan areas."

Then John Bell Williams spoke in a bellicose manner. "We are not yet ready to turn over the state to the leadership of the Kennedys, the Muskies, the McGoverns!"

And Ross Barnett, his voice mellowed, both hands on the podium, his shoulders heaving as he sang praises of William Waller: "A man of *courage*! . . . A *mannnn* of honor! . . . A *mannn* of integrity! A maannnn of fair dealing! . . . A man . . . who will work, and a man who will *make* . . . a great chief executive!"

Waller, a red rose in his lapel, told the crowd, "The opposition in the general election has tried to divide our people —white against black—young against old—and rich against poor. But Mississippians have already sacrificed too much to allow a campaign of divisiveness and distrust to destroy the progress and goodwill of a century."

With emotion, Waller declared, "The Mississippi Democratic Party has guided this state from the depths of economic and political chaos . . . *progress is no accident*! We still face serious problems but we will never solve them through a campaign that seeks to polarize the races! We must work together . . . and without advice from the mayor of the crime-ridden, garbage-bound city of New York!"

Watching Waller on television, I could not help but wonder if a man who had been elected district attorney, a *lawyer*, could honestly believe that kind of rhetoric. He stood on a stage with Stennis, Barnett, Johnson, and Williams— four of the greatest political fools in the history of the South, men who had led Mississippi into ignominy and shame, and who had made the state the laughingstock of the country. Waller, the man who once courageously prosecuted Byron De la Beckwith, stood and praised "the progress and goodwill of a century." I wondered what his grandchildren, studying the history of the civil rights movement, would think of him after reading his speech, given at a moment when the blood and crosses were such a short time gone.

With the election five days off, the office now overflowed with reporters. We had expected the influx of volunteers who suddenly crowded the office, but were not prepared for all twenty-five of them. Suddenly I was spending seven hours a day with reporters, trying to squeeze them in to see The Mayor, and it became difficult with all the new people. Most volunteers had gone to considerable personal expense, leaving jobs or classes in the north for a week, but they were usurping desks, phones, and chairs in the process of getting out a statewide mailing. The new people and the letters were all over the office.

One morning when I came into the office I noticed my desk in disarray. Instinctively, I began to put things in order. A New Jersey voice shrilled at me, "Don't touch that desk! I *need* those things!" Cautiously, I moved away. Magnolia doubled over with laughter as an irritated young woman took over the desk. An hour later, a Massachusetts woman cornered me and asked what plans I had made for parking for the press. "Parking for the press?" I asked. "Yes," she said, "on election night. What arrangements have you made for the reporters' cars?" I said I never made arrangements during the campaign, and had no plans to change that practice now. She told me that that was *not* the way they did it in Massachusetts. I replied that it *was* the way we did it in Mississippi, and when she backed off with a troubled look, I realized that I had bellowed at her.

I stalked off to find a peaceful place, and discovered Barbara Phillips, Joe Huttie, Alec, and Magnolia crowded on the floor of Ed Cole's office. Ed, as usual, was on the phone.

I plopped onto the floor. Barbara, grinning wryly, said, "Welcome to the Evers campaign!" For a moment I began to feel a sense of what the white Southerners originally felt when the civil rights workers came.

Outsiders had swarmed into our office and some Yankee woman was trying to tell me what to do about the press. The volunteers, most of whom were well meaning and deeply committed, were simply carried away with their mission, undoubtedly thinking that in five days they were going to save Mississippi. They had disrupted our fragile order and discipline. Sitting in Ed's office with people I had worked and shared so much with, I was overcome with a feeling of belonging that I had never felt before. Everyone in the office had gone through a long campaign, committed to the notion of personal as well as political change. The RNA, the Neshoba Fair, the wood haulers' strike, the spilled bucket— each was an element of the tender chemistry that had drawn us together. And now there were all these people in the outer office, "campaigning" as it were. Ed got off the phone, commiserated with us briefly, laughed about the "new help we seem to have come upon," and miraculously secured two desks for the group to share.

Thursday night The Mayor returned to Fayette for the weekly mass meeting. This one was important. Rumors of dissension and of Uncle Toms working with the whites had spread like fire. Three hundred and fifty black folks crowded into the sweltering Hollywood Baptist Church. Dwight played "Amazing Grace" and The Mayor evoked memories of Medgar, Klan killings in Jefferson County, the racist administration that had preceded his. Midway through the speech it was evident that the campaign was taking its toll on his emotions. Because of the impending alliance of anti-Evers blacks and Jefferson County whites, the Loyalist slate for November 2 had a tough fight. Evers was furious.

"An' you were out there pickin' *peanuts*, pickin' *cotton*, plowin' mules—all the time sayin', 'Yessum' and 'No'um' to those *meannnn* white folks. And now these *saame* white folks—not the good whites, but the ones who kep' you down—*Are they better than your black brothers?*"

There were no blacks who opposed Evers at the meeting, and these were of course the ones he was condemning. But the crowd was volatile, like him. People were shouting, jumping, yelling, stamping feet; choruses of "Amen," "Say it's so," and "I *know* that's true!" punctuated his speech.

Evers was shouting, stabbing his arm into the air. "Some of you is sayin', 'No, we ain't gonna vote for no more black folks 'cause the ones we got are too stric' on us. They don't allow us to cuss in the streets no more, don't allow us to drink whiskey and beat our women, don't allow us to speed through our town. So we ain't gonna vote for no more black folks!' "

His eyes were wide and glittered like hot coals. "Black folks, they don't say nothin' about all the sufferin' we stopped—the killin', the Klan, that ole man y'all remember what got killed at the ice house. Crippled man sittin' there who couldn't move fast enough for some racist white, so the white devil *shot him dead!* Are we forgettin' *that*, black folks?"

The crowd was yelling, screaming, pounding. "No! No! No!"

He pointed at the black folks. "If you fight against the rights o' black folks in this town, you cain't get no compensation from us. I bite no bones about it! If you gonna get out and canvass against us who're fightin' for the rights of our folks, you cain't work for us. I mean that! If there's *anybody* in this town . . . lemme make it clear now . . . anybody who go out and campaign against us, campaignin' for men who done kep' us down, for men who done mistreated our women, you cain't work in this town."

The crowd was growling, listening to every breath he uttered. "If you think I'm jokin', try me. I do a lot of things, but I ain't ever lied to you! So help me God, if I find out you against us, you ain't got no job! We done struggled too hard. If any o' you don't like our peaches, don't come around shakin' our trees!"

That night, for the last time, the staff crowded into The Mayor's office. He discussed election day plans—the poll watchers to come in, the legal problems to be expected. Evers was very tired when he finished talking. We left the office, trying not to think about what it would be like when we parted ways.

The last tour of the campaign was in the Delta; we left Jackson late Friday afternoon, October 29. We planned to meet Congressman Robert Drinan, (D—Massachusetts), the first Catholic priest elected to the House, and ACLU President Joe Rauh at rendezvous points along the way. The five-car motorcade drove north on Highway 61, an ancient single-laned asphalt that runs roughly parallel to the Mississippi River, raised slightly higher than the vast black earth that becomes a miraculous explosion of milk-white cotton balls every autumn. Cautiously, we followed plantation trucks; cotton snarls spilled out of the vehicles, danced across the road, and rebounded off our windshield. Cars whizzed by us going south.

We drove to Rolling Fork, where fifteen hundred black folks jammed the courthouse in the rain-threatening evening, cheering so loud you could hear it from one end of the tiny town to the other. Next we drove north toward Greenville, and by now a purple curtain was descending on the red horizon. A huge rain cloud was thundering across the river from Louisiana. The only breaks in the darkness were car lights and the endless tiers of cotton, shimmering in the dark twilight. We had spent more time in this region of the state than any other during the campaign. Each time we returned I was filled with awe of the land and its immemorial people. I would see the black earth of the Delta and think of James Eastland and Fannie Lou Hamer: two creatures of the cosmos who had fought relentlessly, one for authority and the other for freedom; each possessed of awesome powers, he of the Senate, she of the soul.

We entered Greenville, a town noted for its civility in race relations, a reputation due in large part to the influence of Hodding Carter, the barrelchested newspaper editor. The courthouse was teeming with black folks. Two reporters from the *Delta-Democrat Times*, a handful of other white reporters, Hodding III, and Wes Watkins, the Loyalists' attorney, had crowded onto the benches in the first row. Hodding was in his late thirties, but looked younger. He squeezed through the crowd and sat next to me. We talked briefly about the campaign, and financial problems Evers would face after it was over. Hodding had given us little help during the campaign; however, I found it hard not to like him. He had worked with and contributed to the campaigns of local candidates in Greenville. An emotional man, Hodding was deeply moved by The Mayor's speech; by the middle of it, one never would have thought the neat young editor in a tan sport coat was a Princeton graduate. He was jumping in his seat, yelling, and trying to hold back tears as Evers conjured images of mean Delta planters, horrible Eastland, and all that the white folks had done to the black folks. Father Drinan, who had met us in Greenville, hung on Evers' words. Evers looked at Hodding at one point and said, "Yeah, but they had some white folks that knew all that badness wasn't right. Had ole Mist' Carter, writin' his paper, and sayin', 'Naw, it's *wrong* to hate black folks and set 'em apart from white folks. It's *wrong* to have Ku Klux Klans and all that.' And Hoddin' and Philip, jus' like their daddy, keep on writin' what they know's true—that black folks and white folks got to work together!"

When Father Drinan spoke he was visibly moved. "I can assure you that you *can* win! It can be done! When I ran for Congress a year ago, people said a priest could never be elected to the House. But in the last hours of the campaign, hundreds and thousands of volunteers canvassed the raining streets in Massachusetts, going door to door and asking those who had not voted to go to the polls before they closed! And we did it, and I know you can do the same—for the courageous Mayor Evers and all the candidates on the Mississippi Loyalist Democratic ticket!"

The next morning the rally was held in Ruleville. Joe Rauh had flown in and was bear-hugging his old friends. Fannie Lou Hamer gave a thunderous speech, outshining everyone else. She was piping hot over the verdict handed down in the case of the killers of JoEtha Collier. "Ah want to know how come they can gun down an innocent, holy li'l chile from Drew, Mississippi, a black girl who is an image of the Lawd, and they call that *manslaughter*—but when a white person gets killed they call it *murder*!" Rauh turned to me after the speech and said wryly, "You know, two years ago they wouldn't even have gotten a guilty on any charge."

Rauh's speech was mostly about the success of the civil rights work in the last decade. He closed snappily, "One thing that makes me feel good here today, is knowing that, on November 3, Mr. Jim Eastland, who lives on a big plantation in Sunflower County, will be represented in the Mississippi Senate by none other than Mrs. Fannie Lou Hamer!" The audience cheered loudly. I was wishing his optimistic statement would come true.

Mayor Evers flew to the Coast for a late night rally, and I drove back to Jackson with sisters JoAnn and Margaret. I ate a quick dinner and hurried over to a church on Fraish Street. The lawyers and students from out of state were being briefed on what to expect two days hence from local election managers who sorely resented the presence of outsiders. Gil Jonas, the peppery fund-raiser from New York who had often kept our campaign alive and breathing, listened intently to a lawyer who was explaining an obscure part of the Mississippi code. The room hung heavy with smoke. I gazed at the three hundred people who had come all the way down here for the last three days. They were black, white, long-haired, some wearing Brooks Brothers shirts, others mini-skirts, still others dashikis. Everyone perused the thick tablet of instructions as the lawyer spoke, looking at the speaker, then at the paper.

Wearily, I wondered what would happen. Despite the change in attitudes we had seen, the election itself was going to be a hard-fought battle. Ed and The Mayor had said they knew votes would be stolen in some counties. I made my way through the crowd to stand in a side alleyway; the door was open and I could still see the lawyer. The night air was cool and from my vantage point I watched the intense question-and-answer period going on inside.

A college student came outside and introduced himself as Dan Kerrigan. He had organized the Georgetown group that had arrived the night before.

"This is some place, Mississippi," Kerrigan said. "You think it's going to be easy on Tuesday?"

"I don't know. There'll be some bad spots. I don't know how bad. I don't think it's going to be terrible. . . ."

Suddenly a figure emerged from the shadows: a big, rotund black man, Reverend Hunter of Macon. He swallowed me in a bear hug, and his voice boomed, "Yeah, indeed, we sho' 'nuf ready in *Macon*, Mississippi!" Reverend Hunter, Kerrigan, and I talked until the poll watchers' meeting ended. Then we went inside to meet some of the lawyers and students. Everyone was impelled by a new sense of urgency. For the first time in the campaign, I began to feel that there was an unknown force in Mississippi, some hidden element of the white folks that would emerge suddenly, inevitably.

The Mayor gave his last speech of the campaign Monday night in Jackson. Afterwards, Ed, Joe Huttie, Alec, Barb, and I found a bar and tried to predict the outcome as we drank our beers. The average vote we came up with for The Mayor was 240,000—210,000 black and 30,000 white. Ed believed about one hundred local candidates would win, including four in the Legislature. Ed, a potential congressional candidate for the following year, reflected that he might just run if Evers got a strong vote. Each of us said we would work for him if he decided to enter the race. We agreed that a different campaign would be necessary for a smaller geographic region: more voter registration, more organization in black communities, more canvasses.

The late news came on the television over the bar. The announcer said that William Waller was expected to defeat Charles Evers tomorrow.

CHAPTER

13

The morning of November 2 was bright and warm. The Evers staff gathered in the office at 6:30 A.M. for the long day ahead. More than 250 poll watchers had been dispatched to counties across the state. The Jackson office was checkpoint for all volunteers; they were to call at prearranged intervals so that we could keep in touch throughout the day.

The day before, Edwin Wiesl, a former Justice Department lawyer in the Johnson Administration, had hammered out a compromise agreement with Mississippi Attorney General A. F. Summer regarding the status of poll watchers. The Mississippi secretary of state considered the Loyalists an "independent" party, despite the official sanction by the national Democratic party. After a lengthy meeting, Summer concluded that two Loyalist representatives could stand at each poll.

The Justice Department had sent its entire voting rights section into twenty-four counties; federal observers from the U.S. Civil Service Commission were in sixteen counties, and federal examiners, empowered to receive complaints, were in thirty-six counties. As a gesture to The Mayor, former Attorney General Ramsey Clark flew in for the election to serve as general counsel in the office. The lawyers Gil Jonas had organized were serving either as poll watchers or as legal advisors in counties where trouble was expected to occur.

It was also the consensus of the Evers campaign, the Delta ministry, and the Lawyers' Committee for Civil Rights that white election officials might attempt to ride herd over illiterates, who were allowed to vote under Mississippi law. Poll watchers could challenge any such suspected chicaneries.

Trouble began almost immediately. When the polls opened at 7 A.M., two New York poll watchers named McAllister and Steingut presented their certificates to the white election official in Midnight, Mississippi, located in predominantly black Humphreys County in the Delta. Kermit James, a black candidate for supervisor, accompanied the two men into the polling place, which was a country store owned by the white incumbent supervisor. McAllister explained that the certificates had the approval of the attorney general of Mississippi, and that, under state law, candidates had the right to have poll watchers. Then three white men in the room told the poll watchers that if they wanted to leave Humphreys County alive, they had better leave now. The two New Yorkers retreated to a car. They left Midnight, driving toward Belzoni, where they hoped to find a phone. Kermit James remained in the polling place, protesting the expulsion, until a white farmer ambled across the room and slammed two hard punches on him. James was arrested by the sheriff and taken out of the poll. The charges were later dropped, however. The poll watchers called Jackson to report that they had not been allowed in the poll; it was nearly eleven by the time Attorney General Summer's office had contacted the Midnight polling place and they were instated. But by eleven, Kermit James knew he had lost, for word of the beating spread like wildfire among blacks.

Ten miles south of Midnight, in Louise, another heavily black town, black folks were scared to vote. In 1970 a fifty-one-year-old black man with one arm had been pummeled to death by eight whites. And on election day one year later blacks had to vote in the gas station where the Klan held its meetings. A hefty white man sat in his pickup truck, replete with gun rack, carefully noting each black person who entered the polling place. Inside, there weren't enough voting booths, so ballots had to be marked wherever blacks could find room. The atmosphere was tense. The turnout by blacks here proved lower than expected.

In Gulfport a Washington attorney named Lester Hyman was having problems. Hyman was a close friend of Evers and had spent part of a summer vacation doing civil rights legal work in Jackson; he was now working for us on the Gulf Coast. The Harrison County Election Commission had rejected the request of a Loyalist poll watcher that he be allowed in the election center to view transferral of cards from voting machine to IBM computer. A skilled man with computers could supplant real ballots with rigged ones. The incumbent sheriff, a man who had given Evers excellent security on Coast tours, had called to warn about an attempt to block the poll watcher. Internal Coast politics had set the sheriff against members of the Election Commission. "If your poll watcher doesn't get in there," the man said, "neither will mine."

At noon on election day a Harrison County judge refused to grant the motion of restraint clause Hyman appealed for. Hyman tracked down the federal judge on the Coast, who also rejected it. In the early afternoon he called Jackson, where the phones were tied up.

Lester Hyman was not the only one having difficulties.

About the same time Kermit James was slugged in Humphreys County, Seth Smith, candidate for constable in Leake County, was attacked by two white men in front of his polling place. An awestruck poll watcher couldn't believe his eyes. John Brittain of the Lawyers' Committee for Civil Rights later said, "Smith's beating had a direct effect on blacks. It scared them away from the polls."

In the Delta counties of Bolivar and Sunflower, black candidates were distraught because of manipulation of black illiterate voters by white poll officials. In Shelby, a heavily black town in Bolivar, election manager James Brown, a white, told poll watchers to "Observe—and don't do nothin' else."

By midmorning, another abuse was taking place in Shelby. When illiterate voters came to vote, the white voting machine operator would inquire if any assistance was desired. Mississippi law gives illiterates the right to such assistance, and most said they did want help. Paul Ryder, a poll watcher from Princeton University, frequently challenged the white manipulations but was always shouted down with threats. At the end of the day, he filed this report:

> Many of these [black] people knew well which candidates they preferred [often they carried a sheet with them diagraming the inside of the booth, with the positions of appropriate levers outlined], but no matter what they said, it was the machine operator and he alone, who decided on and pushed down the levers. . . . Other poll watchers were able to see operators enter false choices for illiterates and indicated by the handouts they carried. The election manager consistently refused illiterates' requests that they be allowed to take friends or relatives into the booth with them. The result of Shelby having many illiterate vot-

ers, combined with the at-best-dubious operator "assistance," was a situation holding, not only the potential-
ity, but the actuality of fraud.

The results of the Shelby vote had even worse implications. There were three other voting officials besides Brown
in the main Shelby poll, however only one, Reverend Fergeson, was trusted by blacks. Reverend Fergeson was in
charge of the fourth machine. At day's end, to the dismay of
Shelby's black candidates and state senatorial candidates
Fannie Lou Hamer and Charles McLaurin, the first three
machine counts showed white candidates scoring impressive
victories over blacks, while in the last machine, blacks won
handily. Consider Mrs. Hamer's vote count: tallies from the
votes with white officials, the first three machines, showed
an average of 75 votes for Mrs. Hamer, and 115 for her opponent, Mr. Crook. Reverend Fergeson's box showed Mrs.
Hamer with 186 votes, as opposed to 59 for her opponent.
Likewise, the count in the gubernatorial race eventually
showed Evers with an average of 150 and Waller 110 in the
first three machines; in the fourth Evers had 239 and Waller
80. Shelby is over 60 percent black.

Meanwhile, in Indianola, the seat of Sunflower County,
election officials at the American Legion hall polling center
had concocted an ingenious obstacle. There were eleven
ballots in eleven different rooms, although there were only
1,200 voters. Thus, with only two poll watchers allowed for
the Loyalists, there was no way of recording all the irregularities. Black folks entered in groups (few wanted to go
vote alone), only to be separated and directed to different
rooms by whites.

With similar reports coming into the Evers office and to
offices of the Jackson Lawyers' Committee for Civil Rights,
Ramsey Clark, Ed Cole, and Ed Wiesl held a noon press
conference. Reporters jammed into the office and in the

back of the room I saw Charlie Hills; his round, red face had finally appeared. Ed charged irregularities: blacks were having a terrible time trying to vote. Clark said it seemed that there was basis in at least one case for a legal challenge. Wiesl elaborated, "We have found there is a pattern throughout the state of Mississippi of making it as difficult if not impossible for black voters to exercise their franchise."

As the afternoon passed, more problems arose. Lester Hyman finally got through from the Coast and explained the plight of his suit. Attorney John Brittain arranged a special hearing with Stokes Robertson of the Mississippi Supreme Court in the judge's Jackson chambers for 6 P.M. Robertson was reputed to be generally tolerant, unlike Brady or Perry. Hyman conferred with Ramsey Clark on the WATS line, then caught a chartered plane for Jackson.

By midafternoon I had drunk what seemed like a thousand cups of coffee. Tension increased in the office each time a phone buzzed. I was taking calls, jotting notes, forwarding calls to the Lawyers' Committee, and trying to detect what, if any, systematic connections could be made among irregularities in various counties. But I could find none; the abuses were widespread and emerged in no set pattern.

In Rankin County a white social worker from Jackson was thrown in jail for protesting a white poll manager's manipulation of an illiterate voter. Another report told of a voting machine that would not register black votes for more than an hour; the entire column was locked! An Antioch student in Adams County challenged an irregularity and was punched in the face by whites.

In Madison County the Ku Klux Klan had disseminated sample ballots in the yards of black voters the night before the election. The ballots were nearly the same as Loyalist ballots in appearance, except that the Klan ballot advocated

X's for an all-white slate of candidates. In Holmes County the same thing happened.

In Canton, the seat of Madison, the Loyalist organization was alarmed to find that ballots on the voting machines had been placed in a horizontal pattern—as opposed to the vertical pattern on the sample ballots and which the Election Commission had originally said would be on the machines. Later, poll watchers' reports said the election managers were telling illiterates how to vote for whites, when the voters wanted to vote for blacks.

A violation of Mississippi election law occurred in Canton when "representatives" of an old folks' home picked up ballots to carry them to shut-in voters who presumably filled them out and had them returned. These "car votes" were done under the authorization of Shed Weeks, the election manager. Flonzie Goodloe challenged the votes, which were then kept in a segregated box. (Absentee ballots for invalids were forbidden in Mississippi; civil rights lawyers said a suit would definitely be filed.) The challenged ballots provided the margin of victory in two races.*

Southwest of Canton, in the heavily black town of Flora (still in Madison County), poll watchers Jim Macera and Anthony Littieri had reached the end of a frustrating day. Macera and Littieri, both college graduates, were volunteers from New York; they had lived in Madison County for three weeks prior to the election, working with Amzie Cotton on a voter canvass for election day. In nearby Flora they were assigned to watch the polls in a place where two muscular whites guarded the door. Several carloads of blacks passed by, afraid to stop. Finally, by midmorning, black folks began slowly to file in. Macera and Littieri were passing out sample ballots to black voters at 10 A.M. when a white official told them it was against the law! They stood

---

* This election contest was ruled legal by the local circuit court; however, at the time of this writing, the case is on appeal to the Mississippi Supreme Court.

their ground, explaining the law, and continued to give out the ballots. A white man sneered at Macera and said, "We knew our colored have the right to vote, so why do you people stand around here watching?" Macera politely explained that he was going to stay, and the man retorted, "We'll find out about this soon."

But the white poll watchers *inside* the polling place were handing out sample ballots for the white candidates—to black as well as white voters. Black folks were shaking, and few were audacious enough to refuse the ballot when handed it. Jim Macera then approached one of the federal observers, a civil service worker from West Virginia. (The other "observer" was a civil service man from Vicksburg, who had smugly told them, "We don't have literacy laws in Mississippi. *Anyone* can vote here!" This, while whites were hustling illiterate blacks within sight of all parties concerned.) Macera explained the situation to one of the federal observers present who stated that he was in Mississippi only to observe and file a report. Even, said the man, if the grossest irregularity occurs, "all I do is write it up and report it." But the shocker came when the man said, "I can't make judgments, really, because I am not familiar with Mississippi voting laws."

Shortly before 4 P.M. a legless black man was driven to the polling center, but his black driver was afraid to get out. Macera and two blacks helped carry the man inside the polls. The election manager hunched over the crippled Negro as he began to vote; the black man was illiterate and confused. The white man said, "Cap, for governor, you can vote for—"

"Evers. I want Evers."

The man scowled, paused for an uncomfortable half minute, and registered the vote for Evers. He skipped the lieutenant governor, secretary of state, and superintendent of education votes, and moved down to the local sheriff's race.

"Billy Noble's runnin' for sheriff. Billy Noble, a candidate for sheriff. That's Billy Noble. Now, that vote would go right here. . . . You want Billy Noble, Cap?"

The invalid was stammering. He looked around the room wide-eyed, and he blurted, "Yess . . . ye-yes . . ."

"Good. Now, you wanna vote some more—or you had enough votin' for today?" The man was shaking uncontrollably. He nodded, stuttered, and said he was through voting. Macera and the blacks carried him back out. As they reached the door a clerk said, "You people would kill that man just to get his vote."

The black man made it back into his car. Macera returned to his position as poll watcher. A white man walked up to him and told him to get into a truck, he was under arrest. There were two other men, and so Macera got in. As the men got in the truck, a poll official chortled, "You got charges ready or you gonna make 'em up tomorrow?"

"Tomorrow," the burly arrester giggled.

Macera later recounted, "When we got in the jail I said to the man who took me in, 'What's the charge?' 'This is an investigation,' he said. 'That's all I got to tell you.'

" 'Can I ask you one question?'

" 'What's that?'

" 'Are you here to enforce the law, or to hurt me?'

" 'If I wanted to hurt you I would have already done it by now.' "

The Shelby situation grew worse, meanwhile, and the two poll watchers drove to nearby Cleveland, Mississippi, where they met two Justice Department lawyers. After listening to their story the lawyers said that they were not in Mississippi to enforce the law. The Justice Department lawyers dispatched two more federal observers, civil service workers from Georgia, back to Shelby. But, as Ryder later wrote:

> Most of the illiterates had already voted by the time
> he came. Enough came so that the civil service men,

Worsham and Meeks, could make reports. Worsham did not see one such instance, however, even though I did. Meeks immediately made himself at home with the white election officials and they spent a great deal of time talking and passing time. Whenever I saw an illiterate having problems and white men there to "help" him, I would quickly point it out to Meeks. He would sort of stroll over and watch it, scribble something *maybe*, and then go back to his conversation, or shuffling some of the papers he had brought with him.

When the vote count began in Flora, Jim Macera was still in jail. A black student from the University of Massachusetts, Sam Davis, was led into the cell adjoining Macera's. Davis had been arrested at another spot in Flora where he had been telling blacks standing in line at 6 P.M. that they should remain there; they could vote as long as they were in line at 6 P.M. But carloads of menacing whites were slowly patrolling the dusty road in front of the polling place; no blacks wanted to stay. Davis entreated them to remain and he was arrested.

As the vote count began, crises multiplied. Back in Humphreys County, a black lawyer named Robbie Dix was standing on a Coke bottle crate trying to watch the vote count, which was taking place in the midst of a sea of white men bunched together in front of him. Standing a dozen feet behind were two federal observers from Stockbridge, Georgia. Suddenly a white man grabbed Dix on the shoulder, twisted him off the crate, and a second man cried, "Tally right, nigger!" as he planted his fist in Dix's mouth, breaking his front teeth. Then he was taken into custody by the sheriff for disturbing the peace.

In Issaquena County, a small though predominantly black region, the sheriff announced on the radio that ballots would be counted privately, due to the "special nature of the election." He put on his gun, walked into the poll, ordered poll watchers fifty feet from the vote count, and told them they would be arrested if they made trouble. At 6 P.M. a highway patrolman picked up the ballot boxes and together with a poll manager transported them to the mayor's house, where they were counted. Although blacks won five races, Evers lost the county to Waller.

At 5:50 Ed Wiesl and I stood in the Jackson airport waiting for Lester Hyman's chartered plane to touch down. Finally, after the two-seater plane wobbled in, we sped down the interstate at eighty-five m.p.h., reaching the capital shortly after 6. Justice Robertson read the brief, heard the argument, and agreed that the poll watcher had the right to be present when the ballots were being placed in the computer. He called Gulfport from his chambers.

Though we did not know it at the time, Fayette was immersed in its own troubles. Both whites and blacks who had sold out were retaliating. The polls had not been open two hours when the election manager at the Harrison store voting place—the owner of the store—ordered the Loyalist representative out of her store. She was backed up by a black youth who was supporting white candidates, presumably for some compensation. Eddie Dunlop, a twenty-one-year-old Alcorn student and the first black to go to Fayette High, quickly cornered a Loyalist lawyer and brought him over to the store. After the lawyer attempted to tell the election manager that what she was doing was illegal, she called a deputy sheriff. But the issue was finally resolved when the attorney explained the law to the deputy, who politely if begrudgingly asked the election manager to acquiesce. Her assistants continued to do their best to keep the registration book as far away from the Loyalist poll watcher as possible.

The importance of the registration book became apparent in the grand jury room of the Fayette courthouse. Bartle

Bull, president of *The Village Voice*, filed the most incisive article on the election. He wrote from Fayette:

> By 9:15 complaints of a new trick were coming in from three polling places. They caught it first in the Grand Jury Room. . . . When a white voter came to vote, the election manager would put the stamp marked "Voted" in the column for a previous election. The space for the present election was then still empty, and the white could come back and vote again. Once the pollwatchers were alerted to this game, a new refinement was developed. When a white voter came to vote, the stamp would be put opposite the name of a black voter, so the white could vote again and the black would be told he had already voted. . . .
>
> Voting was heavy in the two polling places in the county court house in Fayette. Outside, in the 88 degree heat, Evers girls handing out sample ballots were hassled by two young blacks, reportedly leading local Toms. As the girls handed out the sample ballots, the Toms would say to the voters, "You don't need this insult. You can read and vote by yourself. Get along in there and forget it." When a white lawyer told the Toms to lay off the girls, a bulky, middle-aged black in a pink shirt came out of the courthouse and told them to keep it up. This was Early Lott, the local constable, running again on the white slate, this time unsuccessfully. Ed Dunlop went by, on the way to a problem in the courthouse. "Hi, honk," he called to one of the Toms. In a few moments Dunlop sent for the lawyer.
>
> Inside the courthouse, Dunlop and Burnell Walters, the tough black pollwatcher and ex-Fayette cop, were arguing with the election managers and Sheriff Pritchard. The sheriff, an old-timer with thick glasses

and tired eyes, threatened to arrest Walters, who insisted on his right to stand where he could see the registration book. The lawyer said to Sheriff Pritchard, "I'm sure you don't want us to sue you for false arrest. Why don't we just set this up so we can watch as the law requires?" "This here's an FBI man," replied the sheriff, turning to a tan man in a pale blue suit and pale orange shoes. The agent asked the lawyer to see the FBI credentials. After checking the ageless signature of J. Edgar Hoover designating Donald T. Kalady as an agent, the lawyer gave his name to Kalady. The FBI agent and Sheriff Pritchard walked out, saying that the bailiff, one R. M. Truly, who appeared to be partly drunk, would do things "the best he knows how, just like he always done." Walters again took up his position, and the lawyer told Truly that his best was not good enough unless it met the law. Outside, a highway patrol car pulled up, making several black voters hang back from the poll.

Election Commission illegalities were widespread. In Ebenezer, Representative Clark's hometown, a black poll watcher from Fisk University started yelling "Challenge!" when the election manager, accompanying voters into the booth, said, "I wouldn't vote for that one if I was you."

In Port Gibson, votes cast by newly registered eighteen-to twenty-year-olds were impounded by the Election Commission on the basis that they were subject to review as to their legality. By the end of the day it appeared that Mrs. Geneva Collins, the incumbent black chancery clerk who lost, would win if the impounded votes were counted. Civil rights lawyers began laying plans for the legal challenge.

From Clarksdale, where Aaron Henry's race against the White Citizens' Council planter was the key race in the county, a black minister with considerable influence was passing out voting material for white candidates. Blacks in Clarksdale said that he had been bought off.

By 6:45, Justice Robertson granted the motion for a temporary restraining order. He called an election official of the Harrison County Election Commission and told him to let the poll watcher in. But Gulf Coast officials then made their own shrewd interpretation. The poll watcher was allowed in, but was forced to stand behind a glass window over twenty-five feet from the computer. All he saw were the bright dots pop onto the board of the machine. By 8:30, the incumbent sheriff who had called Evers the night before suspecting foul play was defeated.

In Fayette, only seven blacks on the Jefferson slate were winning. Bob Vanderson, the stocky, amiable black man who everyone thought would win, was trailing in his race for sheriff. Eddie Dunlop and a Loyalist attorney reached the county store at Lorman, a small town ten miles north of Fayette; the vote count was going on inside a barn behind the main store. A crowd of unruly whites stood around the barn. Dunlop walked through the crowd slowly; no one spoke. He pounded on the door and the whites began shrieking, "Git away from there, nigger!"

"Anybody can go in there. It's supposed to be a public vote count." The lawyer began explaining to the men that a public count was indeed the law but the men were not interested in his argument. The door opened slightly and Dunlop pushed his way in, only to have a white man yank him from behind. "Ain't no one goin' in there!" the man said. But Dunlop pushed his way in, told the man counting votes that the female poll watcher who had become apprehensive about the crowd outside was legally entitled to watch him count the vote. The lawyer hurried in and backed up Dunlop's statement. The girl moved closer and took her place next to the man counting votes. Dunlop and the attorney moved on to another polling place.

Late that night, with votes yet to be counted, Sheriff Pritchard of Fayette, who had had a hard day, announced he was sick and damn tired of all the challenges, complaints, and black people looking over his shoulder. The rest of the world could go hang, *he* was locking up the remaining ballots; they would be counted in the morning. A black supervisory candidate named Sol Jackson led by 88 votes when the count stopped; he lost by 32 votes the next morning.

A group of blacks stood around in the damp night air. They had stayed throughout the election count, watching the procedures and now realizing that black campaigns were washing away. The men tried to analyze the defeats. No one could say for sure that the entire election had been stolen, but everyone knew that some races had been lost because whites had run the election. The rest of the defeats happened because plans had not been laid well enough. As one man said, "The white folks never hurt us as bad as our own people did today. The Uncle Toms did us in."

By 8 P.M. a large crowd was gathering at the Jackson NAACP headquarters near the Jackson State campus for the Evers "victory party." I arrived in a rather low frame of mind, having fielded calls all day long. By 3:30 my yellow legal pad was filled with notes on violations of the law, people thrown in jail, poll watchers threatened, and God knows how many phone calls I had never managed to return. I had filed three separate reports of incidents with the wire services, Mississippi Radio News, and Jackson stations. After the decision in Justice Robertson's chambers, Hyman, Brittain, and I had gone into the press room of the Capitol to use the telephone. I read the early election returns coming in on the AP wire. In my hand was a notepad with lists of numerous irregularities. Waller had a commanding early lead. Lester Hyman glanced at the wire sheet and asked, "Do they have reporters out in the counties where all that stuff is going on?" "Not exactly," I said. "They have stringers, but I sincerely doubt if they know what they're supposed to do. Obviously, they haven't been watching things very closely." Brittain said somberly, "We're getting the hell kicked out of us."

At the doorway of the NAACP Hall a crowd of reporters was unloading equipment from cars. One man approached me and asked, "What time will Evers get here?" "No earlier than nine," I said.

Then Bruce Payne, the news director for WOKJ, Jackson's AM soul station, stopped me, broadcasting live, and asked what I thought of the election. I had a terrible time putting together an answer but finally came out with, "Well, considering that the attorney general of Mississippi has conveniently managed to let white folks in counties all over the state do whatever they want, I would say that we're not doing well." Payne shook hands with me, nodded sympathetically, and I wandered into the hall where Dwight and the Evers 4 were playing "Watermelon Man." The Mayor was not due for an hour, but the networks had already set up their cameras at the base of the stage. Nearly four hundred blacks were dancing to Dwight's music. All of them were Jackson State or area high school students. Only in the last two weeks of the race had the number of volunteers in our office from the state campus totaled more than a dozen.

I found the anteroom off the side of the stage, which had been set aside for the press and media. Reporters were sitting on tables and chairs, smoking, drinking coffee, talking among themselves, and watching election returns on one of the two color TV's. By 8:15 it was clear that Bill Waller was beating the living hell out of us; he was running up more than a 3-to-1 margin. Whites had voted in a record turnout. Black candidates across the state were trailing in the key local races. From early reports it was clear that of the 285 running, less than 100 (at best) would win.

A reporter tugged at my coat. "Hey, hey man. When's he gonna come?"

"I don't know. An hour, ten minutes, something . . ." I looked at the reporter, who had a bored expression on his face. I pointed to a black man across the room. "That guy over there, that black guy with the bandage on his head, he was a local candidate. Whites beat him up. Why don't you go talk to him?"

The man nodded. "Yeah, that stuff happens here. You know, though, we gotta get Evers. He's the story . . ." Then he muttered something about civil rights being over and he went into the men's room.

I went over to a radio correspondent and told him about the black victim. "Yeah," he said, "I saw that guy. But you know—not that I don't believe it or anything, but we sort of have to have proof." I rattled off a list of irregularities that I had taken notes on. They had been documented by poll watchers' reports that were cascading into the Lawyers' Committee office from nearby counties. He tried to be agreeable, saying that he had to get Evers on tape to feed back to New York, adding that anything regarding irregularities would have to be read from New York off the wire service. Knowing that little of substance was on the wires, I turned and walked out of the press quarters.

I made my way through the crowd. Dwight was crooning a James Brown slow one and the black kids were dancing; the room echoed a soft, delicate moan. I entered the main hallway just as the correspondent for *Time* magazine arrived. He had an attractive girl on his arm; she was a local secretary. He smiled, shook hands, and asked me if Evers had come. "No," I said tersely. The girl peeked into the room. "They dancing?" "Yes," I said, and walked to the front door.

A TV set was propped against the wall directly behind the large glass doorway leading into the hall. Roughly twenty people were crowded around the television, checking the returns. Magnolia and Lois sat on chairs by the doorway, watching intently. The announcer was discussing how large Evers' defeat was and talking about the overwhelming losses on the county and state levels. "And in Coahoma County," he said, "veteran civil rights leader Aaron Henry is losing by five hundred votes, with but a few mostly white precincts left to be counted. In Evers' own Jefferson County only a handful of blacks are winning at this point. . . ."

"They're stealing it," I said. "The only way all those blacks could have lost in Jefferson was if the whites bought 'em off or they stole. It's happening like this all over."

Magnolia replied, "Jason, white folks been stealin' elections and buyin' off scared black folks *all* these years."

Charles Evers was still at his campaign headquarters watching the results come in; he was due at the last rally in a few minutes. In Fayette, meanwhile, Eddie Dunlop was still in trouble. Once the polls had closed in Jefferson County, a Klansman named John Berry, who had been harassing poll watchers all day long, ordered everyone out of the county courthouse. Mississippi election law says that votes are to be counted immediately and in public when the polls close. A Loyalist lawyer read the law to Berry, who nevertheless retreated to his car, after locking the courthouse, and went home to dinner. Two FBI agents witnessed this; when cornered by the lawyer, one of the agents said that the FBI was an investigative agency and was not bound to arrest law-breakers. The agent said that he would be filing a complaint. The white man's car drove into the draining evening and a black man from Mississippi standing in the group said, "That bastard's one of the worst Klukkers in town. If they're pulling this stuff in Evers' town, with the

FBI sitting here, what the hell are they doing all around?"

When The Mayor arrived at the NAACP hall it was clear that they were losing everywhere. The crowd at the hall had grown to five hundred. Reporters were grumbling because Evers was late. The TV sets broadcast the story in a dozen parts of the hall. Alec Berezin and Joe Huttie sat on the steps leading up to the NAACP offices on the second floor. Neither Huttie nor Berezin appeared glum. Huttie was making slow gestures with his hands; but he was too far away and I couldn't hear what he was describing. Barb Phillips calmly smoked a cigarette, listening to Huttie. Across the hall, Magnolia and Lois still watched the TV. Magnolia calmly drank coffee. A few feet from me, Ed Cole was listening to a black minister.

We had all, of course, expected defeat. Despite the rewarding successes of the campaign—the large rallies, the white volunteers, the reception on campuses, the white response to Evers' media exposure—defeat had been in the back of our minds all along. But we had not expected the losses in the counties in such immense numbers. By now I felt progressively bitter at the newsmen who impatiently waited for Evers and plainly were not interested in the counties. The most interested response I had elicited after rattling off the catalog of irregularities was, "Wait'll Evers says it, then it's news." I was bitter at the five hundred black kids who had not campaigned but who showed up for a free dance. I was bitter at the reactionary whites in hamlets, towns, and cities who after a cool summer of letting the press record the "New Mississippi" were now systematically destroying black candidates. The television announcer stoically discussed the black defeats. I remembered an old black man in dusty khakis who had stood on some nameless courthouse lawn now in the back regions of my mind, a man who had said, "It's God's will this day has come. I have hopes. Yes, I have hopes."

The black folks in the tottering churches dressed in their best clothes had fed me fried chicken and talked about how good life could be once the white folks learned a few things they needed to learn; they were drowning somewhere in the huge sea outside of the hall that night. I stood in a corner and bit my fist, remembering the black minister I had stayed with in Clarksdale, a gentle yet firm man who had said that he knew he could like most white folks he knew, only he knew that they didn't even want to like him back. And the old man who had come into the office, the Bible salesman who had told me the young ones needed Christ, *he* came back to haunt me, his eyes shimmering with excitement as he said, "We have to look to our ministers. They have to show us the way, God's way. . . . I came all the way in on the train from Brookhaven."

The infinite motorcades and church choirs and tender people—and then my stormy relationship with Magnolia; it was all Mississippi. Now suddenly everything was pitching back and forth with no central purpose or meaning. *What had it all come to?* What had happened to all of the black folks who had gone to the rallies, collected their quarters, sung their holy songs, gathered on the courthouse squares despite the jitters—where were they going? Like a massive mortal wave, the white farmers and plantation men and cheap cops and rural thugs had inundated the landscape, drowning the hopes and work of the campaign, reclaiming Mississippi for themselves.

I heard horns wailing outside and in another moment fifty people flooded through the doors: security men, volunteers, friends and patrons from up north, and, in the middle of them, flashing the peace sign, kissing and embracing his friends, was The Mayor, looking very much like the governor-elect of Mississippi, and not a man losing by 200,000 votes. Squeaky led him up a flight of stairs and two black policemen began screening people who wanted to follow him. They allowed in only his staff, family, and a special list of friends and contributors who had flown in just for the election.

When I reached the inside of the room my spirits lifted briefly. Everyone was talking, people were shaking hands with him, Mrs. Evers was smiling. Except for the staff, most people there had all along been prepared for the loss. Their only emotions were high spirits. Being with The Mayor to see him concede was indeed an historic moment for them.

After a few minutes I pulled The Mayor over to one side of the room. "Have you seen the reports? We're getting the hell kicked out of us."

He put an arm on my shoulder and said, "Jason, this is the first time, but it ain't the last. You cain't expect to win your first time out."

"Yeah, but what about the black candidates? I've got a whole notepad on poll watchers and everybody who got stomped. I hope you're not planning to go see Waller and congratulate him. These are all the people who voted for him. They might not have all been crooked, but there were sure enough of 'em who knew how to cheat."

His face stiffened. "Yeah, I know all that. The Klukkers and all are gonna keep doin' that, but I got somethin' about concedin'—I can't let him win without personally congratulatin' him. A man beats me three-to-one cain't no one say he cheated. Bill beat me fair and square. I'm gonna go over to the Heidelberg after I speak downstairs. I got to congratulate him."

Then the crowd went downstairs, and I followed everyone into the hall. Dwight's band began playing "Grazing in the Grass," the cameras whirred, the lights shone bright like fireballs, a flank of reporters backed through the crowd of young blacks who were reaching out to soul-shake, to give a pat on the back, to yell, "Right on!" Simmons stood at the base of the stage with Tonny Algood and some pulpwood haulers. Fred Walters, grinning his toothy grin, waved to me from across the crowd.

The Mayor and his wife stood on the stage; he had an enormous smile. He began clapping his hands, tapping feet in time with the music. The crowd was cheering through the roof. Cameras and reporters were five deep, crowded around the base of the stage. The Mayor stopped clapping momentarily. He turned to his wife, and then to Ed Cole, who was now next to him. Then he started calling names. "Where's Elix? My advance man, Elix: where is he? Huttie? Joe Huttie, where's that rascal at? Lois? Magnolia, honey? Where's Jason? I cain't go nowhere without my P.R. man!" We had all flocked to the base of the stage to be close to him when he spoke. When he began calling us, we climbed the stairs. I stood between Alec and Huttie, all of us leaning on one another for balance. The lights were hot in our faces.

Ed Cole stepped in front of The Mayor and held the microphone. "Now, my candidate, your candidate, everybody's candidate, and really our governor! The only man who said all the time he was gonna represent all the people, Charles—" The crowd was explosive. When the applause subsided, The Mayor spoke in a remarkably low voice. He spoke with a tenderness I had rarely heard in him, yet he could be heard in the rear of the hall.

"Thank you very much. . . . Well, you know how them rascals are. They got together on us again. One thing about it—we pulled all the ole skunks out o' the pond. Ole John Bell and all them, they got worried! . . . Big Jim came down and did his little thing. . . . But lemme tell you somethin', my supporters. All of us have done more to change them *meannn* white folks than anything else that ever happened in the past. We haven't lost, we've won."

"Right on! Soul power!"

"Because, you see our job is to make all this possible. . . ." His voice was still gentle. He raised it only slightly for emphasis. There was an almost spiritual ring to his words, strong but compassionate, as though he was relating a parable. "We tricked 'em all down the line. Had 'em scared, spendin' money, doin' their tricks. They wouldn' even give us *half* a chance! They put us in jail, called us dirty names."

The crowd applauded loudly, sensing his wrath, cheering his composure. "But that's all right, white folks, you gonna beat us every time. But we're gonna keep on comin'. This is only the beginnin' . . . Because you take young men like these"—he swept his arm toward us, and then gestured back at the crowd—"young men like these here, black and white. Young women that we've had, black and white— Mississippians, and from across this country, and pull 'em together, and go out and challenge a system that's been corrupt and destructive for nine hundred years, we've *won*! So don't feel bad. . . . We may be beaten, but we ain't defeated!"

The crowd broke into a prolonged cheer, and The Mayor spotted the pulpwood haulers in the crowd. "Where my pu'pwood gang? Come on up, pu'pwood fellas!" Fred Walters gave a yell, and the woodcutters rumbled up onto the stage, the crowd yelling and clapping.

The Mayor was beaming, talking in his soft voice. "So you see, this was a victory. We ran a campaign for the folks. We went to every town we could go to in every county. And we represented *all* the people in this state. We showed no animosity to no one. . . . But today, they beat us in more'n one way. They took it from us in a lotta cases. . . .

"But the most important thing—there musta been over 600,000 Mississippians who went to the polls today, somethin' that never happened before. Because we cared. Whether they voted for me or against me, that's all right. But the one thing that bothers me most, and I don't mind tellin' you, was I had hoped that white Mississippi wouldn' vote against me because I was black, but vote for me because I was the best man. But they didn' do that. . . . But that's all right, white brothers, I'm goin' down to Bill Waller's office right now. I'm goin' right down to where Bill is . . . to prove that we're bigger than they are . . . and say, 'That's all right, Bill, you beat us, but didn't defeat us!' "

"Right on, brother!"

He swept his arm over the pulpwood haulers, then staff. "They cain't stand to see a coalition like this—poor white folks, poor black folks, young white folks, young black folks! And then jus' folks! All gettin' together. They don't want that. But we got somethin' now *ain't* nothin' gonna put out!"

The crowd roared. Dwight blasted three notes on the organ. The Mayor continued, his voice now more forceful. "We're determined to win this state to make it a decent place for all our folks. So, whether Charles Evers goes into the Governor's Mansion or not is not important. What is important is that we are now begun to move ahead as Mississippians. That we are now begun to realize that racists, those who run racist campaigns, are dead and buried once and for all!"

"That's right! Right on!"

An' lemme say this on behalf of my opponent—and I say this without reservations—Bill ran one of the cleanest races, without black folks naturally, of any white gubernatorial candidate that I ever heard of. So let's give the devil his doin'. I think both of us tried to change the attitude of Mississippi. We both tried to raise the standard. But I want all you to know—this ain't the first time I been beaten an' come back!"

The crowd broke into long applause, and then The Mayor concluded, "An' all we got to say here tonight is . . . to all of you who voted for me, thank you so much. To all of you voted against me, thank you so much. To all of you who didn' vote, God help your souls!"

After a long cheer, Evers was grinning. "Is Bill Waller still at his headquarters? Where are they, at the Heidelberg? Are they dancin' down there? Drinkin' champagne? I'm goin' to join them! We're gonna show we're good losers. An' when we win, they better do the same! So, let's keep our chest out, and our chins up, and let's make Mississippi the greatest state in the nation. Thank you so much!"

Squeaky and Woody led him through the crowd. We piled into waiting cars; the press followed behind with great commotion, racing to their own vehicles. We arrived at the Heidelberg, where a drunk Waller supporter met Evers at the door to say the governor-elect had gone to a TV station for an interview. When we arrived at the studio, the press had caught up with us. Evers and his security men entered the lobby of the TV studio; the reporters lugged their equipment in and crowded close behind. A station executive appeared and shook hands with The Mayor. "Bill Waller is being interviewed now, Mr. Evers," he said. "We have a side studio in here. Would you mind waiting until he's off We'll get you on as soon as the commercial goes off after Waller."

The Mayor followed the man down a narrow hall; the reporters, to the shock of the station executive, followed The Mayor. The Mayor, security men, Ed Cole, and the dozen carloads of reporters sat on chairs, tables, and the carpet of the small studio. I found a telephone and called John Brittain at the Lawyers' Committee. "Can you get over here quick? The press is all in one place and The Mayor's going to be interviewed as soon as Waller goes off. If you can make it over in ten minutes, I think we can get a late press conference to air all the poll watchers' reports." He said he was on his way over.

When I returned to the studio, Waller and his wife were on the TV monitor. An announcer was saying, "Governor, there've been some charges of troubles in the counties with Evers poll watchers. What do you feel about those charges?"

Waller drawled, "That's not true. Ah've checked with Attorney General Summer and the only trouble was in Port Gibson. And I don't mind sayin' it, it was started by the outsiders who came in to Mississippi just for this election. Ah think this was a fair election and the overwhelming amount of black votes ah received are indicative of the new attitude in Mississippi. Mah administration will be free of old emotionalisms and one of the first thaings ah intend to do is get Mississippi Democrats back into the national party."

Mrs. Waller told the announcer she appreciated all the prayers of the people throughout Mississippi, and then the announcer thanked the new governor-elect and his wife, saying that the defeated candidate would be on the air shortly. A commercial came on and The Mayor walked out of the small studio. Reporters followed close behind him. But in the minute it took Evers to get from the smaller studio to the main one, Waller's aides had hustled him out of the back door, directly behind the studio set. "Where'd he go?" Evers yelled.

A technician pointed to a small door and The Mayor bolted ahead, leaving the studio crew speechless; the reporters stormed along behind, cameras high and pencils ready. A studio producer yelled to one of his cameramen, "Follow him! We're on the air in ten seconds!" The man picked up his camera and gave chase.

Evers finally caught Waller as he was getting into a limousine. Waller's aides were trying to get him away before The Mayor arrived. Waller saw him and told the driver to wait. Evers approached; the press followed in close pursuit. Waller rolled down the window. The Mayor walked slowly to the car, his arms extended slightly, and gave Waller a firm handshake. "Hey, Charlie!" Waller said. "Whatcha say?" The Mayor leaned over and said a few words to him, waved at his wife, and turned around. The car pulled out in a hurry. The Mayor was engulfed by reporters as he began walking back to the studio for the interview. One journalist was scribbling on his note pad. The Mayor looked at him and grinned. "Ole Bill, he's been running from me all through the election."

The interview was anticlimactic. The Mayor publicly congratulated Waller on running a clean race, and he expressed his distress over the reports of irregularities in the counties. Then the announcer asked him about the campaign. "Do you think it was a failure?"

"No, I wouldn't say it was a failure. In more ways than one, we won. We changed a lotta things. We traveled all over this state, showin' and provin' that the ole days are dead. You won't see no more racist campaigns. We ended all that. Black folks may have got beat this time, but we gonna keep on comin'."

"What will you do now that you've lost, Mr. Evers?"

His head perked up and he looked at the man with a surprised expression. "I'm still The Mayor! I got my work down in Fayette to do. I got my farm down there, y'know. I still got my chickens, cows, my horses. . . ."

At that point a man grabbed me by the arm and said I had a phone call. As I passed into the hall, John Brittain and Frank Parker of the Lawyers' Committee were entering the studio. I pointed to the room where Evers was speaking, then followed the man and picked up the phone. It was Joe Huttie, still at the NAACP headquarters. "There's been some trouble in Scott County," he said. "Two Georgetown kids are inside a barn. They've been watching vote counts, and now they're afraid to leave. We can't get through to any of our Scott County contacts. There's a mob of whites standing around outside, waiting for them to come out. I don't know how much of this is a rumor, but we've received two reports saying the whites have ropes thrown over a tree."

"Oh my God."

"As soon as The Mayor gets off the air, get him to call the FBI."

I raced back into the studio and I caught Ed just as the cameras went off. He delivered the message to The Mayor, who was just taking the microphone from around his neck. Ed whispered in his ear and Evers looked at him incredulously before he bolted out of the studio with the press right behind him. A station executive led us into his private office. The reporters gathered around the door; a secretary politely asked them to move into the lobby. Grumbling, the troops moved. The Mayor picked up the phone and began dialing black leaders in Scott County as Ed stood at his side, feeding him numbers from a notebook. I stepped into the lobby to try to pacify the reporters.

"He'll be out in a few minutes. He's still got a statement to make regarding the irregularities."

"What's the call about?"

"I can't say. It's a report we hope is not true." I stepped back into the office. The Mayor was still dialing.

The next twenty minutes were excruciating. The Mayor placed calls to black leaders in Scott, but none were home. He placed a call to the sheriff in Scott, but could not reach him. Finally he got through to one of the top brass of the Mississippi division of the FBI.

"Me and my staff are worried sick. We cain't have this happen. These kids came down from Wash'ton to be poll watchers and now the Klukkers have surrounded that house. You got to get some men over there."

He listened intently and then his face creased into a huge black frown. He shouted into the phone, "Listen! I don't give a damn *what* FBI policy is! You can observe and take notes all you want. But if I don't hear about those kids gettin' out safe in ten minutes, I'm goin' down there myself, *with* my bodyguards, *in* my campaign cars! I got forty reporters from all over creation sittin' right out here in the lobby who're gonna go with me. An' they'll tell the whole world how y'all never saved those kids after you were tipped off. Now that'll make one damn fool outa J. Edgar Hoover!"

The Mayor slammed the phone down. The station executive touched him lightly on the shoulder. "Excuse me, you have another call on the second line."

Exasperated, he picked it up and answered with a barely audible "Hello." Then his face perked up and he started grinning. "Ohhh, hello, Senator Humphrey! Yeah, we got beat, they sure beat us this time." He looked at the rug, rubbing his toe gently on the carpet, listening and smiling. "Oh, no, I don't feel too bad. Y'know how it is, they got all the ole ducks outa the pond, pulled out a lotta dead white folks to vote this morning . . . ha-ha."

He listened again, and responded, "No-no, we're not defeated. We ain't quittin'. We're stickin' in there. . . . All right, thank you very much, Senator."

When the Humphrey call ended, everyone got anxious again, wondering about the two Georgetown kids in the barn. He put through three more calls, and finally he reached a minister in Scott County. They talked for about five minutes and then, with a look of great relief, he placed the phone gently in its cradle. "The kids are okay. The Rev'nd finally tracked down the sheriff and told him the FBI was gonna come if they didn't get them out."

There was a large sigh of relief. Then I stood up. "The reporters are still outside," I said. "Frank and John are here. Let's get back into the studio and spell out what happened in the counties."

The entourage moved back into the studio and by now it was past midnight. Frank Parker and John Brittain sat next to The Mayor. They enumerated all the beatings, the charges of vote frauds, the irregularities, the poll watchers thrown in jail. Finally a reporter asked Evers if the irregularities "made much difference . . . seeing as how you lost by so much."

"It don't make no difference to my election," The Mayor replied, "but we had three hundred candidates on the local level and these lawyers jus' tole you they had all those tricks and that sho' 'nuf can make a difference in a local election!"

A Mississippi TV reporter asked, "Much of the trouble seems to have stemmed from the outsiders who were brought in to work at the polls. Why *were* the outsiders brought in?"

Evers pointed a finger at him. "I'll tell you why—'cause we cain't *get* fair elections in Mississippi," he said. "What we really need are federal troops! I bite no bones about this —the way whites run the elections, we need help! If Sonny Montgomery, the famous Miss'ssippi congressman, can go flyin' off to Vietnam to see about fair elections, then we ought to go flyin' federal troops down here to make sure we get 'em fair in Mississippi!"

Sometime after two in the morning, I left the campaign office on Mill Street. Ramberg, who had not left the office even for the concession speech, was still on the phone talking with poll watchers and people in the field. I climbed into bed and tried not to think about anything. The last thing on my mind was a radio announcement saying Waller had 480,000 votes, Evers about 150,000. By tomorrow morning Waller would have over half a million votes. By the next afternoon, nearly 600,000.

When I awoke on November 3 it was midmorning. I had what amounted to a dreadful hangover.

CHAPTER

14

The final results of the campaign showed that Waller had defeated Evers by a whopping 424,000 votes: 601,222 (77 percent) to 172,762 (22 percent). Brady got 6,653 (1 percent).

In the other statewide races, Freddie Washington lost to Secretary of State Heber Ladner, 550,343 to 100,816. C. J. Duckworth lost to Superintendent of Education Dr. Garvin Johnston, 546,405 to 128,732.

Of the nearly three hundred candidates who ran for local and county offices on the Loyalist slate, fifty-one were successful. Although far short of our anticipated results, the fifty-one represented a more than 50 percent increase from the number of blacks elected in 1967. Blacks held office in sixteen counties, and in five of the counties the elected officials were the first blacks to hold office in the twentieth century. Five blacks were elected to county-wide posts, and Bob Clark was returned to the Legislature. For the next four years he would be the only Negro in the Mississippi House of Representatives. Forty-five blacks were elected at the beat level, most of them as justices of the peace or as constables. Perhaps the most important elected officials, Representative Clark notwithstanding, were the seven men elected to the crucial supervisors' posts. They would control their own budgets, hire their own employees, and sit in the policy-making convocations of the county boards of supervisors.

The two counties with the highest number of black elected officials were Evers' Jefferson County, with seven, including two supervisors, and adjacent Claiborne County, with nine.

We all knew that blacks had been cheated across the board, but it was soon apparent that this was not the only reason for the defeats. There is no way of telling how many black voters stayed away from the polls because of rumors about the intimidations, beatings, and irregularities. The Justice Department nevertheless concluded that the election was for the most part fair, and Mississippi Attorney General Summer said on television after the results had been counted that "this was the fairest election in Mississippi's history." Perhaps the most incisive statement regarding the election and the irregularities was made by the Delta Ministry, the civil rights steering organization in Jackson. In a report discussing results in key black counties, the sworn affidavits of poll watchers, and the firsthand accounts of black candidates through in-depth interviews, the DM report concluded:

> We do not intend to belabor the election irregularity issue but to merely point out some of the types of cheating that occurred. There were instances of harassment of voters by election officials and by other local whites. There were acts of economic intimidation. There were instances of harrassing [sic] pollwatchers. There were documented several ways that election managers cheated in their "assisting" of illiter-

ate voters. There were improper registration violations. There were other improper procedures with absentee ballots and with assisting incapacitated persons. These occured [*sic*] particularly where the white community was facing what they believed to be a severe challenge to their rule.

Our concern here is the place where such irregularities might have made a difference in the actual election and thereby affected the power relationships. Madison County is the most significant example of that situation. The irregularities in the handling of the ballots constituted approximately 10% of the total vote. Suits have been filed in this case. Should they be successful, Evers will have carried the county, at least one county-wide Black will be elected, and two supervisors will win.

If we use that 10% margin as the "optimum cheating ratio" then irregularities (if they occured [*sic*] and are properly documented) could have made a difference in the following races:

Holmes—five County-wide.

Claiborne—two County-wide.

Coahoma—a Senator and Representative.

Tunica—One County-wide and one Supervisor.

Wilkinson—One County-wide.

At the time of this writing, only the Madison situation is being pressed legally. In Holmes and Claiborne there are not sufficient documentation of the facts to warrant such a suit. It is unknown whether they do in the other three situations. Were the facts clear in all remaining situations and were successful suits pressed, Blacks could come out victors in *eight* new races for important positions. (Italics added)

The press and media coverage of the white backlash was the most depressing part of it. The attitude was typified by the reporter who said that Evers was the story, and then grumbled that "civil rights is over," or the *Time* correspondent who rated the election low enough to bring a date to the concession speech rally, and altogether miss the 1 A.M. press conference. Indeed, all the reporters both from Mississippi and from out of state had one angle to their coverage: the change in the tone of the politics. Of course it was true that the campaign had testified to a changing South. Evers' reception by white Mississippians, the absence of violence throughout the campaigns, and incidents like the standing ovation in the Ole Miss Chapel were new and magnificent milestones. These were elements of the campaign, but not of the election. The election disturbances were either ignored altogether in press and media reports, or they were significantly downplayed. There were no reporters in the counties to cover the election process in the most racist state in the nation. The Washington *Star* headline of the UPI story from Jackson is typical of the November 3 reportage: "Waller Routs Evers, Both Hail Progress." The article quotes Evers' and Waller's speeches, but it does not do Evers justice. It ignores everything he said about the beatings, intimidations, and false charges on which poll watchers were jailed:

> Evers, the mayor of Fayette, sounded an optimistic note.
>
> "Whites and blacks are going to look at each other differently now, as citizens," Evers said. "I've proved that a black man can run for office in Mississippi without getting shot, without getting killed."
>
> Evers praised the "clean campaign" of Waller, who first gained national attention in 1964 with his vigorous, but unsuccessful prosecution of a white man for

the sniper slaying of NAACP leader Medgar Evers, Charles' brother.

Waller told a cheering crowd of 650 supporters here last night that the election marked a "historical transition in Mississippi" in that the campaign was "void of any emotionalism or any negative political persuasion."

Press, TV, and radio reports presented Evers and Waller as sympathetic opponents, and Waller emerged as a hero, the man who brought the New South to Mississippi. This was hardly the case, for Waller had never really addressed himself to problems of race. Indeed, he never even mentioned race, and said that his administration would be for *all* Mississippians. The candidates and the issues were real, of course, but the press and media chose to turn Waller and Evers into the symbols in the story of the Mississippi elections. A CBS correspondent, for example, filed a film story including the 1 A.M. press conference and Evers' statements. The New York editors, however, opted for Cronkite's reading a script giving only the basic details of the story: Evers beaten by the moderate Waller, blacks fail to vote. *Time*, in analyzing the defeat, wrote: "The massive setback to black hopes resulted from (1) huge turnouts of white voters, and (2) an apparently large number of black voters who supported white candidates." Of the documented violence that had a marked effect on black voters, *Time* gave this one terse mention: "There were scattered reports of intimidation, harassment and other irregularities during the vote count."

Perhaps the most disappointing treatment of the irregularities came in the normally reliable *New York Times*. Tom Johnson, the award-winning black reporter highly regarded for his reportorial savvy, wrote a story about the election violations the day after the election—only to have it stashed away in the end of the first section.

The best piece of election reporting I read was by Bartle Bull, President of *The Village Voice*, who went to Mississippi as a volunteer in Fayette and became incensed by the irregularities he observed there. He wrote a penetrating account of what he saw.

There is no way of telling how many votes were stolen from Evers or other black candidates. An even more alarming result of the violations was the attitude the Justice Department held toward the election; that it was a fair one. In my opinion, that is simply false. While some poll watchers' reports were not properly written, many more reports vividly described what happened. Evers' comment about Mississippi Congressman Montgomery going to Vietnam to inspect "fair" elections precisely states the problem that remains in Mississippi: despite blatant white cheating, the federal government refuses to ensure that fair elections are held. The federal observers, most of whom were white Southerners or even Mississippians, were soul mates with the white election officials, and they had no power other than to observe and file a report. In many cases they did not even do that. The problems Jim Macera discussed in the Flora situation are disgraceful: a southern observer, admittedly unfamiliar with Mississippi election laws, was more interested in making small talk with whites like himself who happened to live in Mississippi. The Justice Department lawyers were in Mississippi not to enforce the law but to observe the process. The FBI's presence was all but irrelevant, as the bureau is mainly a fact-finding agency; further, as everyone in Mississippi knows—especially veterans of the civil rights movement—the FBI always checks in with the local law enforcement officials, white men, in order to touch base. The election may have been the fairest in Mississippi's history, but it was still crooked. In 1975, unless the Justice Department undergoes a significant change in philosophy, the election in Mississippi will be even less encumbered with observers and federal officials for the elections. One might ask why federal troops should not be sent in to see that the elections are held fairly.

The Delta Ministry properly deduced that intimidations were not the major cause of the defeat. Indeed, in many cases, as the press correctly reported, blacks defeated themselves. From an organizational standpoint, the counties—having no firm experience in political campaigns and elections—were ill-prepared. As Reverend Harry Bowie of McComb observed, "We have a civil rights hangover . . . we can't depend on leaflets and mass meetings to get out the vote. We need a strong, well-balanced organization to make sure the vote gets out . . . and that it votes black."

It was indeed true that many blacks crossed over and voted for whites. The Delta Ministry analysis was that Evers had 12,000 white votes, while Waller had 10,000 black votes. Evers, however, led the county slate in votes received in all but five instances. In other words, local black candidates lagged behind Evers in black votes in their own counties. Moreover, it is estimated that 20,000 blacks who voted mismarked their ballots, thus making them null and void.

The reasons for these failures stem from historical and cultural factors. The 1971 election was the first for many black voters. The very process of marking the ballot was difficult, since voting—the fear factor notwithstanding—was something many blacks had no experience in. The illiterates were at an added disadvantage. Many blacks' actual perceptions of the ballot and machine prior to the election were vague at best. In a Voter Education Project survey, a social worker spent six weeks in various counties before the election, using a series of slides and tapes explaining the process of voting and how actually to cast a ballot. After meeting with groups in over ninety communities, she said that the participants were deeply confused and baffled about the act of voting. "It was apparent from the presentations," she wrote, "that very little information had ever been made available or accessible to voters on the voting process."

Of representative Clark County she observed:

Of the two ballot boxes for two precincts in Lexington (each containing approximately 400 ballots) there were at least 30 mismarked ballots in each box. These mismarked ballots appeared to be voted by Blacks because of the candidates marked. In Lexington the turnout was approximately 50% Black for these two boxes. Therefore, it appears that 30 out of 200 Blacks voting at each of these boxes did not know how to mark the ballots properly, making the percentage 15%.

In Holmes County, the fact that some voters did not know how to vote properly accounted for the loss of some of the offices for Black candidates.

Moreover, black voters often didn't vote the entire slate. Father Luke Miscel of Madison County explained this: "Our people turned out like never before. But we didn't anticipate the problems with the ballots. We ran a slate of thirty candidates, and I don't think more than half of our voters made a decision on all the offices in question. The drop-off was usually from governor to sheriff and then down to a supervisor and a local candidate, like constable or J.P. They'd skip all the rest." This problem appeared in other counties in Mississippi. Blacks had little trouble voting for Evers. His name was recognizable and they had him on their minds when they entered the booth. But after voting for him, black voters frequently skipped down to vote for offices with some pertinence to their own interests, omitting other key races. Ignorance, confusion, fear, misconceptions as to what the ballot would look like, impatience over the length of the ballot—these were definite factors accounting for black losses. As Father Luke soberly added, "Next time if we can get the same turnout but with only one third as many candidates, we can concentrate on electing a small but powerful number of black elected officials in Madison County."

There were also grave political mistakes made by the black candidates themselves. Reverend Bowie's reference to the "civil rights hangover" is a case in point. Numbers of black candidates went to Evers' rallies where the turnouts were the largest ever. The Mayor also brought a dynamism and legitimacy to the campaigns. But black candidates themselves apparently did not politick hard enough. It is difficult to be critical on this point. There was no more honest statement about the situation, however, than that of Representative Clark. Repeating his story about giving the pig to a man who was going to oppose him, the Holmes County legislator added, "What black folks got to learn is that to win, you gotta go out and meet everybody, campaign everyday. From May to November I saw every one of my constituents *at least* once a month. Went by their farms, called 'em on the phone, stayed behind after church. Look at me—I worked like that for six months, and I barely squeaked back in. You can't speak at a rally in summer and then in fall and expect to win. . . . You got to do more than that—go after it!"

Evers' own vote, when compared with the defeated candidates' votes in black counties, illustrates one of the most complex problems. At each rally he tried to dispel deep-seated feelings blacks had about their own peers, that they were not as qualified as the white incumbents. The Mayor's fears that blacks would consider the white man from a *political* perspective and the black man from a *personal* perspec-

tive proved true. A supervisor who gave patronage or repaired roads in the black community prior to the election
for the first time ever—even if he was a racist who made
money from lucrative corrupt dealings—beat a black man
who might not have been unanimously supported by blacks
because he missed church too much. One voter registration
worker even concluded that in some instances blacks voted
for whites although they knew they were racists. If the voters held certain reservations about the personal aspects of
the racist's black opponent, they would rather not vote for
the black man *for fear he would embarrass the black community*! Evers' high vote in comparison with black candidates' disappointing results materialized because he became
a legitimate politician through statewide media exposure—
unlike local blacks who were everyday neighbors with those
vying for local offices.

The effect of white politicians in their campaigning before black folks was equally imposing. Most blacks had
never been approached by a white man asking for a vote.
When a white man stood in front of a black church handing
out his cards, black folks felt a surge of pride. It was a break
with tradition, a subtle symbol. The white man was asking
the black man for something and this had a social importance; it was a step up. An additional problem was the attitude of over 95 percent of the some 615,000 whites who
voted—and who voted for whites right down the line. As
the sheriff of Port Gibson said after the election, "I didn'
even bother campaignin' before the whites. I knew they'd
vote for me. I only campaigned before the coloreds. . . . I
had to get some o' their votes to win. I did." Whites voted
most consistently for key offices of sheriff and supervisor;
blacks voted least consistently for them.

In numerous counties the selection process by which
black candidates were chosen to run on the Loyalist slate
was ill-conceived. A mass meeting was held and different

people announced their intentions, filed their papers, and became candidates—regardless of their standing in the community or their ability to fill the political office in question. In conversations after the election with blacks in counties up and down the Mississippi River, I came away with the unanimous conclusion that black candidates should be more carefully screened for the next election. As one successful supervisor put it, "If blacks are gonna win we gotta run people that are popular, men and women folks respect. You run a weak candidate he'll run a weak race. One o' the things that goes with politics is internal fightin'—but we gotta get that outa the way before we put our folks up, not at the polls after they're there. That's the way white folks do it. That's the way we gotta do it."

Factionalism was also a crucial deterrent to black victories at the polls. Evers' own Jefferson County was badly divided on election day. The Evers forces were opposed by whites who had secured the support of Uncle Toms. While bribery was an elemental factor, some blacks were nevertheless not satisfied with the choice of certain candidates on the Evers slate, and so they did not vote for them. Claiborne County was also split. For example, the incumbent chancery clerk, a black woman, had clearly alienated segments of black voters before the election. The Port Gibson sheriff later remarked, "I didn' understand some o' the choices the black folks themselves made. They went and put up people that members o' their own race didn' like. You can't expect to win if you got candidates your own folks don't see eye-to-eye with."

Perhaps the worst problem was the election procedure itself. Though election commissioners were elected, due to a change in the law in 1968, nearly all were white. Blacks were nominally included in administrative election roles; however, most were clerks or had inconsequential roles in which they were unable to view the actual voting. Many black electioneers were uninformed about the laws—or, if informed, found great difficulties with white election managers. The circuit clerk, who handles all records of voter registrants in the county, had run the elections in the past. In many counties, despite the fact the Election Commission was charged with checking the duties of the circuit clerk and running the election, the circuit clerk nevertheless was in charge and did not always act scrupulously. The Election Commission is supposed to hear appeals of those denied registration and to eliminate the names of dead citizens from the books. But many Election Commissions did not check the circuit clerk's records before election day.

A further complication was that of racist party affiliation. The Regular Democrats of Mississippi did not recognize the Loyalists as Democrats, but rather as "independents." Whites did not want to recognize the Loyalists as an official party. This caused much consternation regarding the legality of the poll watchers and whether white officials felt the poll watchers could challenge votes or judgments of the election commissioners.

Many black election appointees were unable to enforce a correct by-the-rules election. The crucial issues were the election process, election laws, and the correct procedures election managers should follow; the whites ran the elections in much the same fashion as they'd done over the years. And it must be conceded that many whites were likewise ignorant of the stipulations under the new law. They simply didn't know that this election was not going to be run "like we've always run them." Some whites actually thought they were running the election legally since the election commissioners who had secured their services had not informed them about changes in the rules.

The greatest problem whites faced in the actual election was posed by the poll watchers, most of whom were from out of state and white Mississippi election officials felt that an "outsider" bused in just for the election had no right challenging the process that had always been used.

While poll watchers are a necessity in the battle to win fair elections for blacks in Mississippi for the future, it is clear that blacks must do more than band together cohesively in their political organizations. Ultimately they must also shoulder the burden of their poll watchers. There is little reason to suspect that in 1975 white officials will treat outsiders who come into the state for five days at election-time any differently than they did in 1971. The dilemma, of course, is that blacks are still frightened at the very thought of doing it themselves and most are still economically beholden to whites. The transition will be painful.

The morning after the election the campaign office was stripped of its vitality. Posters, ribbons, banners, fliers, and envelopes were strewn about the floor; the walls were naked and white. Volunteers collected small fliers or posters for The Mayor to autograph as keepsakes. Suitcases were lined against the wall on one side of the doorway. People had planes to catch, long car journeys or bus trips to begin. One by one, volunteers filed in and out of The Mayor's office. Some had been with us six months, working in various counties—others had been with us only five days. People chatted, exchanged addresses and phone numbers, hugged and kissed, and said goodbyes. A few reporters milled around the front to record impressions of the aftermath. Outside, a Jackson cop wearing a black uniform methodically wrote out tickets and placed them on the cars parked in front of the office; no tickets had been given during the campaign.

As the volunteers trickled out of the office and the chill November afternoon grew colder, I started cleaning out my desk. Magnolia was talking on the telephone at the next desk, politely explaining to someone that The Mayor was making no more appointments, that he was leaving for Fayette in a few minutes. Joe Huttie, surveying the chaos of a filing cabinet in which he had kept contracts with the TV stations, puffed patiently on his pipe. I wondered what was going through his head: he had quit a good job in Minnesota to work in Mississippi for peanuts. Although his media program had been good, some blacks were already saying that Evers had spent too much money on TV, had gone on an ego trip, and that the overexposure had scared the living hell out of the whites so that they voted for the opposition in record numbers. Ramberg, the forelock of auburn hair drooping over his forehead, sat on his desk talking with a New York lawyer preparing to fly back. Ed Cole, looking relieved not to be stuck in his office or cradling a telephone, was playing with his three-year-old son Peter off in a corner of the room. Alec Berezin sat next to Ed, a faint smile on his face. Alec had no more schedules to map out, no more trips into densely wooded hamlets to advance. The two men said nothing; they tranquilly watched Peter. But I was disturbed. It was weeks before my head cleared, and only then, sitting alone at three in the morning in a farmhouse in Poplarville, I was able to agree with Harry Bowie's pragmatic assessment: "We got in fifty-one candidates, more than twice what we had before. We had a record turnout, though. Sure we lost, but we made a powerful first step. Four years from now we'll win more. We learned a lot."

Now sitting at my desk, I watched Barb Phillips, who had worked so diligently organizing campuses and counties and was Xeroxing a list of home phone numbers of the staff. She finished the work and began to hand them out. "Here," she said as she gave one to me, propping her bifocals back on her nose and grinning. "We have to keep in touch, you know. All of us."

The last volunteer left The Mayor's office and I tore a

poster off the wall and went in to see him. He started laughing when I handed him the poster. "All we been through and all you want's an autograph? Lawd, lawd, Jason. I got the phone company sayin' I owe 'em three thousand and I got a meetin' in Fayette tonight, I got everything comin' down at me at once." He signed the poster, slid it across the table to me, and sat back in his chair. The picture of his brother was directly behind him.

I looked at him and for the first time since the night we met over fried chicken I realized I had nothing to say. I couldn't think of a word. He looked at the ceiling briefly and the silence between us was strange. Finally he chuckled. "Well, you got a lotta stories to tell all your folks down in Loosiana. You sho' was green when you started, but you came in flyin' with rest of us." His eyes darted to a corner of the desk where a mosquito audaciously whizzed about a pile of papers. He took a book and slammed it onto the table, blotting the mosquito into the back cover. With the end of a pencil he carefully removed the mosquito and deposited it into the wastecan. He put the book down and looked at me. Still, neither of us spoke. And so I knew it was time to say goodbye.

I stood up and offered my hand. His huge forearm shot forward and we clasped palms. He held on, looking me in the eye. I saw my face in his pupils. For some bizarre reason I was grinning like a fox. His eyelids fluttered and he whispered, "Keep in touch now, hear?"

"Oh yeah, I'll be in touch."

He came out of his office about ten minutes later, Squeaky hurrying in front of him. Only a few of us were still around, cleaning out desks and talking. He had already said goodbye to each of us, and when he emerged from the back his gaze caught a large table in one corner of the room. "That table—that table belongs to the NAACP. We gotta get it back over there, tomorrow." He walked to the door.

"Squeaky, make sure we get that table back tomorrow." He looked at the front desk. "The phone . . . lawd, lawd. The phone company wants to take me for everything I got. . . ." He was reaching into his pocket when he finally made it to the car and none of us could hear what he was saying as Squeaky shut the door and then they drove off.

The next morning I piled most of what I owned in the world into my battered Volkswagen and drove south on Interstate 55 toward Louisiana. I thought about the people I had worked with and what they were planning to do. Ed, Joe Huttie, and Barb Phillips would remain in Jackson to conduct a study on black factionalism. Ramberg had passed the Mississippi bar and was joining the Hinds County Legal Services Committee. Alec was returning to Cleveland to continue law school. Sister JoAnn was going to Fayette to work in the Town Hall; Sister Margaret was going to Grand Coteau, Louisiana, to teach. Woody was returning to New York and his duties with the police department. Martin Lias was going to work in Fayette, and Squeaky was returning to Jackson State. I was going to my parents' farm in Poplarville to write. And The Mayor was going to Fayette.

The metal signs that had now become familiar marks in my memories floated past as the car spun along the highway. Terry, Raymond, Hazelhurst, McComb—each sign evoked the memory of some gentle black person I had known when we visited there. For months after the election, any Mississippi license tags I saw made me remember black folks in that county—the men and women in the churches, on the courthouse lawns, the uplifted faces, the eyes that glowed when the sad sweet songs hummed in murky Mississippi nights.

Suddenly, like lightning, a huge 1971 Cadillac roared

past. A well-dressed white man and his plump wife silently stared at the road. The license tag read "Coahoma County, Mississippi." Mentally I added, "Home of Aaron Henry."

And then, with uncontrollable passion, I began to weep.

Epilogue

The world breaks everyone and after many are strong at the broken places.

—Hemingway, *A Farewell to Arms*

I

Shortly after the election the Masonite plant in Laurel announced an increase in wages for the pulpwood haulers. The price of a unit of wood rose from $20 per 7,100 pounds to $23 per 7,100. Even more important was the new designation for the price of a cord, the standard demanded by the Gulf Coast Pulpwood Association. The cord was set at 5,400 pounds and the price at $18. The following telegram was sent to the Laurel woodcutters from a man who had kept a continued interest in their struggle.

November 23, 1971
James Simmons,
President, Gulf Coast Pulpwood Association
Box 74, Laurel, Mississippi

Congratulations on your great victory. I understand the woodyards of Laurel and the Masonite Corporation have come to terms and that these terms amount to about $45 a week per man. You and your 6,000 members of the Gulf Coast Pulpwood Association deserve tremendous credit. Your victory is another proud chapter in the history of the American Labor Movement. I know that you will now continue your struggle until total victory has been achieved and I stand ready, as in the past, to offer any assistance I can.

> George McGovern
> Chairman, Senate Committee on
> Nutrition and Human Needs

William Waller was inaugurated on a cold January afternoon. Evers was not invited to the ceremony, nor were any members of the Loyalist Democrats. Waller's speech, while void of the "old emotionalisms" he had condemned in his campaign, was nevertheless lackluster. He was sworn in by Judge Tom Brady. In his speech he discussed progress and the new period Mississippi was entering; the word "black" was not mentioned.

Waller did destroy some old symbols. He made good his promise to include all Mississippians in government. He appointed a black man to the ETV board, and a black educator was elevated to the state's highest education board, ousting a Hederman in the process. He hired a black man to his personal staff as a consultant on minority employment. And he announced a special B. B. King day in Mississippi honoring the blues singer. Cleve McDowell, a defeated candidate for the Legislature from the Delta, was appointed to the Penitentiary board.

Waller's legislative work in the first session was marked by few high points. (Indeed, most of the elected officials had supported Sullivan.) His attempt to have the State Sovereignty Commission turned into a public relations department for the governor failed. This was a laudable effort; the fault must not be laid to Waller. As Representative Clark observed after his colleagues sang praises of an anti-busing bill one afternoon, "In a lot of ways, this Legislature is worse than the last one." But the illegal activities of the Sovereignty Commission remained dormant. Its very existence was a symbol of white resistance. Like the past, it proved less effective.

A Tallahatchie County legislator called for a bill to require that poll watchers be Mississippi residents. His county, he said, "had a bunch of wooly-headed people and a bunch of long, string-haired people come in to watch our elections!" Civil rights attorneys observed that the bill could not be effective if passed, since the Voting Rights Act would probably render it illegal. How could elections have any chance of being held fairly without poll watchers who would not be fired from their jobs or beaten later by praetorian whites?

The Legislature did pass Waller's highway program. The sorely needed four lanes would be paid for by a revenue from a one cent sales tax on gasoline. And so, in the poorest and most overtaxed state in the land, the highways would be paid for by the little man who could not afford to be much of a consumer to begin with. To Waller's credit there was an admirable veto of a bill that would have allowed banks to raise their credit interest rate. As the governor himself put it, it was a "veto for the average man." Waller also took firm steps to integrate the highway patrol, and black people liked that.

Waller, riding the crest of publicity as a New South governor, soon showed himself to be a politician with one foot in the New South and one lagging behind in the Old. By February 1972 it was clear that if the Regulars wished to go to Miami Beach for the convention, a union would have to be forged with the Loyalists. He went on the *Today* show and lied, saying that Evers and Aaron Henry were not on speaking terms. This was at the time when Evers and Henry and Loyalist leaders were mapping strategy for their delegation's reseating at the July convention. Moreover, Hodding Carter, III, had sat on the McGovern-Frazier Commission for party reform. Waller had no idea of how to challenge the Loyalists.

The Loyalists and the Regulars would have to bargain. The Loyalists had the national sanction that the Regulars wanted. Not only were white Democrats anxious for a voice in the national party, but the Mississippi congressional delegation had, when their years of service were combined, over a century in seniority. Eastland (Judiciary) and Stennis (Armed Services) were Senate chairmen; Jamie Whitten chaired the powerful Agriculture Committee in the House. The Regulars wanted to ensure the congressional delegation's seniority by reacceptance into the Democratic fold.

At best it can be said that Waller's position on the struggle between the Loyalists and Regulars was shortsighted. Since the Loyalists had the sanction, they received the official party call. For the record, Aaron Henry had requested use of the Regulars' polling places for Loyalist caucuses. But Leon Bramlett, chairman of the Regulars, said in no uncertain terms that his executive committee members weren't interested "in meeting with those people." At this juncture—in February—a logical move by Waller would have been to flood his supporters into Loyalist precinct and county caucuses, and thus through sheer numbers simply take over control of various delegations. Why Waller didn't take this measure is not altogether clear. Indeed, had he sought to outnumber the Loyalists and failed, it would look bad for him statewide. Also, by the mere attempt he would be playing the blacks on their own field. But had he been successful even partially—say, winning five key county delegations—he would have been in a position to bargain. But as Charles Ramberg perceptively noted at the time, "Waller's not sending his folks to our meetings. To be honest, I don't believe the man even understands the party guidelines for delegate selection."

This apparently was the case. Waller publicly stated his conviction that a unified party should go to Miami. Then he told the Regulars to hold their caucuses separately from the Loyalists; however, he suggested that both sides attend each others' meetings. The Loyalists did precisely that, and to Waller's chagrin, five of the Regulars' county delegations were Loyalist-dominated. (Hodding Carter, III, was chairman of the Regular *and* Loyalist delegations from Washington County.) The Regulars, meanwhile, held some party caucuses in the good old Mississippi way, completely violating the party rules. One white county leader told blacks flatly that they would not be selected as delegates. Judge Brady was elected to a county delegation that did not allow proper minority representation. And for the Loyalist dossier, there was also Simms Luckett, a Delta planter who, upon adjournment of his county caucus, told a reporter, "We wanted to make sure none of our delegates were committed to Humphrey, Muskie, McGovern, Lindsay, or the likes of those boys."

By March the writing was on the wall. Waller knew his delegation had little chance. Thus, the Regulars and Loyalists recessed their state conventions to consider compromise and union. A special committee was formed to pursue conciliation; members of both sides sat on it. Ed Cole was one of the Loyalists. He told me, "The bargain was simple. We had the sanction that they wanted. They had the in-state power, especially at the county level, that we wanted a share in." Waller explained to his recessing party, "We must affiliate with the national party and help our [congressional] delegation in Washington."

After much preliminary thrashing about, the Loyalists laid down the terms for a conciliation. These included an

official merger of the two parties under the Loyalist constitution. An equally proportioned biracial state executive
committee would serve as an advisory board for all agencies,
commissions, and federal patronage. County party committees would be apportioned on the basis of racial breakdown.
Waller would have to support the single-member-district
reapportionment, crucial to black opportunities for election
in future races. The Miami delegation would have to be
chosen under the McGovern guidelines; Loyalists would
have to compose 60 percent of the delegation.

Various offers and rebuttals were made. The Regulars
stood fast on one proposal: simply to send a unified delegation to Miami. As Ed Cole later mused, "I could tell from
the start of the sessions that all they wanted was to go to
Miami as easy as possible. I understood that, but I didn't understand how they took us to be so naive. They refused to
offer us anything in return! It was as if we didn't have anything to offer *them* . . . all they were willing to do was *go*
with us! They simply said they'd go to Miami and we could
take a full delegation each, just give everyone a half a vote.
That was ridiculous."

No agreement was reached. The Regulars reconvened
and Governor Waller addressed them, saying that the Loyalist demands went "far beyond the realm of possibility."
The governor then served notice that the Loyalists had ten
days to accept the Regulars' "offer" or else face a court suit
in Mississippi that would seek to expel the Loyalists as the
official party, and thus prevent them from going to Miami.
But this could hardly have had much effect, since the Credentials Committee of the Democratic Party would decide
which delegations represented which states and whether
they had conformed to party law. "We won't give up till we
get to Miami!" Waller declared. "And we'll get to Miami
fighting!"

Writing in the *Delta-Democrat Times*, Hodding Carter, III, analyzed Waller's move:

> The governor, dipping into the pages of a history book which the state's politicians should forget, had to play to the galleries. He described the Loyalists' negotiating points as 'demands'; then made some demands of his own. He gave the Loyalists 10 days to accept a ridiculous offer, which is that they give up half of the state's delegation in return for nothing. The governor then played what he apparently thinks is his trump card, which is a threat to contest the Loyalists' seating first in Federal court and then at the national Democratic Convention in Miami.
>
> We trust both efforts will be financed out of his own pocket, since using anyone else's money would amount to fraud at best and at worst. . . . There is no possible way for a Federal suit to succeed, since the courts have historically stayed far clear of intra-party warfare. As for the national convention, the Loyalists are already seated on the temporary roles, and the Regulars failed to challenge within the required time following the Loyalists' selection of convention delegates. It would take the credentials' committee approximately 10 minutes to dispose of the Regulars' challenge, such as it is. . . .

It took the Credentials Committee a little more than one hour to dispose of the Regulars' challenge. The governor himself pleaded the case at the hearings in Washington. But by then even he knew his trump had turned out to be a joker. The night before the hearing he pursued Carter and Henry in a hotel hallway, trying to renegotiate, suddenly offering to agree to some of their terms. But with no way to hold him to the bargain, they refused. The next day, as Waller pleaded his case, Carter sat as vice-chairman of the Credentials Committee. The Loyalists retained the sanction. Waller later told a Mississippi reporter who asked if he would accept Lawrence O'Brien's invitation to be an honored guest of the convention that he would not go because he didn't "think it would be altogether proper."

The lawsuit settled little if anything. Judge Dan Russell observed that the court could not prevent the Loyalists from going to Miami; he asserted, however, that the Loyalists did not represent the rank-and-file Mississippian, as the Regulars did. An appeal was lodged in the Fifth Circuit Court of Appeals, although it had no effect on the Miami convention. The Regulars subsequently found the party campaign chest sorely depleted. Waller was in the uncomfortable position of leading a state party that was now sending out letters requesting financial contributions to pay the lawyers' court fees.

The Mississippi delegation to Miami divided its votes among McGovern, Chisholm, Sanford, and Humphrey. Hodding Carter condemned Waller on national television for vetoing a vital HEW grant to a Mound Bayou, Mississippi, hospital: "You can have your delegation, Governor Waller, just give us that hospital grant!" Waller's veto—which Loyalists saw as a form of revenge for the loss of party representation at Miami—was overriden by OEO.

II

The progress of the election lawsuits was discouraging. The Lawyers' Committee for Civil Rights in Jackson was successful in two reapportionment cases, but by midautumn 1972 suits on the Canton and Midnight irregularities had gone into moves and countermoves. The Justice Department, according to Frank Parker of the Lawyers' Committee, "has absolutely no interest in the cases." But in Leflore and Issaquena counties, lawsuits voided supervisory elections, which had been conducted on an at-large basis; the areas of black concentration in black majority counties had been diluted. A flagrant malapportionment created beats that zigzagged through the black community, nullifying voting strength. Attorney Parker observed, "The Justice Department had originally objected to the Legislature's 1966 amendment giving counties the right to hold at-large elections. The objection was based on predictable dispersing of the black vote [see Chapter 2]. But Issaquena and Leflore simply ignored the Justice Department and went ahead. We—the Lawyers' Committee—ended up filing the lawsuit that knocked the election out. The Justice Department refuses to enforce its own verdicts. They wouldn't even file the suit." The elections were voided.

By winter 1972 it was clear that the Justice Department's attitude was steadfastly cynical. John Brittain of the Lawyers' Committee noted that the election day violence of 1971 "was directly proportionate to black political strength or possible potency," yet no action was taken by Washington on the irregularities. I wrote to David Norman, head of the Civil Rights Division of the Justice Department, asking permission to read election observers' reports, and received no reply. In Washington, just before turning in the final draft of this book, I was informed that such reports were off-limits to journalists and nondepartment personnel.

Similar gerrymandering has occurred in Warren, a river county whose seat is Vicksburg, a town with a sizable black population. A redistricting plan was conceived to severely cut black voting strength. Warren County officials ignored an early Justice Department complaint, and attorney Parker commented bitterly, "The Justice Department has yet to file a suit objecting to *its own complaint* being ignored!"

I asked him for his view on the apparent malfeasance on the part of the Justice Department. He said, "Southern strategy." As of 1972 over half of Mississippi's counties were mapping reapportionment plans. The Lawyers' Committee has its work cut out.

The Nixon Administration's posture toward Mississippi became appallingly clear in the wake of the ITT controversy. During the Senate Judiciary Committee's investigation, Chairman Eastland abstained on key votes, abstentions that in effect were votes *for* the Administration. Once the investigation had been railroaded through and Kleindeinst confirmed, the new Attorney General announced that he would visit Mississippi in October. He stayed at Eastland's home in Sunflower County, campaigning for the senator in his bid for reelection against a moderate Republican. Agnew later visited Mississippi and endorsed Eastland, who was re-elected in 1972.

Both statistics and "the system" in Mississippi show that the future for blacks will be a long uphill battle. Black emigration, especially by the young, is eroding voter strength in certain areas. Half of the black population is also under voting age. White voting strength, on the other hand, remains stable, which is tantamount to an increase, given the black drop. Nixon's sweep of the South in his reelection has led many to believe that he will throw even heavier weight against renewal of the Voting Rights Act than he and John Mitchell did in 1970. The Voting Rights Act runs out in August 1975, three months before the state elections are to be held.

And the establishment in Mississippi is still mostly white. The judges are all white and, with a few stalwart exceptions, they are bigots. Of the 410 important supervisory positions, only seven are held by blacks. The State Senate is all white; Representative Robert Clark is the lone black in the House. The FBI in Mississippi, always on amiable terms with white law officials, is still a white agency. Waller did little in his first year to bring in more of the sorely needed legal services

programs to help blacks and poor whites, nor did the governor enact any sweeping antipoverty program, elemental to
any improvement. These federal and state agencies are
heavily white.

As for elections in the years to come, George Taylor, director of the Lawyers' Committee, explained, "It is absolutely essential that Section 5 of the Voting Rights Act be
renewed for ten years. If counties are given a free rein to
reapportion, or if the Legislature changes election laws any
way they want, we're sunk. We also need strict rules allowing illiterates help when they vote. The manipulation is
so flagrant now it's disgusting. . . . Illiterate voters should
have the right to help from anyone they choose, not who the
poll manager tells them they have to follow."

Another essential law would demand that polling places
be manned by federal officials in nonpartisan polling places:
schools, firehouses, and so forth—not in white-owned stores
or cotton warehouses. The change to multimember legislative seats needs to be wiped away so that black voting
strength based on population distribution can be justly realized. With the retreat on domestic policies in the Nixon Administration, blacks beholden to whites stand little chance
of freeing themselves through job corps programs and the
like. Given the looming malapportionments, the crisis of the
seventies will not be how the black vote is cast but whether
it is diluted. It will be a hard fight.

III

I last visited Jackson in late October 1972. It was a changing city, now exploding in an unparalleled business boom.
People had moved to the suburbs, new restaurants and bars
abounded, shopping complexes expanded. Bill Minor commented that he was going to write a piece for the *Times-Picayune* just on Jackson: "The last time I wrote a story on the

city was just after World War II. Now it's a city growing like never before."

I drove down the streets I remembered from the campaign summer and fall, and many of the old discomforts were not as acute. The place seemed more peaceful, as though it had forgotten about the past and joined the twentieth century. The campaign office was empty, the owners unsure what to do with the building. On the side of the wall the "Evers for Everybody" sign was still bright—only now cars did not slow down to look at it. The paint, in any event, had been good.

Even the State Capitol had a new look. Waller, the brash country boy who defeated the Hedermans, had the portraits of the beauty queens removed from the second-floor rotunda. In their place was a display on Mississippi progress. The Jackson papers were most indignant.

Evers himself was changing, or at least moderately so. Remembering the man who had helped him, he supported Lindsay for President. His subsequent feeling toward McGovern was lukewarm, since the candidate's aides had arrogantly snubbed both The Mayor and Aaron Henry at Miami Beach. After the convention he told a Mississippi reporter he had his doubts about the McGovern candidacy. When the Clarksdale *Press-Register* ran a front-page headline saying Evers supported Nixon, Evers announced he was backing McGovern. Shortly before my trip to Jackson, I saw Evers in Buffalo, where we spoke together at the state university. Now, for the first time, he was visibly concerned about Vietnam. During the campaign he had not talked about the war, as it was not an issue in Mississippi. He was asked about it only once, and he replied that he was against all wars, which was a convenient answer. But late in the campaign he had said to me, "I couldn't understand all those kids mad at LBJ. Domestically, he was the best President we ever had. So what if he had that war? All Presidents have had wars." But at Buffalo he asked me before his speech if I understood how people could so easily accept the inhuman bombardment of the North. I said I didn't know, and could only reply that the country was in a spiritual shambles. Addressing the students, he said, "And this war, this turrible, turrible war . . . I been readin' all about that bombin'. If we had been at war with France or England, against white-skinned folks, you think we'd be bombin' like that? Not hardly. It's because the Vietnamese are yellow-skinned people that Nixon doesn't care about all the bombs. The Bible says, 'Thou shalt not kill.' And we're doin' that each night over in Vietnam. Why should we kill all them Vietnamese? I never seen a Vietnamese, have any of you?"

In Mississippi, where McGovern's campaign was being run by a handful of white liberals, Evers was the centrist figure of the Loyalists. That is to say, the party was bitterly divided into two factions, and he was on relatively civil terms with both. Aaron Henry's health was deteriorating, and the white liberals had control of what little party power there was. At the Democratic National Convention, the bitter divisiveness had surfaced when some Loyalists initially opposed a Hodding Carter for Vice President drive. Less than a joust for party power, the Loyalists' rift stemmed from incredible ego battles. But the Loyalists still held the party sanction. Ultimately, the Regulars will have to bargain with them. Therein lies hope for the future.

Evers' political work will bear watching. He still maintains strong ties in the national Democratic Party. In Mississippi he is a pivotal force that white politicians will have to reckon with. Should he run in 1975—or later—his presence ensures a base of at least 150,000 votes a white candidate would lose. The black vote will become more and more important to whites. In neighboring Louisiana, gubernatorial candidate Edwin Edwards adopted a reform platform and made firm commitments to black leaders. Receiving 80 percent of the black vote, he was elected by a mere 6,000 votes. Louisiana has no black leader like Evers, but the black vote is more unified. In Mississippi, a moderate white —even a tacit liberal—can be elected, but he will have to make his deals with blacks. It will be most difficult for a white politician to win broad-based black support without Evers' endorsement or political help.

To accomplish real change, black folks in Mississippi must organize. The 1971 campaigns of more than three hundred Loyalist Democrats were first signs of such organization and they were crucially important campaigns. With experience comes sophistication, and the work over the next five years must be based on political techniques, not on civil rights rituals. In the 1973 municipal elections, political effort will go into counties with heavy black voting strength and nonfactionalized organizations. In 1975 in the key black counties— Jefferson, Claiborne, Wilkinson, Coahoma, and Madison— leaders must work on grass-roots organizing. They will field smaller slates of candidates, men and women chosen with more political discrimination. The lessons of 1971 will be remembered. As Evers said the night of his defeat, "We may be beaten, but we ain't defeated."

Perhaps the most important factor in Evers' career is that he has produced remarkable results in Fayette. This is most important for black Mississippi, because it is a tangible reality whites cannot deny. Small as it is, Fayette is prospering. The Mayor has brought in over $10 million HEW, HUD, and foundation programs. The Robert F. Kennedy Memorial center, a multipurpose complex, is nearing completion. The health facilities in Jefferson County upgraded under Evers are better than in most counties in the state. The town payroll has tripled in four years, the white automobile salesman in Fayette is realizing more business than ever before, and with a modern shopping complex being built, the town will have a number of new employment opportunities in the seventies. Evers' success in Fayette has not been ignored by whites. The college newspapers frequently send reporters to do stories on Fayette and its bustling new programs. Eventually, the daily newspapers will do the same.

But there is promise in an even deeper realm. The old order of Mississippi is changing; slowly, perhaps, but unmistakably. Busing is the residue of the old tradition. The basis of the new style with its moderate tone is something that each race has known all along through all the years of fear and fury: that whites and blacks in the South have lived in close proximity for a century and are remarkably similar human beings. The racist paternalism remains, but it is slowly giving way to a thin bond between blacks and whites of an altogether different fiber. The closer whites look, the more they see reflections of their own joys and sorrows in the faces of black folks. The common denominator of survival and dignity was felt in the Laurel courthouse at the wood hauler's rally. Young whites are now growing up more acutely aware of the fallacies that they inherited. In a deserted laundromat in Jackson, a white boy from a remote county told me the story of his spiritual growth since high school. Many like him are yet to come. Significantly, integration is working well in rural counties, where whites outnumber blacks on an average of 65 percent to 35 percent. More recently, desegregation plans have begun to take root in Jackson, Hattiesburg, and Meridian—places where a half-dozen years ago the white opposition to integration took its cues from members of the Citizens' Council, but where now one often finds moderation and attempts at peaceful conciliation.

Shibboleths continue to dissolve in Mississippi. In April 1972 the elder Hodding Carter passed away. The man denounced by the Legislature in the late fifties for "selling out for Yankee gold" was accorded adulatory eulogies on the floor of the Capitol. Governor Waller praised him as a "great Mississippian" and attended the funeral. It is even possible that—eventually—even the Bilbo statue in the Capitol will go.

The old culture is not bursting at the seams, but it is losing elements of its power. False glorification of the redneck at the expense of the black was the cornerstone of the past tradition. It was the myth of farmers who plowed long fields and hunted deep woods and drank hard whiskey and told legends of boys who were men and the best halfbacks their counties produced. But now the myth is falling short, unable to satisfy the men who once believed in it. The farmers slowly die; more people move into cities, and Mississippi now has a burgeoning middle class that it never had in the mid-fifties; the farmers' sons sip beer, watching a modernized ritual that pits the bodies of black and white football players against one another with reckless abandon each Sunday. Perhaps the most crucial transition will come, as Peter Schrag has suggested, when the white cheerleader for Ole Miss kisses the black quarterback after he has won the big game. That will be a corner turned.

The task of the coming generation of Mississippi politicians is to substitute a new myth—or at least the trappings of one—for the old. As a political tool, the old myth won't work. The remnant of the past yet to be tackled is, of course, poverty. There is no place more ripe for a populist than Mississippi. Here he can draw together his folks, black and white, and get himself elected on the platform that he will get something done for the betterment of men and their families. Charles Evers tried, but a black campaign was the product of an idea whose time had not yet come.

I believe that Charles Evers' campaign will be of enduring importance to Mississippi and her people. He was the first man to articulate the visceral problems from which *all* Mississippians suffer. In his time, a black man will probably not be elected governor. But perhaps his grandchildren will see the portrait of the burly black mayor hanging in a special niche on a wall in the Mississippi Legislature. For one day, when we are old or dead, a black man will be elected governor of Mississippi. He will come when our current struggles have seeped deep into the past. And by then there will be a true reformation of the spirit, which will be necessary in the face of new dilemmas of the day. It will be a long time from now, but at least that campaign has begun.

Poplarville, Mississippi
New Orleans, Louisiana

November, 1972

Notes

By including sections about Mississippi history, it was not my intention to shed new light on old material. Rather, I felt that to write about the Evers' campaign as a phenomenon in a period of historical transition, it was important to present the past in a brief and readable way, so that the developments of 1971 could be clearly seen as a departure from the past.

Moreover, I have always been disturbed about the stereotypes of the South—the crosses, the evil rednecks, the supposedly ingrained furies of the region. The Old South was spoon-fed on fear and cynicism. Without belaboring the point, I sought to show how Mississippi came to be the society it was, what changes began during the civil rights movement, and the extension of those changes in 1971.

The following books were helpful to me in preparation and research for this book:

Belfrage, Sally. *Freedom Summer.* New York: Viking Press, 1965.
Carter, Hodding. *The Angry Scar: The Story of Reconstruc-*

tion 1865–1890. Garden City, N.Y.: Doubleday, 1959.

———. *Southern Legacy.* Baton Rouge: Louisiana State University Press, 1950.

Carter, Hodding, III. *The South Strikes Back.* Reprint of 1959 ed., Negro University Press.

Cash, Wilbur J. *The Mind of the South.* New York: Alfred E. Knopf, 1960.

Cook, Fred. *The Nightmare Decade: The Life and Times of Senator Joe McCarthy.* New York: Random House, 1971.

Cruse, Harold. *The Crisis of the Negro Intellectual.* New York: Morrow, 1971.

Du Bois, W. E. B. *Souls of Black Folk.* New York: NAL, 1969.

Evers, Charles. *Evers.* Edited by Grace Halsell. New York: World, 1970.

Franklin, John Hope. *From Slavery to Freedom: A History of American Negroes.* New York: Alfred E. Knopf, 1967.

Green, A. Wigfall. *The Man Bilbo.* Baton Rouge: Louisiana State University Press, 1963.

Halberstam, David. *The Unfinished Odyssey of Robert Kennedy.* New York: Random House, 1969.

Herbers, John. *The Lost Priority: What Happened to the Civil Rights Movement in America.* New York: Funk & Wagnalls, 1970.

Hilton, Bruce. *The Delta Ministry.* New York: Macmillan, 1969.

Holmes, William F. *The White Chief: James Kimble Vardaman.* Baton Rouge: Louisiana State University Press, 1970.

Huie, William Bradford. *Three Lives for Mississippi.* New York: NAL, 1968.

Kirwan, Albert D. *Revolt of the Rednecks: Mississippi Politics (1876–1925).* New York: Peter Smith, 1964.

Lewis, David. *King: A Critical Biography.* New York: Praeger, 1970.

Lord, Walter. *The Past That Would Not Die.* New York: Harper & Row, 1965.

Louis, Debbie. *And We Are Not Saved: A History of the Movement as People.* Garden City, N.Y.: Doubleday, 1970.

McGill, Ralph. *The South and the Southerner.* Boston: Little, Brown, 1963.

Michie, Allan A., and Ryhlich, Frank. *Dixie Demagogues.* New York: Vanguard Press, 1939.

Moody, Anne. *Coming of Age in Mississippi: An Autobiography.* New York: Dial, 1968.

Morris, Willie. *Yazoo: Integration in a Deep Southern Town.* New York: Harpers Magazine Press, 1971.

———. *North Toward Home.* New York: Dell, 1970.

Navasky, Victor. *Kennedy Justice.* New York: Atheneum, 1971.

Newfield, Jack. *Robert F. Kennedy: A Memoir.* New York: Dutton, 1969.

Percy, William Alexander. *Lanterns on the Levee: Recollection of a Planter's Son.* New York: Alfred E. Knopf, 1941.

Salinger, Pierre. *With Kennedy.* Garden City, N.Y.: Doubleday, 1966.

Sherrill, Robert. *Gothic Politics in the Deep South.* New York: Grossman, 1968.

Silver, James W. *Mississippi: The Closed Society.* New York: Harcourt, Brace & World, 1966.

Sorenson, Theodore. *Kennedy.* New York: Harper & Row, 1965.

Watters, Pat. *Down to Now: Reflections of the Civil Rights Movement.* New York: Pantheon, 1972.

Watters, Pat, and Cleghorn, Reese. *Climbing Jacob's Ladder: The Arrival of Negroes in Southern Politics.* New York: Harcourt, Brace & Jovanovich, 1970.

White, Theodore H. *The Making of the President 1960.* New York: Atheneum, 1961.

———. *The Making of the President 1964.* New York: Atheneum, 1965.

———. *The Making of the President 1968.* New York: Atheneum, 1969.

Witcover, Jules. *Eighty-Five Days: The Last Campaign of Robert F. Kennedy.* New York: Ace Books, 1969.

Woodward, C. Vann. *The Burden of Southern History.* New York: NAL, 1969.

Zinn, Howard. *The Southern Mystique.* New York: Alfred E. Knopf, 1964.

———. *SNCC: The New Abolitionists.* Boston: Beacon Press, 1964/65.

Also, material from the files and observations of Wilson Minor, of attorneys for the Lawyers' Committee for Civil Rights, and from poll watchers' reports.

Index